# MASONS
# and
# BUILDERS
# LIBRARY
# Vol. II

## by Louis M. Dezettel

**THEODORE AUDEL & CO.**
*a division of*

**HOWARD W. SAMS & CO., INC.**
4300 West 62nd Street
Indianapolis, Indiana 46268

**FIRST EDITION**

SEVENTH PRINTING—1978

International Standard Book Number: 0-672-23183-2

Library of Congress Catalog Card Number: 78-186134

# Foreword

There are numerous factors that must be taken into consideration when designing or constructing any type of building or small project around the house. Among these factors are terrain, geographical location, the type of material to be used, and the cost of placing or using this material.

Brick, concrete block, and structural clay tile have been gaining popular use over the past years as a basic building material for homes and industrial buildings. Many hours can be saved, and labor costs cut when single-wall construction is erected with concrete block or structural clay tile. Masonry walls can be faced with brick which not only beautifies the structure but adds insulation automatically.

So far, no automatic method for laying brick has been devised. It is a hand operation, depending entirely on the bricklayer's high degree of skill and efficiency. Years of experience have developed a pattern or technique in handling the trowel and in mixing the proper ingredients used in mortar.

The purpose of this book is to aid the builder, whether he is a man who does occasional masonry work around the house, a contractor, or an apprentice, by supplying the information needed to avoid or correct many common building faults that are directly affected by poor workmanship or improper mixing of various materials.

The author is indebted to the *Portland Cement Association* and its members for their permission to use their abundance of literature for much of the information contained in this book. Thanks is also given to the *Sakrete Corp.* for the many photographs they furnished for one of the projects described in Chapter 13.

Louis M. Dezettel

# Contents

## Chapter 15

## Chapter 16

## CHAPTER 1

# Brick

As structural material, brick has reached a high state of art in strength, appearance, and other factors. Not only is it the most popular basic material for building homes and industrial buildings, but it is highly regarded for its architectural and aesthetic possibilities, as shown in Fig. 1.

Fig. 1. Brick has ornamental as well as structural value. The floor is a rough brick which can withstand foot traffic.

Methods for making basic brick have not changed much over the years. Even handmade adobe brick is still used to a limited extent. Yet, brick is probably only second to wood in its long history of use. The art of brickmaking dates from very early times. Sun-dried, or adobe, brick were used thousands of years before the earliest recorded date of history, as given on a brick tablet of the time of Sargon of Akkad, 3800 B.C., founder of the Chaldean empire.

It was very natural for the dwellers along great rivers, such as the Euphrates and Tigris, to notice on the banks the sunbaked and irregularly cracked clay blocks which, after a little crude shaping, proved suitable for building a wall. Later, and about the time when the Tower of Babel was built, the Chaldeans learned how to burn brick, thus converting the clay into a hard substance. In the time of Nebuchadnezzar (604-562 B.C.), the Babylonians and Assyrians had acquired the art not only of making hard burnt brick but of beautifully enameling them. The Chinese claim great antiquity for their clay industries, but it is probable that the knowledge of brickmaking travelled eastward from Babylonia across all of Asia.

The Great Wall of China was partly constructed of brick both burnt and unburnt. This was, however, built at a comparatively late period (210 B.C.) and there is nothing to show that the Chinese had any knowledge of burnt brick when the art flourished in Babylonia. The first brick buildings in America were erected on Manhattan Island in the year 1633 by a governor of the Dutch West Indies Company. The bricks for these buildings were made in Holland, where the industry had long reached great excellence. For many years brick were imported into America from Holland and also from England.

In America, burnt bricks were first made in New England in about 1650. The manufacture of brick slowly spread throughout the New England states. The Colonial days produced five types of brick architecture from New England to Virginia. In the nineteenth century up to about 1880, American brick building was confined largely to the use of common brick for ordinary construction or for backing stone-faced walls. From that date up to the present, a growing taste has demanded and secured artistic effect in the brick wall by the use of specially selected or manufactured brick of various shades and finish.

By definition, *clay is a common earth of various colors, compact and brittle when dry, but plastic and tenacious when wet.* It is a hydrous aluminum silicate generally mixed with powdered feldspar, quartz, sand, iron oxides, and various other minerals. The various kinds of clay are named for their suitability to a particular use—brick clay, fire clay, potter's clay, etc. All clays are the result of the denudation and decomposition of feldspathic and siliceous rocks, and consist of fine insoluble particles which have been carried in suspension in water and deposited in geologic basins according to their specific gravity and degree of fineness.

These deposits have been formed in all geologic epochs from the Cambrian to the recent, and they vary in hardness from the soft and plastic alluvial clays to the hard and rock-like shales and slates of the older formations. The alluvial and drift clays which were used alone for brickmaking until modern times, are found near the surface, are readily worked, and require little preparation; whereas the older sedimentary deposits are often difficult to work and necessitate the use of heavy machinery. These older shales or rocky clays may be brought to a plastic condition by crushing and grinding in water, and they then resemble ordinary alluvial clays in every respect.

The clays or earth used in modern brickmaking may be divided into two classes according to chemical composition, as:

1. Clays or shales containing only a small percentage of carbonate of lime.
2. Clays containing a considerable percentage of carbonate of lime.

The first mentioned class consists chiefly of hydrated aluminum silicates, which is the true clay substance. Clays of this class usually burn to a buff, salmon, or red color. The second class known as *marls* may contain as much as 40% chalk. Marl burns to a sulfur yellow color which is quite distinctive. The color of brick depends on the composition of the material and the manner in which it is treated in the kiln. The chief colorant is the iron oxide in the clay, which does not show until the material has been heated, and which cannot be determined from an inspection of the raw material. It should be remembered that brickmakers often speak of clays as red clay, white clay, etc., according to the color of the brick made from them, without any reference to their color in the unburned state.

The strongest brick clays, or those possessing the greatest plasticity and tensile strength, are usually those which contain the highest percentage of the hydrated aluminum silicates. All clays contain, in greater or lesser amounts, some undecomposed feldspar. The most important ingredient other than the clay and sand substance is oxide of iron for color and to a lesser extent for hardness and durability. A clay containing from 5% to 8% oxide of iron, will, under ordinary conditions of firing, produce a red brick. If the clay contains 3% to 4% alkalies or the brick is fired too hard, the color will be darker, approaching purple. Fenugenous clays generally become darker as they approach the fusion point. Alumina acts to make the color lighter.

All clays when heated sufficiently lose their plasticity and cannot regain it, so that on burning, they are converted into rigid bodies. Thus, when a clay is heated, the first effect is to drive off the water of formation. The clay then becomes dry, but is not chemically changed; it does not cease to be plastic when cooled and moistened. On continuing to raise the temperature, the chemically combined water is separated and the clay undergoes a molecular change, which prevents it from taking up water again, except mechanically.

With the loss of the chemically combined water, the clay ceases to be plastic. On further heating, clays tend to undergo partial fusion. When this has occurred to a sufficient extent for the fused material to fill the pores completely, the brick becomes impervious to water and is said to be *vitrified*.

The varieties of clays used in brickmaking are very numerous. Of these which may be mentioned are:

1. **White burning clays.** These are composed chiefly of alumina, silver, and water, and are used to a very limited extent in brickmaking since cheaper materials are available.
2. **Marls.** Marls contain a considerable proportion of lime in the form of chalk or limestone. Brick made from these materials are almost white; this is not due to the purity of the material, but to the combination of the iron oxide with the lime in the clay. Marls are easily fusible and give a characteristic effervescence when a little hydrochloric acid is poured on the surface.

3. **Loams.** Loam consists of clays containing a large proportion of sand, rendering them easier to work than tougher clays.
4. **Shales.** Shales are underrated clays which have been subjected to so much compression that they are almost semi-rock in characteristics. They have little plasticity. Red burning materials obtained from impure shales are largely employed in brickmaking.
5. **Fire clays.** Fire clays are the refractory clays, or those capable of resisting very high temperatures in furnaces. They are, accordingly, used for making fire brick which are employed in lining boilers, furnaces, and fireplaces.
6. **Boulder clays.** Glacial action produces these clays, and they are distinguished from other clays by the number of rounded stones they contain. With careful selection and preparation, boulder clays make satisfactory common brick.

In addition to the foregoing classes, there are other designations of clays such as:

1. **Brick earth.** The term brick earth is used to distinguish clays which can be made into brick without much mechanical treatment, from the harder rock clays and shales which must first be ground. Accordingly, the machinery necessary to manufacture brick from brick earth is reduced to a minimum.
2. **Fat clays.** Fat clays are those which are strong or plastic, containing a high percentage of true clay substance and a low percentage of sand. Such clays take up a considerable amount of water in tempering, dry slowly, shrink considerably, and lose their shape and develop cracks in drying and firing. Fat clays are improved by the addition of coarse sharp sand, making the brick more rigid during the firing.

The presence of organic matter gives wet clay a greater plasticity. In some of the coal-measure shales the amount of organic matter is considerable, which renders the clay useless for brick making. Other impurities, which frequently occur are the sulfates of lime, magnesia, chlorides, nitrates or soda, potash, and iron pyrites. All of these except the pyrites are soluble in water and are undesirable, because they give rise to scum which produces patchy color and pitted surfaces. The most common soluble impurity is calcium sulfate, which produces, in drying, a whitish scum on the brick surface. Such brick are of inferior quality because the scum becomes permanently fixed in burning.

Scumming is an important item in the manufacture of first-class brick. When a clay containing calcium sulfate must be used, a certain percentage of barium carbonate is usually added to the wet clay. This converts the calcium sulfate into calcium carbonate, which is insoluble in water, so that it remains distributed throughout the mass of the brick instead of being deposited on the surface.

Efflorescence is a white powder of crystallization caused by

Courtesy Structural Clay Products Inst.

**Fig. 2. Plastic clay material is placed in a compressor and squeezed into a long bar.**

water-soluble salts, which are sometimes present in the brick or mortar. Water, such as rain, will sometimes leach the salts out of the brick, and they appear as white powdery-like patches on the surface. Currently, only a small percentage of brick produced in the United States contains enough salts to produce efflorescence.

## HOW BRICK IS MADE

Because of the weight of the raw material and the finished product, transportation economy dictates that processing plants be located near the material source, and near the markets. As a result, there are several hundred brick processors, both large and small, throughout the United States. Even a smaller plant requires a considerable capital investment in earth shovels, trucks, crushers, compressors, kilns, and drying sheds. The illustrations accompanying this section were taken at the Kinney Brick Co., near Albuquerque, New Mexico.

Clay is dug from nearby pits and trucked to the various plant locations. It is dumped into a crusher at which point other chemicals may be added. The right amount of water is added to make the material into a heavy plastic "mud." The plastic material is then placed into a compressor. A compressor is shown in Fig. 2. The material, under great pressure, is squeezed out as a long rectangular-shaped tube, much like toothpaste is squeezed out of a tube. This can be seen near the center of the illustration. Near the left

Fig. 3. A taut-wire cutting machine cuts the plastic bars into brick sizes.

side of the illustration is a cutter, which cuts the extruded material into long bars, about 20 brick-lengths long. The cutter moves with the extruded material, making the operation a continuous one.

Each bar is moved over to a taut-wire brick cutter (Fig. 3). It cuts the bar into standard sized bricks. The brick is cut slightly oversize, to allow for shrinkage during drying. The bricks are then piled, with air spaces between each brick, onto pallets with rail wheels. Because of the high compression of the extrusion, the plastic bricks are hard enough to support the weight of several layers. The pallets are moved by rail to one of many drying sheds (Fig. 4) where they are held several days under moderate heat. This removes all moisture, leaving a brick that is dry but crumbles easily.

Fig. 4. Drying sheds remove moisture from the bricks.

When dry, the bricks are moved to a kiln, where they are baked for 24 hours at high temperature. The kilns, or ovens, which are gas fired (Fig. 5), are long and have doors at both ends. The pallets are wheeled into one end and removed from the other end. This makes the process almost continuous—with fresh brick going in one end as the cured bricks are removed from the other end. It is in the kiln that the bricks become hard.

Fig. 5. Bricks are kiln-cured in long ovens for at least 24 hours.

Fig. 6. Common brick has no chemical treatment for color. It is hard, has less
water absorption, and is the basic structural brick

Time and temperature determine hardness and water absorption. Common building brick is made of the natural clay or shale. Their outside color is not uniform. Although not normally used as face brick, some people prefer this effect for fireplaces and other purposes. Barium additives will prevent this discoloration and produce a single-colored brick for face brick. Other additives, or other types of clay or shale, produce colors other than the common "red" brick, as explained before.

## COLOR AND TEXTURE

The color of brick is the function of the material, the curing time, and heat of the kiln burning. Most color is caused by the amount of iron in the mix which is part of the clay dug from the earth. The heat oxidizes the iron to form iron oxide, which is red.

The lighter colors (the "salmon" colors) are the result of underburning. If a higher and longer heat is applied, the brick will be harder; therefore, the lighter-colored, or underburned brick, will generally have less compressive strength and greater water absorption. These are used for decorative purposes as face brick, backed up by other tiers of harder brick. The sides are smooth as the plastic clay is extruded from the die. If the clay is not chemically treated, the brick cut from the extrusions forms the common brick which is the backbone of all brick structures (Fig. 6). While color treatment is accomplished by chemical additives added to the clay and by the control of heat in the kiln, the texture is added after extrusion and before baking. Some deep-textured bricks are made by molding, rather than by extrusion.

Brick textures may be stippled, water or sand struck, or have horizontal or vertical markings or a host of other finishes. Fig. 7 shows two unusual finishes. Fig. 7A is vertically scored after the brick is cut from the extrusion. Fig. 7B looks like natural stone, but is the result of molding brick in special forms.

## STRENGTH AND WATER ABSORPTION

Strength is usually a measure of the compressive strength in lbs. per sq. in. of the flat surface. Compressive strength (and water

(A) Vertical scored.

(B) Molded brick in special forms.

**Fig. 7. Brick texture.**

absorption qualities) is a result of time and temperature in the kiln baking process, as mentioned before. Compressive strength is a serious consideration only when multistory walls of load-bearing types are to be built. Otherwise, the compressive strength of brick is usually more than adequate for normal use.

Most brick throughout the country are made with a compressive strength between 3000 and 7000 psi (lbs. per sq. in.). About 8% of all brick are below and about 25% are above this figure. Water absorption is expressed in percent to total weight, and is the percent of weight increase after the brick is soaked in water for a given period of time. Two soaking methods are used: either 24 hours in distilled water or 5 hours in boiling water. Absorption is based on the following formula:

$$\text{Percentage of absorption} = \frac{100\,(B-A)}{A}$$

where,

A  is the weight of the dry brick,
B  is the weight of the saturated, or wet, brick.

A dry brick is first weighed. It is then soaked in water for 24 hours, or boiled in water for 5 hours. It is weighed again. Substi-

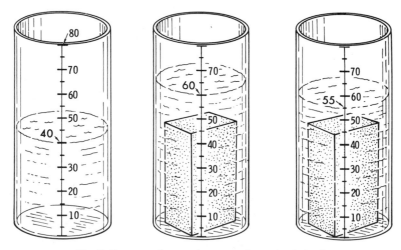

Fig. 8. One way of measuring water absorption in bricks.

tuting in the above formula will give the percent of water absorption.

Another method of measuring water absorption is shown in Fig. 8. A glass cylinder is marked in arbitrary but evenly divided marks on the outside. In the example shown, water is poured into the cylinder to the 40 mark. When a brick is placed in the water, the water may rise to the 60 mark. This means 20 units of water have been displaced. After 24 hours the water may drop to the 55 mark. The 5-division lowering of water means the brick has absorbed 25% of the displaced water.

Compressive strength and water absorption is considerably less important than good workmanship and proper mortar. For example, brick with a high-water absorption figure will soak some of the water out of mortar when laid up, but dampening the brick before using it will overcome this.

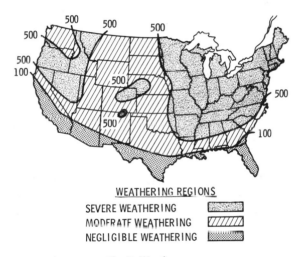

WEATHERING REGIONS
SEVERE WEATHERING
MODERATE WEATHERING
NEGLIGIBLE WEATHERING

Fig. 9. Weather map.

An important factor in providing years of good strength to brick structures is weathering. Freezing and thawing of water caught in the cracks and crevices of brick and openings left due to poor workmanship in the mortar can result in a faster deterioration than any other factor. In addition to good workmanship, brick texture selection and proper mortar pointing is important. Where weathering conditions are bad, deeply textured bricks should be avoided.

Fig. 9 is a weathering index for the United States. It is based on the number of times winter rains may go above or below the freezing temperature of 32°F.

## STANDARD BRICK SIZES

Nominal brick sizes are based on 4″ modules; actual sizes are slightly smaller, to allow for mortar thickness. This is illustrated in Fig. 10. The 4″ squares are the module standard and an "economy" brick is used to illustrate the concept. Generally the nominal size of "economy" brick is 4″ × 4″ × 8″, but its actual size is 3⅝″ × 3⅝″ × 7⅝″. This allows for a ⅜″ mortar thickness on all 3 sides of the brick.

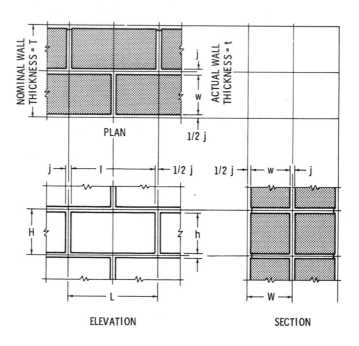

Fig. 10. Illustrating the modular nominal dimensions of standard brick.

The precise actual brick size varies from maker to maker, depending on his ability to control shrinkage during baking. Fairly close tolerances are maintained by most makers and differences are easily adjusted by mortar thickness at the time of use. The most frequently used brick has a nominal size of 4″ × 2⅔″ × 8″ in thickness, height, and length. A three-course high layer consists of three bricks measuring two modules high, or 8″. This size and its weight are handy for one-hand laying up.

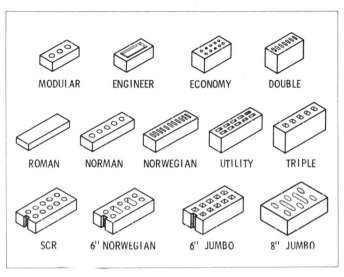

Fig. 11. Brick names indicate sizes as listed in Table 1. The brick may or may not have hollow cores.

Brick sizes are given names to identify their size and shape. Fig. 11 shows the shape of those in popular use. Table 1 lists the sizes of these bricks. These are nominal sizes, rather than actual. Not all of these are available from all brick makers. Since the user is dependent on local suppliers, sizes should be checked before planning any brick structures.

Locally available brick may or may not have hollow cores. The hollow cores do not significantly reduce their strength or water absorption ability. The hollow cores are used primarily to reduce weight, and make life a little easier for the brick mason. Bonding

23

## Table 1. Nominal Brick Sizes

| Unit Designation | Dimensions | | | |
|---|---|---|---|---|
| | Thickness | Height | Length | Modular Coursing |
| Standard Modular | 4″ | 2⅔″ | 8″ | 3C = 8″ |
| Engineer | 4″ | 3⅕″ | 8″ | 5C = 16″ |
| Economy | 4″ | 4″ | 8″ | 1C = 4″ |
| Double | 4″ | 5⅓″ | 8″ | 3C = 16″ |
| Roman | 4″ | 2″ | 12″ | 2C = 4″ |
| Norman | 4″ | 2⅔″ | 12″ | 3C = 8″ |
| Norwegian | 4″ | 3⅕″ | 12″ | 5C = 16″ |
| Utility(1) | 4″ | 4″ | 12″ | 1C = 4″ |
| Triple | 4″ | 5⅓″ | 12″ | 3C = 16″ |
| SCR brick(2) | 6″ | 2⅔″ | 12″ | 3C = 8″ |
| 6″ Norwegian | 6″ | 3⅕″ | 12″ | 5C = 16″ |
| 6″ Jumbo | 6″ | 4″ | 12″ | 1C = 4″ |
| 8″ Jumbo | 8″ | 4″ | 12″ | 1C = 4″ |

(1) Also called Norman Economy, General, and King Norman.
(2) Reg. U.S. Pat. Off., SCPI.

Courtesy of Structural Clay Products Inst.

to the mortar is also improved because more surface is exposed to the mortar. The nominal dimensions of hollow-core load-bearing structural clay tile also follow the 4″ module design. These will be treated at some length in a later chapter.

## ADOBE BRICK

The oldest form of brick is the adobe brick, dating back to 3800 B.C., as mentioned at the beginning of this chapter. It was the principal method of dwelling construction by the Indians of the Southwest and by the first Mexicans settling into the southwest territories, then owned by Spain. It is still in limited use and an attempt is being made to standardize and promote its use in some areas of the San Joaquin Valley of Southern California.

Adobe is made of mud, finely chopped straw, and water. Clay occurs in good percentage in the natural earth of many regions in the Southwest, and forms the bond which holds the materials into a solid brick when dry. There are no large-scale processors of adobe brick which makes the manufacturing of adobe brick a do-it-yourself project. The well-mixed ingredients are placed in molds and are sun-dried until hard.

It has been assumed that an adobe home is cool in the summer and warm in the winter. Tests have shown that it takes a 3 ft. thick adobe wall to equal the insulation qualities of a frame house with 2″ × 4″ construction. Adobe absorbs water easily, unless specially treated, and is a hazard in areas subject to flooding.

Because of their weight (30 lbs. or more per brick) and limited demand, it is not economical to ship adobe brick more than 50 miles, nor to use professional masons for adobe home construction. While there are a few home builders who would be willing to construct adobe homes, what home building remains is confined to areas where the homeowner's "sweat-equity" is in the work he puts into it by making the brick, putting in his own footings, and laying up the brick.

## CHAPTER 2

# Mortar

The weakest part of a brick wall is the mortar used to bond the bricks together. Well-baked brick has tremendous compressive strength and has low water-absorption qualities. Not so with mortar, whose quality depends on the proportions of the ingredients and the workmanship in using it.

## INGREDIENT PROPORTIONS

Mortar is basically concrete and could have all of the durability qualities of concrete as described in the volume on concrete. Fundamentally, the ingredients would be the same, except for one factor, and that is workability. Because mortar is applied to brick, and the brick laid up into a wall by hand, the operation is much slower than pouring concrete. Mortar must be treated to reduce its initial setting time. Because it is troweled to provide a given thickness of mortar joint, and bricks must hold many layers or courses above it without settling down by weight, it must hold a shape. These requirements make mortar different from concrete.

Mortar workability is a function of the amount of hydrated lime used in the mix. Final strength is greatest when there is no hydrated lime. Table 1 shows the relative strength of mortar, varying with the amount of hydrated-lime content and the flow, which is a measure of the water content. The flow after suction is the flow after one minute of contact with the brick—the brick withdrawing some of the water from the mortar. Note the greater strength where the difference between the initial flow and the flow

## Table 1. Compressive and Tensile Strength of Mortars

| Mortar No. and Mix[1] | Initial Flow Percent | Flow After Suction, Percent of Initial Flow | Strength, psi[2] | |
|---|---|---|---|---|
| | | | Tension | Compression |
| 1 | 100 | 87 | 457 | 5492 |
| 1:¼:3 | 120 | 87 | 425 | 5153 |
| | 133 | 87 | 420 | 4830 |
| 2 | 100 | 89 | 300 | 2758 |
| 1:½:4½ | 120 | 88 | 277 | 2408 |
| | 133 | 88 | 268 | 2175 |
| 3 | 100 | 92 | 180 | 1173 |
| 1:1:6 | 120 | 93 | 165 | 905 |
| | 133 | 91 | 145 | 793 |

[1] Proportions: Cement, lime, sand by volume.

[2] Tension specimens, briquets; compression, 2-in. cubes; both cured in water, tested at 28 days.

Courtesy of Structural Clay Products Inst.

## Table 2. Recommended Mortar Mixes

### Proportions by Volume

| Type of service | Cement | Hydrated lime | Mortar sand in damp, loose condition |
|---|---|---|---|
| For ordinary service | 1—masonry cement* or 1—portland cement | — 1 to 1¼ | 2 to 3 4 to 6 |
| Subject to extremely heavy loads, violent winds, earthquakes or severe frost action. Isolated piers. | 1—masonry cement* plus 1—portland cement or 1—portland cement | — 0 to ¼ | 4 to 6 2 to 3 |

*ASTM Specification C91

Courtesy Portland Cement Association

after suction is the least. This points up the importance of using brick with a minimum of water absorption. It is very important to first wet the brick if there is some suspicion the brick has high water-absorption qualities.

27

Masonry cement is portland cement with the necessary additives to improve workability. Masonry cement does not require the addition of hydrated lime. For increased strength, masonry cement may be added to straight portland cement. Table 2 shows the recommended mixes for two general services.

Mortar is also known by type number for specific service needs. The following are the type numbers, the proportions of ingredients recommended, and the services for which they are intended:

**Type M**—1 part portland cement, ¼ part hydrated lime or lime putty, 3 parts sand; or 1 part portland cement, 1 part Type II masonry cement, and 6 parts sand. This mortar is suitable for general use and is recommended specifically for masonry below grade and in contact with the earth, such as foundations, retaining walls, and walks.

**Type S**—1 part portland cement, ½ part hydrated lime or lime putty, 4½ parts sand; or ½ part portland cement, 1 part Type II masonry cement and 4½ parts sand. This mortar is also suitable for general use and is recommended where high resistance to lateral forces is required.

**Type N**—1 part portland cement, 1 part hydrated lime or lime putty, 6 parts sand; or 1 part Type II masonry cement and 3 parts sand. This mortar is suitable for general use in exposed masonry above grade and is recommended specifically for exterior walls subjected to severe exposures as, for example, on the Atlantic seaboard.

**Type O**—1 part portland cement, 2 parts hydrated lime or lime putty, and 9 parts sand; or 1 part Type I or Type II masonry cement and 3 parts sand. This mortar is recommended for load-bearing walls of solid units where the compressive stresses do not exceed 100 lbs. per sq. in. and the masonry will not be subjected to freezing and thawing in the presence of excessive moisture.

The information in Table 3 is based on proportions to 1 cu. ft. of cement, whether regular portland or masonry cement is used. Cement is purchased by the sack, which contains 1 cu. ft.

## Table 3. Quantities of Materials Per Cubic Foot of Mortar

| Mortar mixes | | | | Quantities | | | |
|---|---|---|---|---|---|---|---|
| Cement sack* | Hydrated lime cu. ft. | Sand** cu. ft. | Masonry cement sack | Portland cement sack | Hydrated lime cu. ft. | Sand* cu. ft. |
| 1 Masonry cement | — | 3 | 0.33 | — | — | 0.99 |
| 1 Portland cement | 1 | 6 | — | 0.16 | 0.16 | 0.97 |
| 1 Masonry cement plus 1 Portland cement | — | 6 | 0.16 | 0.16 | — | 0.97 |
| 1 Portland cement | ¼ | 3 | — | 0.29 | 0.07 | 0.86 |

*1 sack masonry cement or portland cement = 1 cu. ft.
**Sand in damp, loose condition.

## SAND

The aggregate (sand) used in mortar should be well-graded and clean. It must not contain any organic material, such as salts, or alkalies. These will weaken the mortar. All sand must pass the ⅛ " square sieve, and be gradually graded from that size down, but not smaller than that which passes the No. 100 sieve. The better the grading of sizes between those two, the better the voids between sand grains will be filled and the lesser the amount of cement that will be needed. It is a matter of economy rather than strength.

## WATER AND PLASTICITY

The lesser the lime content of mortar is, the greater the strength will be; but lime improves workability. The lesser the amount of water used (down to a limit) the greater the strength of the mortar will be, as it is with concrete. But water, too, is important to workability. For this reason, there is no recommended ratio of water to cement, as there is for concrete.

The amount of water in mortar is more a matter of experience than of any rule. Since some water is lost due to absorption by the brick, some allowance is made for this. More important is the effect on the ease with which mortar is applied to brick when a wall or other structure is laid up. The water content must not be so great that the mortar slides off the trowel when picked up, nor oozes off the end of a brick when it is laid up.

If too much water is absorbed by the brick, it will leave too little for proper hydration of the cement, and the mortar will lack strength. A rough test for excessive water absorption in brick is as follows: Sprinkle a few drops of water on the flat side of a brick. If the water is absorbed in less than one minute, absorption is too fast. If this is the case, a hose should be used to water the pile of bricks to the point where water runs off on all sides. However, do not use the brick immediately. They must be dry on the surface before use. Any water you can drink is usually good for use with mortar. Avoid water with alkalies or salt.

## HOW TO MIX

From a time and labor saving standpoint, mixing is best done in a power mixer of the kind used to mix concrete. A revolving drum powered by an electric or gasoline engine is used.

Small quantities may be mixed by hand. A flat board structure or box is used. The board or box must be tight to prevent the loss of water. If built well, it may be used over and over again. A shovel for turning the dry ingredients and a hoe for mixing when water is added, are essential. For either method, mix the dry ingredients first. Turn the ingredients over three or four times until thoroughly mixed. Add water to the dry ingredients until the proper plasticity is obtained. Use a hose or bucket. If mixing is done by hand, make a depression in the center of the dry ingredients. Pour water into the depression. With a hoe, bring the dry ingredients at the edge over into the depression and stir. If more water is needed, make another depression and add more water, as before.

All of the ingredients, including the water, must be thoroughly mixed to a mud-like consistency. Usually, there is enough water when the hoe can be shaken free of mortar mix, but it must not be too wet, as explained before.

## RETEMPERING

Retempering means the adding of water to mortar when it becomes too stiff while in use. Water may be added to keep it plastic if stiffening is due to water evaporation. Mortar that has stiffened because it has begun to set must not be retempered, but must be thrown away and new mortar mixed.

A rule of thumb to decide if stiffening is due to evaporation or hydration is as follows: Mortar beginning to stiffen before 2½ hours at temperatures of 80°F or higher may be retempered. At temperatures of under 80°F, the time may be extended to 3½ hours. Any mortar older than these allowed times should be discarded since it will have begun to set due to hydration, and retempering will only weaken the mix.

## COLORING MORTAR

Masonry cement may be purchased in a number of colors. Since they are premixed under careful control, the color from batch to batch will be consistent. When mixing your own, only mineral colors must be used with white portland cement. The following are the color ranges and how they are obtained:

Pink to red—Red iron oxide
Browns—Brown iron oxide
Yellow to buff—Iron hydroxide
Gray to blue slate—Manganese dioxide, black iron oxide or 1% to 2% carbon black
White—White cement, white sand and white stone.

Mix all dry ingredients first. Mixing must be thorough. When the water is added, stir until there are no streaks visible.

## EPOXY

No mortar is as strong as the bricks which are used. However, where strength is needed, as for load-bearing walls, an additive called epoxy may be purchased. Epoxies, and the amounts to be used, vary with the manufacturer. Your supplier can tell you what to buy and how to use it. Epoxy adds somewhat to the cost of mortar and should be used only where the extra strength is needed. It can make mortar even stronger than the brick used and has tremendous bonding power to the brick.

## CHAPTER 3

# Tools Used

The number of tools used by a brick mason are not numerous nor are they expensive. The essential ones are shown in the sketch

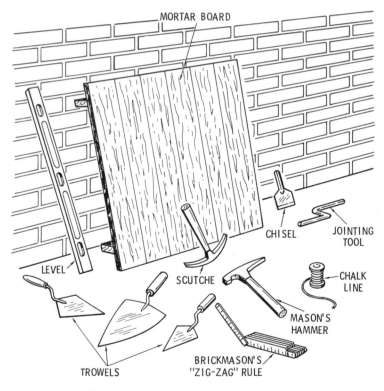

Fig. 1. Principal tools used by the brick mason.

of Fig. 1. In addition to these, some masons carry a hoe and shovel for preparing and handling the mortar, a large carpenter's right angle, other sizes of spirit levels, and jointing tools.

Many contractors will find it a worthwhile investment to purchase a power-driven mixer for the mortar. Contractors for large projects may also invest in a fork lift, or elevator, for carrying brick to a higher level. Generally, the old hod-carrying days using man power to carry brick and mortar on his shoulder up a ladder are practically gone.

## SPIRIT LEVEL

The most important job in laying brick is the first or starter row. To lay a perfectly vertical wall, with true corners, and equal spacing of mortar joints, laying of the corners and first course are most important.

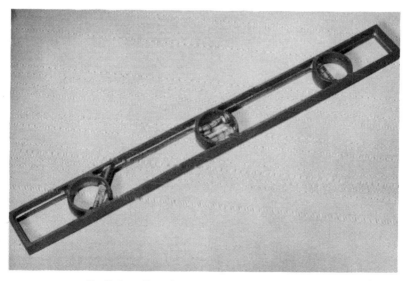

Fig. 2. A medium size magnesium spirit bubble level.

A brick wall starts with two corners raised part way. The distance between corners must be precisely measured, to follow the 4″ module concept. The first course of brick is laid on a bed of mortar over a concrete footing. The spirit level is used to make sure this first course is perfectly horizontal, as it will affect all of the courses above it. Fig. 2 illustrates a magnesium spirit level, with glass bubbles for both horizontal and vertical checking. Included is a 45° bubble for those few occasions where it may be needed. Longer levels may be made of wood, aluminum, or magnesium.

Several courses of each corner are laid and the spirit level used to make sure they are perfectly vertical. A large carpenter's square is used to make sure adjacent sides are square. From that point on, a taut line is used between corners to set the mark for succeeding courses of horizontal brick rows. An occasional check with the spirit level assures that rows are horizontal.

## MEASURING

Essential to a good start is accurate measurement, as explained before. Fig. 3 shows two popular types of measuring devices. One is a folding metal rule, opening to 72″. The other is a 50-ft. tape with a hand rewind.

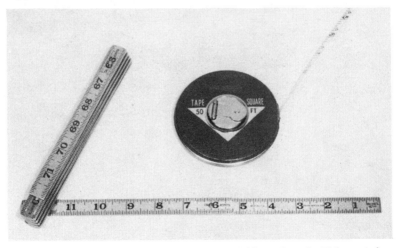

Fig. 3. Two popular measuring tools; the metal folding rule and a 50-ft. rewind measuring tape.

The tape is used to establish the corners based on multiples of the 4″ module. The rule sets the position of the taut line for each course as the wall is laid up. The vertical measurements also follow the module concept, using the standard brick sizes described in the first chapter of this volume. For example, three courses of the standard module brick will lay up a wall 8″ high including the thickness of the mortar.

## T-ANGLE

The adjustable T-angle, shown in Fig. 4, is used to accurately transfer one angle to another. For example, a corner other than 90° may be transferred to another corner to match. The tool has a thumb nut for adjusting the angle to the first corner. Tightening the screw holds the angle for transfer to another corner, either as an identical angle or one that is 180° greater. Thus, a third adjacent wall will come out parallel to the first.

Fig. 4. An adjustable T-angle.

## TAUT LINE

The next, and most used, measuring tool, is the taut line. It is fastened from corner to corner to establish the height of the next course of brick. The best line is made of linen, approximately 84 ft. long (Fig. 5). As shown in Fig. 6, the line is drawn tight from

35

corner to corner, mortar is laid along the lower course of brick, and a new row of brick is pushed or tapped into place to match the line. Fig. 7 shows masons laying in a mortar line, just below the taut line. The next step will be the placement of brick for the next course.

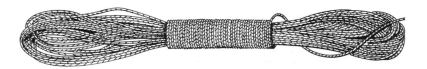

Fig. 5. A good grade of linen taut line is important in accurately laying up a brick wall.

## TROWELS

The large trowel (top of Fig. 8) is the most used tool in the mason's kit. It is in constant use in handling mortar when laying up

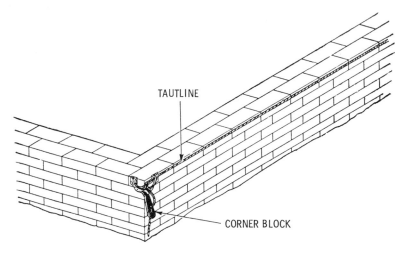

TAUTLINE

CORNER BLOCK

Fig. 6. Illustrating the use of a taut line from corner to corner as a guide for the next row of brick.

a wall. The next smaller size is convenient for buttering the ends of brick when the mason has a helper who does nothing but butter the brick. The smallest size is ideal for tuck pointing which is repairing mortar in an old brick wall. Fig. 9 shows a medium-size trowel, ideal for the do-it-yourself home handyman with only occasional brick work to do.

The large trowel should be the best that money can buy. Being in constant use with abrasive material, it must stand up under long

Fig. 7. Masons laying a mortar line on which a row of brick will be placed even with the taut line.

Fig. 8. Three sizes of trowels.

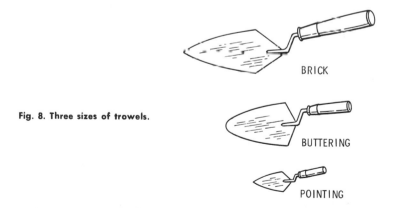

BRICK

BUTTERING

POINTING

periods of use. It is also used by experienced masons to cut brick into smaller sizes by hitting the brick with the edge of the trowel. If it is not made of well-tempered steel, the edges will soon become badly marred. Handles on the trowel are usually wood. The end is used to tap the brick into position, but the tapping is light, and the wood is not badly damaged, even with long use.

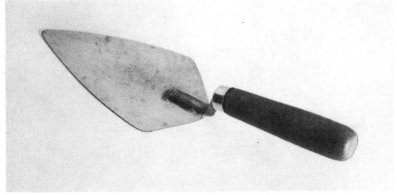

Fig. 9. A small trowel good for home handymen.

## BRICK CUTTERS

The module method of construction reduces the need for placing a short or half brick. Sometimes circumstances require a brick less than the standard size and this is done by cutting. A sharp blow with the edge of a trowel, in the hands of an expert, will break a brick pretty close to the size desired. Hard brick is not easily done this way. Two tools are used for cutting brick.

The mason's hammer (Fig. 10) has a curved chisel-like edge on one side. With practice, one soon learns to cut brick close to the desired size with a few whacks of the chisel side. This side is also used to clean the face or edge of the brick if the break is rough. The chisel side of a mason's hammer is used to knock off old mortar when an old wall is being repaired with new sections.

The other side of the hammer has a square flat side somewhat like a hammer. It is *not* used as a hammer in conjunction with a chisel. A wide-edged chisel (Fig. 11) is the most accurate method for cutting brick, but it should be used with a wood mallet or a

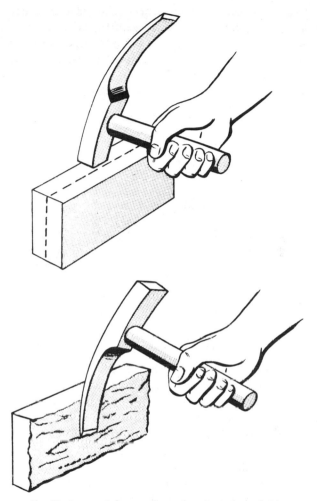

Fig. 10. A mason's hammer is used to cut and trim brick.

hand-sledge type hammer, not the mason's hammer. Often the chisel is used to score a line at the break point and the brick is subsequently broken into two parts with the mason's hammer.

Large contractors use a carbide-toothed power saw to cut brick to the exact size, with square sides, and with greater overall economy than can be done by hand. A brick broken into a piece smaller than its standard size is called a "bat". A half brick is called a half bat. Anything between a half size and full size, but not including full size, is called a three-quarter bat.

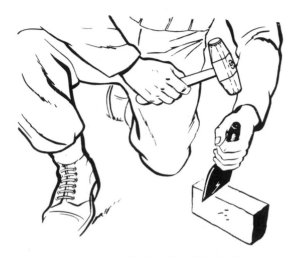

Fig. 11. Scoring brick with a wide chisel.

## THE MORTAR BOARD

Whether mortar is mixed by hand or by a power mixer, quantities of it are carried and placed on a mortar board for use by the mason when laying up a brick wall. Mortar boards are generally wood and are easily homemade.

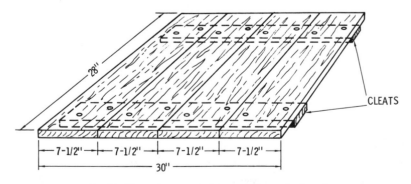

CLEATS

7-1/2"   7-1/2"   7-1/2"   7-1/2"

30"

28"

Fig. 12. Illustrating a typical homemade mortar board.

Sections of 1″ × 8″ wood are cleated together into a board about 28″ × 30″ (Fig. 12). The cross cleats are of the same material. Close-grained, hard wood should be used. It is important that the wood absorb only a minimum amount of water from the

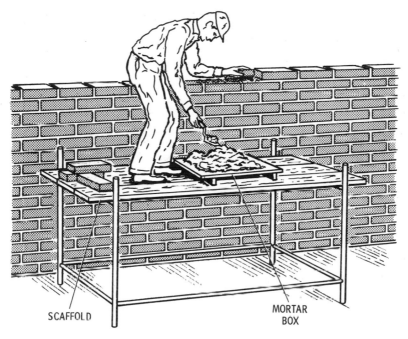

SCAFFOLD             MORTAR BOX

Fig. 13. A small mortar box may be more convenient for some jobs.

mortar, and that there is no leak through the edges of the boards. Plane the edges true or use wood that is not warped. The mortar boards are placed on platforms for easy access to the mason or are constructed with legs. The less the mason needs to bend over, the less tiring the job and the more efficiently he can work.

In confined spaces, the mortar may be contained in a box (Fig. 13) smaller than the regular mortar board. Sides make it possible to hold a fair quantity of mortar. However, a flat board with no sides provides easier access for the mason and there is no waste from mortar caught in corners.

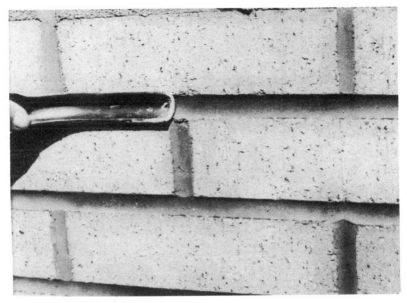

Fig. 14. A jointing tool is used to press the mortar into a tight concave joint.

## JOINTING TOOL

Any curve-faced tool of metal may be used to press the mortar into the joints of brick after the excess has been struck off. Tools are made in various sizes for different joint thicknesses. They are S-shaped and curved on one side. Bent solid round metal rod may also be used but it adds unnecessary weight. Fig. 14 shows a jointing tool used to put a concave joint into brick mortar.

## CHAPTER 4

# Bonding

To bond means to bind or hold together. Bonding is important in brick construction to make a solid and secure structure. There may be three different meanings to the word bond, as it refers to masonry. These are:

**Structural bond.** The interlocking of masonry units by overlapping bricks or by metal ties.

**Pattern bond.** Interlocking and overlapping brick work following a fixed sequence. Pattern bonds for structural purposes have become standardized and are given names. Some pattern bonds are used for appearance purposes only, or combined to provide a special appearance plus structural bonding qualities.

**Mortar bond.** The adhesion of the mortar to the masonry or to steel reinforcement ties placed in the masonry. Mortar alone is not strong enough to provide sufficient bonding for secure structures.

In overlapping brick construction, most building codes require that no less than 4% of the wall surface consist of headers, with the distance between headers no less than 24″ vertically or horizontally. Headers are bricks laid with their longest dimension perpendicular to the front or facing tier of brick, and overlap into the second row or tier behind, for a double-thick wall. Steel ties are finding wider use, with codes requiring at least one tie for each 4½ sq. ft. of surface.

## TERMS APPLIED TO BONDING BRICK

Common names have been applied to the brick depending on their position in the structure. Fig. 1 is a sketch of their names and positions.

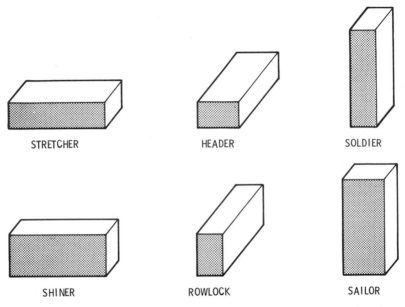

STRETCHER      HEADER      SOLDIER

SHINER      ROWLOCK      SAILOR

Courtesy Structural Clay Products Inst.

**Fig. 1. Bricks are given names, based on their use and position.**

Most wall construction is with *stretchers*. Stretchers are bricks with their largest surface horizontal and longest edge facing out. *Headers* have their smallest dimension facing out and are used to interlock with a wall of brick behind. A *soldier* is a brick standing on its end, and is often used as the top course of a wall, forming a sill for the support of ceiling or roof joists (Fig. 2). When a soldier is placed with its largest face forward, it is often called a *sailor*. A *rowlock* is a header standing on edge. A rowlock with its largest surface facing out is sometimes called a *shiner*. Rowlock placement reduces the number of bricks in a double-thick wall but it is not as strong.

Fig. 2. How soldiers are used for the top course as a sill. Generally its main purpose is decorative.

Fig. 3 illustrates the method used to bond the bricks shown in Fig. 1. Each layer of brick is called a course. Stretchers are laid overlapping and provide the interlock between courses. Rowlocks are placed as stretchers or headers for interlocking. The dimensions are such as to leave a cavity between vertical tiers. Wythe (or withe) is the term generally applied to the grout between brick faces. The grout used is a thinner mortar to permit its flowing completely into every crevice and irregularity of the brick surfaces. The word wythe also refers to the wall between flue cavities of a chimney.

## OVERLAPPING AND THE MODULE CONCEPT

As mentioned in an earlier chapter, nominal brick dimensions are based on the 4″ module concept. The face and long edge are a multiple of 4″, while the thickness is a simple fractional part of 4″ (usually ⅓ of 8″). Actual dimensions are slightly less to allow for mortar thickness. Modular dimensions permit placing brick in

45

## BONDING

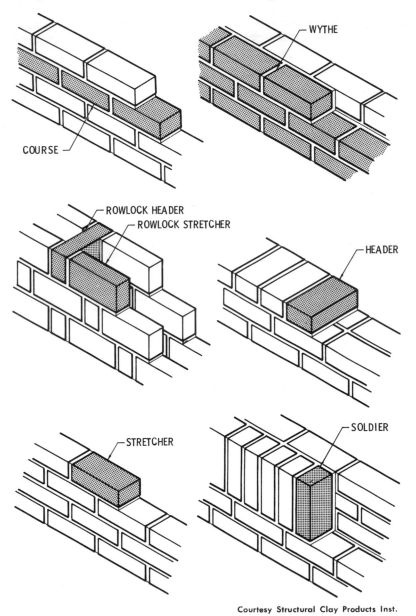

Fig. 3. How various bricks are used in overlap **bonding.**

walls with both stretchers and headers to result in a fixed pattern in appearance, without the need for cutting brick into small pieces, except in a few cases.

Fig. 4 shows how a stretcher is twice the width of a header and, conversely, headers are one-half the width of a stretcher.

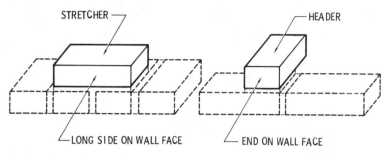

Fig. 4. The nominal length of a brick is just twice that of its width.

## MODULAR LAPPING

Modular dimensions have resulted in standard overlapping techniques, and the expressions of ½ lap, ¾ lap, ¼ lap, and ⅓ lap have developed.

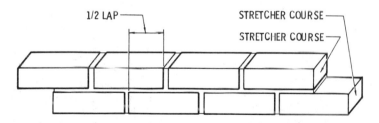

Fig. 5. Showing ½-lap bonding commonly used in stretcher courses.

The most common method of laying brick with stretchers, most used in walls, is the ½-lap method. This is clearly shown in Fig. 5. One-half the brick length in each successive course overlaps ½ the brick length below it. On occasion, for a change of pace in appearance, ⅓ lap is used. One-third of the brick length overlaps ⅔ of the brick below it. However, with each reduction in overlap, the strength of the mortar bonding is reduced. The limit of reduction is no overlap at all, sometimes used for garden walls. To retain strength in such cases, a number of metal ties are used for bonding.

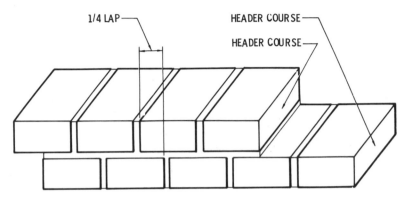

Fig. 6. Best bonding for courses of all headers is the ¼ lap.

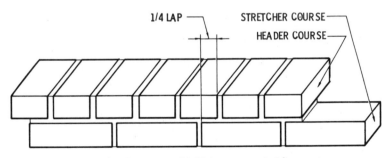

Fig. 7. A header course with ¼ lap over a stretcher course.

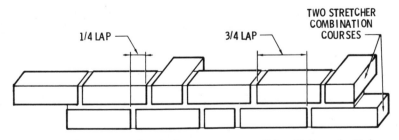

Fig. 8. Headers and stretchers in the same course result in a ¼ lap and a ¾ lap.

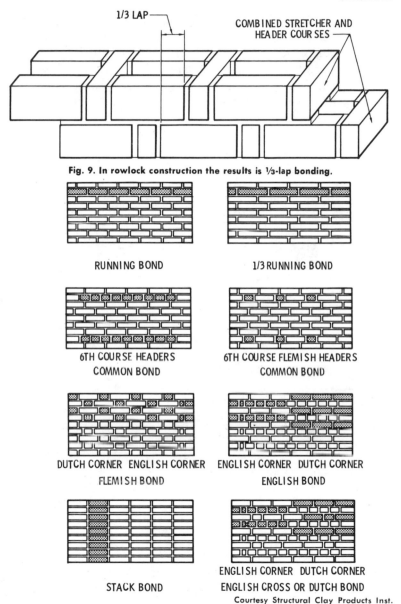

Fig. 9. In rowlock construction the results is ⅓-lap bonding.

RUNNING BOND

1/3 RUNNING BOND

6TH COURSE HEADERS
COMMON BOND

6TH COURSE FLEMISH HEADERS
COMMON BOND

DUTCH CORNER   ENGLISH CORNER
FLEMISH BOND

ENGLISH CORNER   DUTCH CORNER
ENGLISH BOND

STACK BOND

ENGLISH CORNER   DUTCH CORNER
ENGLISH CROSS OR DUTCH BOND

Courtesy Structural Clay Products Inst.

Fig. 10. The most popular bonding pattern in general use.

The use of ¼ lap is usually with headers, or headers and stretch-ers. Fig. 6 shows two courses of headers with ¼ lap. This provides the maximum bonding for the shorter width of headers. The bond-ing is between half widths of headers but the ¼ lap is the width of a stretcher. Fig. 7 shows the ¼ lap used between courses of headers and stretchers. This is the method commonly used for a full course of headers. Where headers alternate with stretchers in the same course, the ¼ lap will look like Fig. 8. Note that headers have a full ½-lap bonding surface with facing stretchers above and below, but stretchers are reduced to ¼-lap and ¾-lap bonding. In rowlock construction, with alternate headers and stretchers, the result is ⅓ lap at all bonding surfaces (Fig. 9).

Fig. 11. Here ⅓-lap running bond is used in a single-tier brick-veneer form.

## STRUCTURAL PATTERN BONDS

When brick is laid with good bonding in mind, a pattern is formed which, when repeated consistently, results in an appearance that is pleasing as well as being strong. This is especially true when header bricks are involved in the structure.

Over the years standard patterns have been established, and each is given a name for identification. About six are in wide general use. They are illustrated in Fig. 10.

**Running Bond.** All brick are laid in ½-lap stretcher bonding, without headers. A variation is the ⅓ running bond, as mentioned before (Fig. 11). Because there are no headers for bonding to a second thickness of brick behind, metal ties must be used between thicknesses. The metal ties allow for an air cavity between sections. The air space provides extra insulation against the transmission of heat through the brick wall. If strength is more important than insulation, the cavity may be filled with concrete. The running bond is also used for homes of brick-veneer construction, which are homes of $2'' \times 4''$ framing and a single layer of facing brick, essentially for appearance. A common method of home construction in some areas is an all-frame home with brick veneer in front and wood or stucco on the other three sides.

**Common or American Bond.** Perhaps the most frequently used bond pattern is the common or American bond. The pattern consists of several courses of stretchers only and headers every 5th, 6th, or 7th course, depending on the needs for structural strength. A continuous course of headers is used. A variation is the Flemish header course in which headers alternate with stretchers.

In the common-bond pattern, each row of headers must start their corners with a ¾ length of brick, to come out even with a symmetrical pattern, on the $4''$ module system. The half-size brick appearing at the ends of some stretcher courses is a full stretcher starting the adjacent wall around the corner.

**Flemish Bond.** This bonding pattern is obtained by using alternate header and stretcher bricks with each header on one course centered with a stretcher in the course below and above. Where the strength of so many headers is not needed, many of the headers shown can be clipped brick or ½-bat size. However, there is no reduction in total brick used and labor can be saved by not clipping the brick.

**English Bond.** This pattern is formed with alternate courses of running stretchers and running headers. As with the Flemish bond, many of the header brick may be clipped if preferred.

**English Cross or Dutch Bond.** Similar to English bond, except the stretchers are spaced so each header faces the middle of a stretcher on one side and a joint between stretchers on the other. The joints form a series of overlapping X's, thus the name English "cross."

**Stack Bond.** Bricks stacked vertically and horizontally with no overlap form a stacked bond. Bonding strength between bricks and to the layer of brick behind is by means of metal straps or ties. This pattern is seldom used for a load-bearing wall, where the extra strength of overlapping is a must. Where stack bond is specified for load-bearing walls, a liberal use of steel reinforcing bars is important. This is also called block pattern.

## CORNERS

Fig. 10 shows two types of corners for the English-, Flemish-, and Dutch-bond patterns. In the Dutch corner, the corners start with a ¾ bat. In the English corners, they start with a ¼ bat. The ¼ bat, however, must never be placed at the corner, but at least 4″ from the corner. These corners allow for proper spacing to make the pattern come out as intended.

## QUOINS

Brick that are cut for use on corners are called *quoins,* a word that is slowly passing out of popular use. Fig. 12 illustrates the various quoin shapes and how they are used. The diagonally clipped, or king quoin, will have the appearance of a ¼ bat visible in the brick face, but the structural strength of a larger size. Fig. 13 shows two methods of making the English corner. With a king closure or quoin, the brick will have the appearance of a ¼-lap brick at the very corner, without the attendant weakness.

Fig. 14 shows the relation of the cut brick to the whole brick. Brick is easily cut by first scoring it with a chisel having one straight side and one beveled side (Fig. 15). After scoring, a whack with the flat of the mason's hammer head will break the brick off even with the scored lines. It takes experience to obtain the precision needed for making clean breaks.

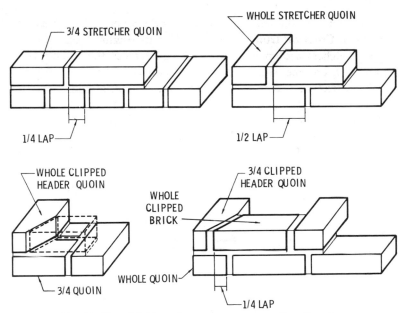

Fig. 12. Clipped brick used at corners are generally call quoins.

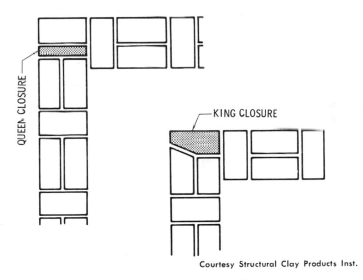

Courtesy Structural Clay Products Inst.

Fig. 13. Two methods of making an English corner.

53

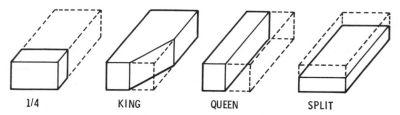

| 1/4 | KING | QUEEN | SPLIT |

Fig. 14. Cut brick used for closures and corners.

## CLOSURES

All brick work starts with the corners. The last brick placed to complete a course is called a *closure* or *closer*. Most often the

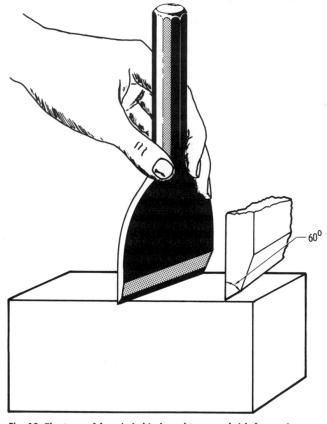

60°

Fig. 15. The type of beveled chisel used to score brick for cutting.

closure is a full stretcher somewhere in the middle of the course. For many structural pattern bonds, closures require cutting brick as described above. Fig. 16 shows some of the frequently used closures, in addition to the full stretcher.

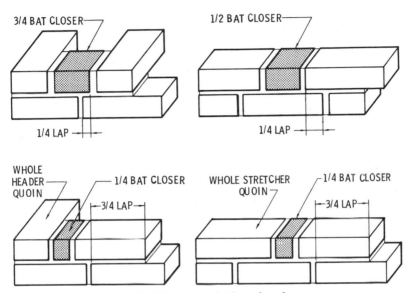

Fig. 16. Variations of cut brick used as closures.

## GARDEN WALL

A variation of the Flemish pattern bond was given the name of garden-wall pattern. If two or more stretchers are used between headers, the back and front of the brick wall will have the identical appearance. An early use of this design was for garden walls. Fig. 17 shows how brick is laid for two-, three-, and four-stretcher garden-wall construction.

Figs. 18 and 19 show two garden-wall patterns with intentional appearance design. Note the free use of ¼-bat closures to make the diagnoal designs come out even. Part of the design results from the use of brick with differing textures and shades of colors. See Chapter 8 for more information on special design patterns.

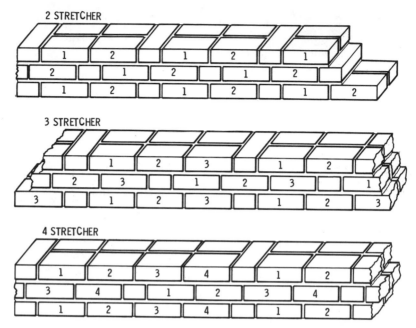

2 STRETCHER

3 STRETCHER

4 STRETCHER

Fig. 17. A variation of the Flemish pattern which is called garden wall. It has the same pattern on each side.

Fig. 18. Garden-wall design emphasizing diagonal lines.

## METAL TIES

There are certain conditions in which the use of header brick for bonding to the rear brick wall section is not appropriate. Metal ties are then used instead of header brick.

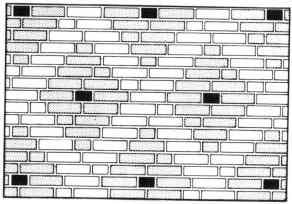

Courtesy Structural Clay Products Inst.

**Fig. 19. A dovetailed garden-wall design.**

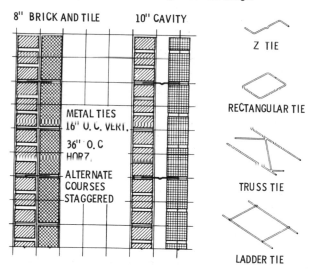

Courtesy Structural Clay Products Inst.

**Fig. 20. Metal ties bonding together two walls. Various metal ties are also shown.**

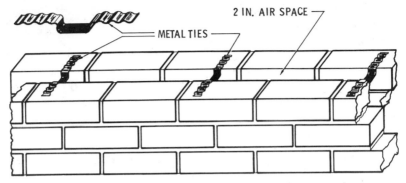

Fig. 21. Metal strap ties between two tiers of brick with an air cavity between.

Fig. 20 illustrates the method of bonding a brick facing wall to a tile backing. Also shown are some of the shapes of metal ties available. While clay tile sizes follow the 4″ module design concept, their larger size eliminates the use of headers for bonding. Metal ties do the job.

Where an air cavity between layers of brick is desired, metal ties provide the best means of bridging across the cavity for bonding. The center illustration of Fig. 20 shows this application with clay tile as the backing wall. Fig. 21 illustrates the use of metal ties in an all-brick wall with a cavity between.

While a flat metal tie is shown in Fig. 20, most ties are formed of round steel reinforcing rods. The diameter of the rods must be small enough to be fully embedded in the mortar. Since metal is subject to possible rust, a careful job of mortar work is necessary to reduce water seepage to an absolute minimum.

## CHAPTER 5

# How To Lay Brick

So far, at least, no automatic method for laying brick has been devised. It is a hand operation and it depends almost entirely on human effort except for the use of power equipment to deliver and place the bulk material and to mix the mortar. For this reason, contractors must require that the bricklayer develop a high degree of skill and efficiency, to make the business a profitable one and the mason's job a secure one.

Years of experience have developed a pattern or technique in handling the trowel and brick that has become most efficient. This chapter will describe that method, as well as other important steps in laying brick. Whether you are a homeowner doing his own work, one mason among many on a job, or the contractor himself, this method will result in the most amount of work done with the least amount of fatigue.

## ESTIMATING NEEDS

Table 1 shows the amount of brick and mortar needed for various areas of brick wall surface and at several common thicknesses. This table is based on ½″ thick mortar which, with the use of standard brick sizes, will result in the 4″ modular dimensions. Since actual brick sizes will vary slightly from processor to processor, it will be necessary to adjust the mortar thickness to achieve the modular dimensions.

## Table 1. Amount of Brick and Mortar needed for Various Wall Sizes

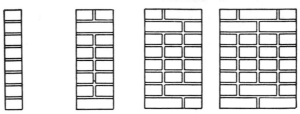

| Area of wall in (sq. ft.) | 4-inch wall | | 8-inch wall | | 12-inch wall | | 16-inch wall | |
|---|---|---|---|---|---|---|---|---|
| | Number of brick | Cubic feet of mortar | Number of brick | Cubic feet of mortar | Number of brick | Cubic feet of mortar | Number of brick | Cubic feet of mortar |
| 1....... | 6.2 | 0.075 | 12.4 | 0.195 | 18.5 | 0.314 | 24.7 | 0.433 |
| 10...... | 62 | 1 | 124 | 2 | 185 | 3½ | 247 | 4½ |
| 20...... | 124 | 2 | 247 | 4 | 370 | 6½ | 493 | 9 |
| 30...... | 185 | 2½ | 370 | 6 | 555 | 9½ | 740 | 13 |
| 40...... | 247 | 3½ | 493 | 8 | 740 | 13 | 986 | 17½ |
| 50.... | 309 | 4 | 617 | 10 | 925 | 16 | 1,233 | 22 |
| 60...... | 370 | 5 | 740 | 12 | 1,109 | 19 | 1,479 | 26 |
| 70...... | 432 | 5½ | 863 | 14 | 1,294 | 22 | 1,725 | 31 |
| 80...... | 493 | 6½ | 986 | 16 | 1,479 | 25 | 1,972 | 35 |
| 90...... | 555 | 7 | 1,109 | 18 | 1,664 | 28 | 2,218 | 39 |
| 100.... | 617 | 8 | 1,233 | 20 | 1,849 | 32 | 2,465 | 44 |
| 200.... | 1,233 | 15 | 2,465 | 39 | 3,697 | 63 | 4,929 | 87 |
| 300.... | 1,849 | 23 | 3,697 | 59 | 5,545 | 94 | 7,393 | 130 |
| 400.... | 2,465 | 30 | 4,929 | 78 | 7,393 | 126 | 9,857 | 173 |
| 500.... | 3,081 | 38 | 6,161 | 98 | 9,241 | 157 | 12,321 | 217 |
| 600.... | 3,697 | 46 | 7,393 | 117 | 11,089 | 189 | 14,786 | 260 |
| 700.... | 4,313 | 53 | 8,625 | 137 | 12,937 | 220 | 17,250 | 303 |
| 800.... | 4,929 | 61 | 9,857 | 156 | 14,786 | 251 | 19,714 | 347 |
| 900.... | 5,545 | 68 | 11,089 | 175 | 16,634 | 283 | 22,178 | 390 |
| 1,000.. | 6,161 | 76 | 12,321 | 195 | 18,482 | 314 | 24,642 | 433 |
| 2,000.. | 12,321 | 151 | 24,642 | 390 | 36,963 | 628 | 49,284 | 866 |
| 3,000.. | 18,482 | 227 | 36,963 | 584 | 55,444 | 942 | 73,926 | 1,299 |
| 4,000.. | 24,642 | 302 | 49,284 | 779 | 73,926 | 1,255 | 98,567 | 1,732 |
| 5,000.. | 30,803 | 377 | 61,605 | 973 | 92,407 | 1,568 | 123,209 | 2,165 |
| 6,000.. | 36,963 | 453 | 73,926 | 1,168 | 110,888 | 1,883 | 147,851 | 2,599 |
| 7,000.. | 43,124 | 528 | 86,247 | 1,363 | 129,370 | 2,197 | 172,493 | 3,032 |
| 8,000.. | 49,284 | 604 | 98,567 | 1,557 | 147,851 | 2,511 | 197,124 | 3,465 |
| 9,000.. | 55,444 | 679 | 110,888 | 1,752 | 166,332 | 2,825 | 221,776 | 3,898 |
| 10,000 | 61,605 | 755 | 123,209 | 1,947 | 184,813 | 3,139 | 246,418 | 4,331 |

Note: Mortar joints are ½" thick

The dimensional volume of brick to mortar is about 7 to 1. A ⅜" mortar thickness would mean a 25% reduction in mortar volume and about a 3% increase in brick numbers for the same

## Table 2. Ratio of Cement, Sand, and Lime
## for Various Mortar Mixes

| Mix by volume, cement-lime-sand | Cement, sacks | Lime, lb. | Sand, cu. yd. |
|---|---|---|---|
| 1—0.05—2 | 13.00 | 26 | 0.96 |
| 1—0.05—3 | 9.00 | 18 | 1.00 |
| 1—0.05—4 | 6.75 | 44 | 1.00 |
| 1—0.10—2 | 13.00 | 52 | .96 |
| 1—0.10—3 | 9.00 | 36 | 1.00 |
| 1—0.10—4 | 6.75 | 27 | 1.00 |
| 1—0.25—2 | 12.70 | 127 | .94 |
| 1—0.25—3 | 9.00 | 90 | 1.00 |
| 1—0.25—4 | 6.75 | 67 | 1.00 |
| 1—0.50—2 | 12.40 | 250 | .92 |
| 1—0.50—3 | 8.80 | 175 | .98 |
| 1—0.50—4 | 6.75 | 135 | 1.00 |
| 1—0.50—5 | 5.40 | 110 | 1.00 |
| 1—1—3 | 8.60 | 345 | .95 |
| 1—1—4 | 6.60 | 270 | .98 |
| 1—1—5 | 5.40 | 210 | 1.00 |
| 1—1—6 | 4.50 | 180 | 1.00 |
| 1—1.5—3 | 8.10 | 485 | .90 |
| 1—1.5—4 | 6.35 | 380 | .94 |
| 1—1.5—5 | 5.30 | 320 | .98 |
| 1—1.5—6 | 4.50 | 270 | 1.00 |
| 1—1.5—7 | 3.85 | 230 | 1.00 |
| 1—1.5—8 | 3.40 | 205 | 1.00 |
| 1—2—4 | 6.10 | 490 | .90 |
| 1—2—5 | 5.10 | 410 | .94 |
| 1—2—6 | 4.40 | 350 | .98 |
| 1—2—7 | 3.85 | 310 | 1.00 |
| 1—2—8 | 3.40 | 270 | 1.00 |
| 1—2—9 | 3.00 | 240 | 1.00 |

area coverage. A ⅝″ mortar thickness calls for a 25% increase in mortar and 3% decrease in brick numbers. If face brick is used on the first thickness of wall and common brick on other tiers, adjust the number of different brick accordingly. Remember to allow for extra face brick depending on how many face-brick headers are to be laid.

Table 2 shows the amount of cement, lime, and sand, to use for batches of a little over 1 cu. yd. of mortar. The lower amounts of lime are to be used when portland masonry cement is used. The higher sand ratios are permitted only if the sand is well graded. Higher volumes of poorly graded sand can only result in a weak mortar with poor bonding qualities.

## SCAFFOLDING

Equally important to the handling of the trowel for reduction of worker fatigue and improved production, are the placement of the material and the amount of physical movement required to lay brick. The mortar board and supply of brick should be immediately behind the bricklayer so he has a minimum amount of steps to take for material. An apprentice should be kept busy supplying the mortar from a mixer and seeing that the brick pile is always supplied.

A brick wall up to about 4 ft. high can be erected with the brick mason standing at ground level. Above 4 ft., it is necessary that he and his material be raised to reduce the amount of reach. Scaffolding for raising the brickmason and his material takes on many forms, from simple to complex. One- or two-man operations on low walls will find a simple wood scaffold sufficient. Contractors with a variety of jobs will make a worthwhile investment in adjustable tubular-metal scaffolding.

Fig. 1 shows the dimensions for making a wood scaffold out of homemade or ready-made saw horses. It is important that the top planks be secured with nails to the trestles, to allow freedom of movement without worry about loose planks. Mortar board and a supply of brick are also kept on the scaffold. The scaffold structure should be no closer than 3″ from the wall, to be sure it does not bear against the wall and push it out of alignment.

Fig. 2 shows a typical tubular-metal scaffold structure. It allows for considerable adjustment of the working platform for a minimum amount of bending and reach. The mason's platform does not bear against the brick wall, as it appears to do in the illustration. It is counterbalanced by the weight of the brick and mortar and needs no front support. This type of scaffolding may be used on multistory structures if brick is laid from the inside. At the finish of the first story of the building, a rough floor is placed and the scaffolding is used on the floor for second-story brick work.

## FOOTINGS

It is important that the weight of brick walls, especially those which carry a load, be supported by a base that will provide an

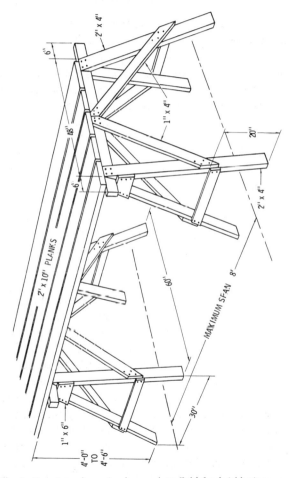

Fig. 1. How to make a simple wood scaffold for bricklaying.

## How To Lay Brick

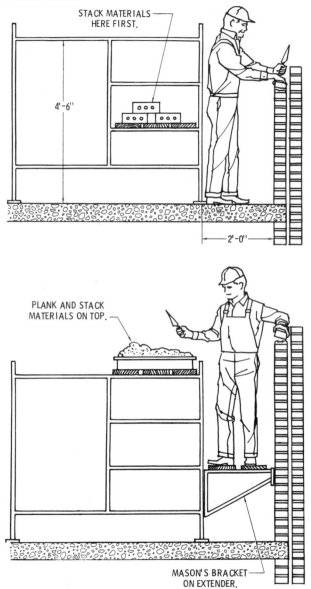

STACK MATERIALS HERE FIRST.

4'-6"

2'-0"

PLANK AND STACK MATERIALS ON TOP.

MASON'S BRACKET ON EXTENDER.

Courtesy Structural Clay Products Inst.

Fig. 2. An adjustable tubular-metal scaffold provides greatest flexibility for material placement and height adjustment.

even distribution of weight. Otherwise, any settling will result in cracks in the mortar.

Although some firm well-packed earth foundations will be sufficient, the usual practice is to pour a concrete foundation in which reinforcing rods have been embedded. The concrete foundation or footing should be twice the width of the wall and have a depth below the frost line. This is particularly important in areas of colder climates, where there is considerable freezing and thawing, which can produce some heaving of the earth. The footing can be poured into a dug trench, with fairly straight sides, with or without forms.

The importance of a perfectly straight and horizontal footing cannot be overemphasized. The footing and the first course of brick will establish the accuracy of a horizontal wall rising course by course above it. After the concrete of the footing has set enough to support the weight of brick above it, usually about seven days, place a line of 1″ thick mortar along it and lay an entire course of brick along the length. Use a spirit level and tap the brick into place to make a perfectly horizontal first course. Thereafter, the taut line method of measuring, described later, will keep the wall going up with horizontal accuracy.

## MIXING THE MORTAR

The structural strength of a brick wall depends more on the ingredients and mixing of the mortar, and the workmanship in applying it, than on the strength of the brick itself. Mortar must have the proper plasticity for easy handling, yet the correct mixture of ingredients for strength over a long period. This was thoroughly covered in Chapter 2.

A large proportion of sand, while economical, will result in weak mortar, unless the sand is well-graded. Since well-graded sand costs more than ordinary sand, it may be just as economical to use less sand and more cement to keep the mortar quality good. Mortar must be constantly mixed fresh. If it is more than two or three hours old, depending on weather, it will begin to take a set and become harder to handle. If the mortar begins to stiffen before that time it is probably due to water evaporation and some water may be added (called retempering). If stiffening is due to hydration, retempering will only result in weak mortar.

## WETTING THE BRICK

Always give brick the sprinkle test before using. It only takes a minute. Sprinkle a few drops of water on a brick. If it is absorbed by the brick within one minute, the brick has too much absorption and should be wetted before using. If left untreated, the brick will absorb water from the mortar leaving less in the mortar for complete hydration.

If wetting is called for, pour water from a hose on the entire pile of brick until the water runs down the sides. Let the water soak in and the surface water evaporate from the faces of the brick before using them.

## PROPER USE OF THE TROWEL

Since the laying of brick is a hand operation, and the trowel is in the bricklayer's hand constantly, there is probably no more important operation in laying up a brick wall than the proper use of the trowel. How it is held in the hand and how it is turned as mortar is applied affects efficiency and fatigue.

The student of bricklaying must first learn how to handle the trowel in picking up, throwing, and spreading mortar. The practical way for the apprentice to acquire this knowledge is to practice on the mortar board during lunch periods and before working hours. In this practice he should learn how to pick up a trowelful of mortar cleanly, and to spread sufficient mortar to lay at last three brick with one trowelful of mortar. Some bricklayers throw, in one operation, enough mortar to lay four or five brick, depending on the thickness of the joint.

In order to use a trowel properly, it should be held firmly, yet loosely, with the full grasp of the right hand and applied with the play of the muscles of the arm, wrist, and fingers. Only actual practice can give the various necessary mechanical movements. Lifting a trowelful of mortar from the tub or mortar board, up to

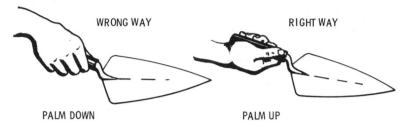

Fig. 3. Wrong and right way of holding a trowel. Note the position of the thumb.

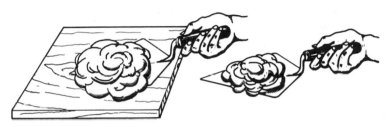

Fig. 4. How mortar is taken from the board. The trowel is always held with the thumb up for easier turning.

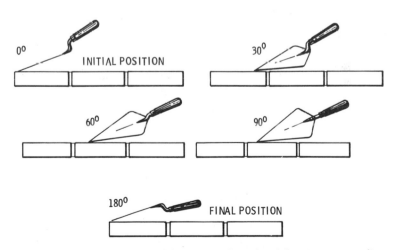

Fig. 5. How the trowel is turned during a single stroke of throwing a mortar line.

67

the courses of brick on the wall and throwing the mortar the length of three or more brick, is done with the muscles of the forearm.

In throwing the mortar, *the trowel is turned through an angle of 180° (that is, turned upside down) while the trowel is being moved the length of three or more brick.* In order to turn the trowel upside down, evidently it must be held as shown in Fig. 3, because the hand, unlike the owl's head, does not work on a pivot and 180° is about the limit it will turn without elevating the elbow. Fig. 4 shows how the mortar is "picked up" from the mortar board preliminary to throwing it on the brick.

In order to fully understand how the bricklayer throws the mortar, the operation is first shown by the diagrams in Fig. 5. Here, only the trowel is shown without hand or mortar so its various positions may be seen as it travels the length of the spread of a three-brick length, and back again to begin the spreading stroke.

## APPLYING THE MORTAR

The placing of the mortar before laying the brick consists of four distinct operations.

1. Throwing
2. Spreading.
3. Cutting off.
4. Buttering end joint.
5. Jointing.

The operation of throwing the mortar results in a rounded column of mortar along the central portion of the brick leaving the outside portions bare, as shown in Fig. 6. In order that the brick shall have a full bed of mortar to lie on so that the load will be distributed over its entire face, the mortar after being thrown should be spread by going over it with the point of the trowel as shown in Fig. 7.

When the operation of spreading the mortar has been perfectly done no cutting off is necessary. If, however, too much mortar was thrown, or too much pressure exerted on the trowel in spreading the mortar, some of it will hang over the side of the brick as shown in Fig. 8. In this case it must be cut off so that it will not

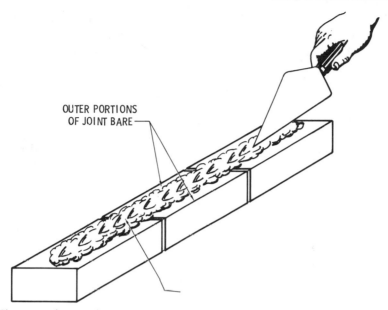

OUTER PORTIONS
OF JOINT BARE

Fig. 6. As the trowel is turned the mortar is spread over the center of a row of three to five bricks.

at any point project over the side of the brick, as shown in Fig. 9. In addition to laying a bed of mortar for the brick to lie on, the end of each brick, when laid, must be covered or "buttered" with mortar so there will be a layer of mortar in the vertical joints as well as in the horizontal joints.

## LAYING THE BRICK

In lifting a brick from the pile on the ground or scaffold, in order to place it on the bed of mortar, the bricklayer grasps the brick in his left hand, as shown in Fig. 10. He butters one end, and in "laying" the brick, first places it on top of the bed of mortar (previously spread) a little in advance (to the right) of its final position as shown in Fig. 11A. He presses the brick into the mortar with a downward slanting motion as indicated by positions M, S, in Fig. 11B, so as to press the mortar up into the end joint. During this operation the brick moves from its initial position M, shown in

69

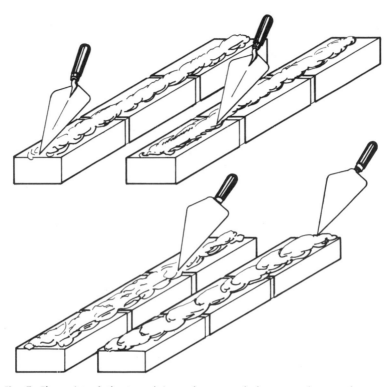

Fig. 7. The point of the trowel is used to spread the center furrow of mortar over most of the brick surface.

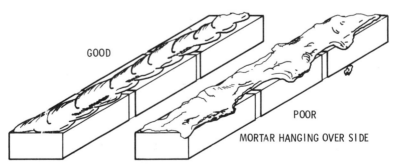

Fig. 8. Good practice is to spread the mortar over the brick surface without any excessive overhang.

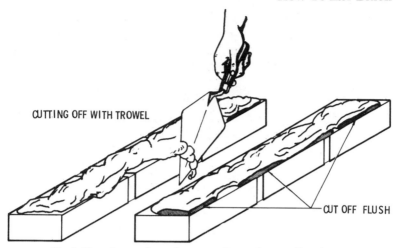

CUTTING OFF WITH TROWEL

CUT OFF FLUSH

Fig. 9. If mortar overhang does occur it must be cut off as shown.

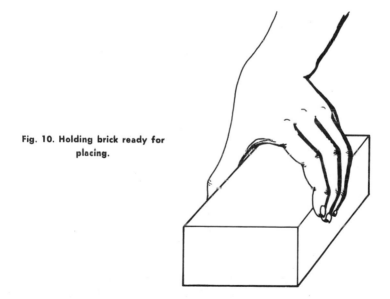

Fig. 10. Holding brick ready for placing.

dotted lines M, (corresponding to the position shown in Fig. 11A) to some intermediate position S, as shown in Fig. 11B.

This is the shoving method of bricklaying, and if the mortar is not too stiff and is thrown into the space between the inner and outer courses of brick with some force, it will completely fill the upper part of the joints not filled by the shoving process. After shoving the brick down and against the mortar in the end joint, it is forced home, or down until it aligns with the brick previously

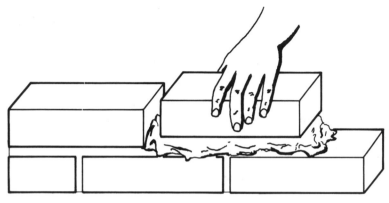

(A) Placing the brick on the wall.

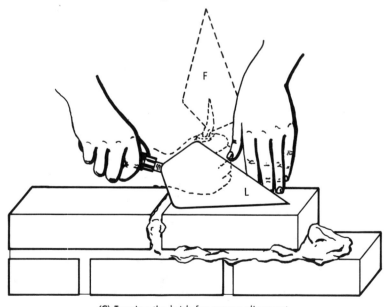

(C) Tapping the brick for proper alignment.

**Fig. 11. Four steps in**

laid by tapping it either with the blade of the trowel, as shown at L (Fig. 11C), or with the handle butt of the trowel in position F, shown in dotted lines. During the operation just described, more or less mortar is squeezed out through the face and end joints as

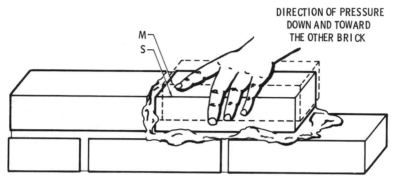

DIRECTION OF PRESSURE
DOWN AND TOWARD
THE OTHER BRICK

M—
S—

(B) Shoving the brick into position.

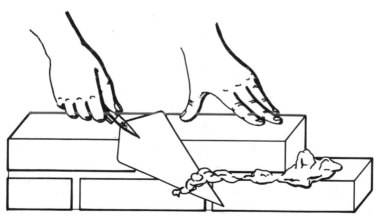

(D) Cutting off excess mortar.

placing a brick into position.

73

shown in Fig. 11D. For appearance and to save mortar it is cut off flush with the trowel. This mortar on the trowel thus cut off should be used for buttering the end of the next brick. It should never be thrown from the trowel back onto the mortar board. When thrown back onto the mortar board, a large portion may daub up the brick instead of landing on the board, and the operation results in an unnecessary motion each time.

Fig. 12 shows the laying of a course of rowlock header brick. At point (A) the largest face of the brick has been buttered and is ready to be shoved into position. At point (B) a closure is placed as the last brick in the course. Both faces are buttered and the brick is shoved down into place. If the measurement of total length and thickness of mortar has been correct, the closure brick should result in the two facing vertical mortar lines being the same thickness as the others in the wall.

## USING THE TAUT LINE

Evidently if no guide is provided and the brick is laid by eye, a true wall surface could not be obtained as some of the brick would be laid too far out and others too far in. In order to guide the bricklayer so that the brick will lay straight, a taut line secured by pins is used, or the equivalent. In order to have supports for the line, a corner of the wall is first built up several courses, and then a lead or support is placed at some point along the course.

The line is made fast around the end or corner, stretched taut and wound around a brick on the lead, as shown in Fig. 13. This is better than using a nail or pins because if the latter pulls loose, the nail may hit a bricklayer in the eye, resulting in injury to or loss of his eye.

The line should be placed 1/32″ outside the top edge of the brick and exactly level with it. In order to hold the line at 1/32″ distance outside the top edge, make two distance pieces out of cardboard, or preferably tin, shaped and attached to the line as shown in Fig. 14. The reason for this offsetting of the line is that the brick should be laid without touching the line—the 1/32″ marginal distance being gauged by the eye.

Obviously, if the brick are laid so that they touch the line, the

(A) Buttering the wide part of the brick.

(B) Placing the closure or last brick in place.

**Fig. 12. Rowlock leader brick placement.**

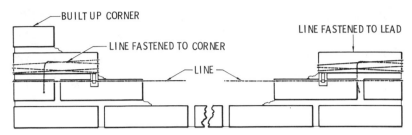

Fig. 13. With corners built up, a line is drawn taut to establish a level for each course of brick.

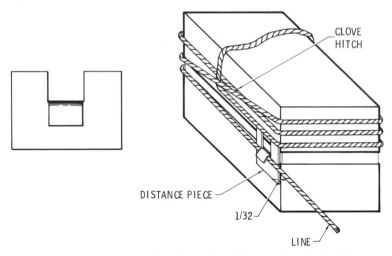

Fig. 14. A spacer made to hold the taut line ⅟₃₂″ away from the brick face.

latter would be shoved out of place resulting in irregularities in the wall. Hence, see that no brick touches the line. The tendency of inexperienced bricklayers is to "crowd the line" or as it is called laying brick *strong* on the line. This effort to work with precision does not accomplish the desired result for the reason just given.

The student who works with precision will not be satisfied with the instruction to set the line level with the top face of the brick. He

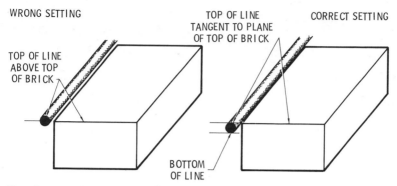

WRONG SETTING

TOP OF LINE
TANGENT TO PLANE
OF TOP OF BRICK

CORRECT SETTING

TOP OF LINE
ABOVE TOP
OF BRICK

BOTTOM
OF LINE

Fig. 15. Correctly set the line ⅟₃₂″ out from the edge of the brick and the top surface even with the top of the brick.

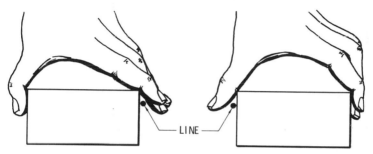

LINE

Fig. 16. Placing the brick into position without disturbing the line.

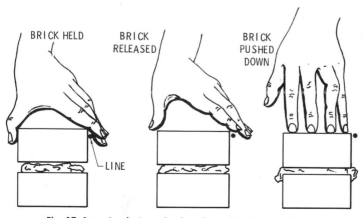

BRICK HELD

BRICK
RELEASED

BRICK
PUSHED
DOWN

LINE

Fig. 17. Steps in placing a brick without disturbing the line.

77

(A) The brick is placed and shoved to the right aligning it with the string.

(B) A closure brick put into place.

Fig. 18. Brick place-

will want to know whether the top or bottom of the line should be level with the top of the brick, especially if it is a thick line. Of course, bricklaying is not a machinist's job and one is not expected to work with machinist's precision, however, precision methods cannot be criticised when they can be used without any extra effort or loss of time. Fig. 15 shows the wrong and right ways to set the line when precision is considered.

A skillful bricklayer *will never touch the line even in applying the mortar or laying the brick.* There are two ways of holding the brick, as shown in Fig. 16, so the line will not be disturbed. It should be understood that even the fingers must not touch the line —otherwise it will be pushed out of place while other workmen are using it as a guide. The method of laying the brick without touching the line is shown in Fig. 17. Of course, practice is necessary

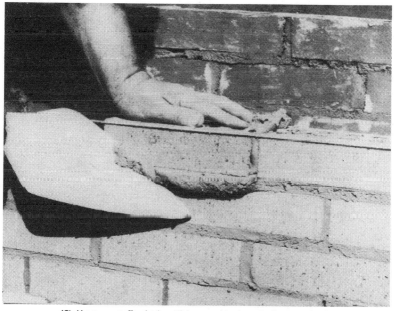

(C) Mortar cutoff which will be used to butter the next brick.

ment and mortar cutoff.

(A) Mortar is layed over several bricks.

(B) Bricks in place and aligned.

Courtesy Structural Clay Products Inst.

Fig. 19. Laying the rear tier of

to do this successfully. The student should practice before laying to the line so that he will acquire the habit of bringing his thumb and fingers up as the brick goes down near the line.

Fig. 18 shows the laying and cutting off of the front tier of a wall. At point (A), the end of a brick has been buttered, placed in position, and shoved toward the brick already in position, to the correct vertical mortar-joint thickness. If the mortar is plastic enough, the pressure of the hand on the brick will align it with the taut string. At point (B), a closure brick is placed and pressed down to the level of the line. Point (C) shows a brickmason cutting off the squeezed out mortar. With experience this can be done without touching the line.

In Fig. 19, a second layer of brick, with a shallow cavity between, is laid and mortar cut off. At point (A), the line of mortar is thrown and readied for a few bricks of a course. At point (B), the bricks are in place, properly aligned to the string. The only difference between the two series of illustrations is the final cutting off

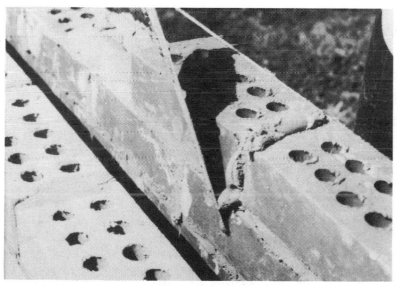

(C) Mortar cutoff is downward allowing excess to drop into cavity.

brick with a cavity between.

(A) With a line in place, mortar is thrown across several bricks.

(B) A ½-bat header is being tapped into place.

**Fig. 20. Laying up a**

of excess mortar. With a shallow cavity, cutting off excess mortar upward is difficult because of the small amount of room. It is more economical to cut off downward and let the excess mortar fall into the cavity, as shown at point (C).

The three illustrations in Fig. 20 show a tier of bricks being laid up for the front of a frame home. Because only one tier is used, this is called brick-veneer construction. At point (A), the taut line is in place and a layer of mortar is being thrown across between two halves of a course, with a few brick in place near the center. Two brickmasons will be working one at each half of the course. At point (B), one mason is working on the short course around the corner. He is tapping a ½-bat, with header end showing, into place, with the constant use of a spirit level. Note the vertical board temporarily nailed into place. This board has been carefully aligned with a vertical level and serves as the guide for the corner. At point (C), the closure brick has been placed and excess mortar has been cut off. The line will now be moved up (⅔ of 4″ for modular brick), checked for horizontal accuracy, and the next course laid.

(C) A closure brick has been placed to complete one course.

brick-veneer wall.

Fig. 21. Using a pointing tool to press mortar into the joints.

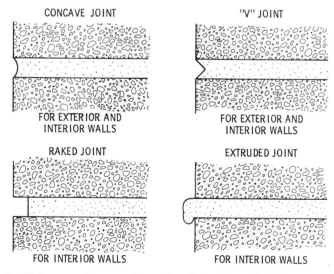

CONCAVE JOINT

"V" JOINT

FOR EXTERIOR AND
INTERIOR WALLS

FOR EXTERIOR AND
INTERIOR WALLS

RAKED JOINT

EXTRUDED JOINT

FOR INTERIOR WALLS

FOR INTERIOR WALLS

Fig. 22. Four popular mortar joints. The raked and extruded joints are not
recommended for exterior walls in cold climates.

## TOOLING THE JOINTS

Tooling consists of compressing the squeezed out mortar of the joints back tight into the joints and taking off the excess mortar. The tool should be wider than the joint itself. Jointing tools are available in a number of sizes and shapes. They are generally made of pressed sheet steel or solid tool steel, S-shaped, and are convex, concave, or V-shaped. The convex side is pressed against the mortar.

By pressing the tool against the mortar you will make a concave joint—a common joint but one of the best. Tooling not only affects appearance but it makes the joint watertight which is the most important function. It helps to compact and fill voids in the mortar. Fig. 21 shows concave-joint tooling.

## TYPES OF JOINTS

The concave and V-joints are the best for most areas. Fig. 22 shows four popular joints. While the raked and the extruded styles are recommended for interior walls only, they may be used outdoors in warm climates where rains and freezing weather are at a minimum. In climates where freezing can take place, it is important that no joint permits water to collect.

In areas where the raked joint can be used, you may find it looks handsome with slump style brick. The sun casts dramatic shadows on this type of construction.

## CHAPTER 6

# Wall Types, Thickness, and Anchoring

Brick construction is used for many purposes, but, by far, the greatest use is in wall construction. Brick features great strength, fire resistance, and good insulation.

Chapter 1 includes information on the compressive strength of brick. Because of this strength, for years multistory structures were made of all brick with the brick carrying the loads of upper floors and their contents.

Perhaps the best example of all brick construction is the Monadnock Building, in Chicago, which was built in 1893 and still stands. Six-foot thick walls at the bottom are tapered to 12″ walls in the top floor. However, with the advent of the modern skyscraper, steel skeletons carry the loads and brick or other types of walls are used on the outside as well as for interior purposes. As a result of the popularity of skeleton construction, solid brick buildings have been specified only for buildings of three- or four-story heights and less. Claims are made for the space-saving factors in steel skeleton design, but the loss of better insulation afforded by brick has been somewhat overlooked.

In recent years, engineers in Europe have developed brick-wall designs of only 6″ thickness capable of carrying the loads of buildings up to 16 stories in height. This design is beginning to show up in buildings in the United States. Fig. 1 shows the design used to

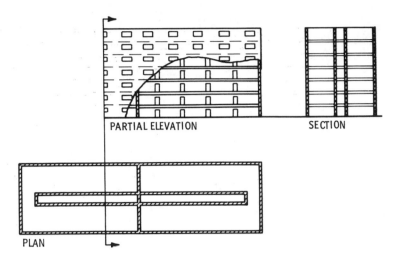

PARTIAL ELEVATION        SECTION

PLAN

**Fig. 1. Design for longitudinal bearing walls offering high strength. A 6" wall can bear the load of a 16-story building.**

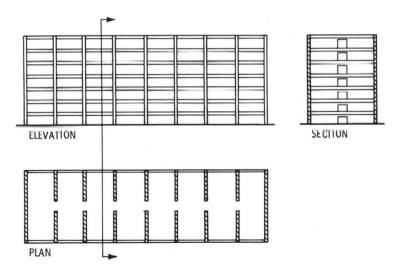

ELEVATION        SECTION

PLAN

**Fig. 2. Design for high-strength transverse bearing walls.**

provide good longitudinal strength. Fig. 2 shows the method for achieving good transverse strength. In actual practice, both methods are combined.

## TYPES OF BRICK WALLS

There are three basic types of walls in common use. These are the *veneer* wall, which is one tier of brick and does not carry a load, used only as a facing on frame homes. The *solid* brick wall is from 8″ to 24″ thick, depending on the load they may carry. The *cavity* wall includes an air cavity between the first tier of brick and succeeding tiers of different thicknesses. Cavity walls may consist of brick in all tiers or a combination of brick and hollow clay tile.

## VENEER WALLS

A typical home with a brick-veneer facing is of frame construction, using 2″ × 4″ wall studding. Ceiling joists and roof rafters are supported on the sills over the 2″ × 4″ walls. The brick facing provides superior insulation and better appearance. The wide choice of brick textures and colors, and the beautiful patterns used in brick overlap, make it the most varied of home finishes. Many homes now use one or more interior walls of brick, especially the wall on which a fireplace is located.

There are two generally accepted methods of placing a brick veneer wall against the frame construction of a home. These are shown in Fig. 3. The most frequently used method is to space the brick tier away from the sheathing on the frame studs. About a 1″ air space is the usual practice. The brick wall is secured to the frame by corrugated metal tabs. There should be a metal tie for each 2 sq. ft. of wall area. The other method is the use of a paper-backed wire mesh against the studs, instead of sheathing. The brick is grouted right up against the wire mesh. A special grout or the regular mortar may be used.

Fig. 4 is a cutaway view of brick veneer with the metal ties plainly shown. Fig. 5 is a side view. The ties should be corrosion-resistant, and should be placed with a slight slope downward to

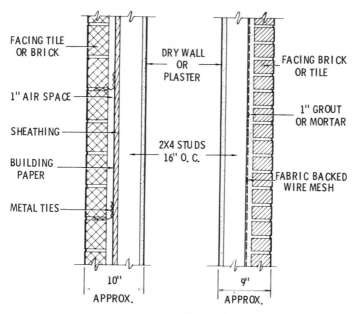

FACING TILE OR BRICK

DRY WALL OR PLASTER

FACING BRICK OR TILE

1" AIR SPACE

SHEATHING

1" GROUT OR MORTAR

BUILDING PAPER

2X4 STUDS 16" O. C.

METAL TIES

FABRIC BACKED WIRE MESH

10" APPROX.

9" APPROX.

Courtesy Structural Clay Products Inst.

Fig. 3. Two methods for placing brick veneer on a frame home.

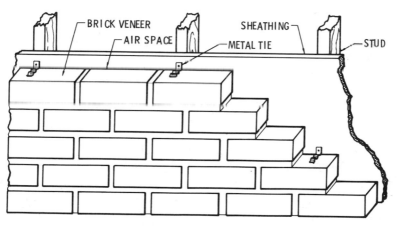

BRICK VENEER

AIR SPACE

SHEATHING

METAL TIE

STUD

Courtesy Structural Clay Products Inst.

Fig. 4. Illustrating metal tabs securing the brick to the sheathing.

89

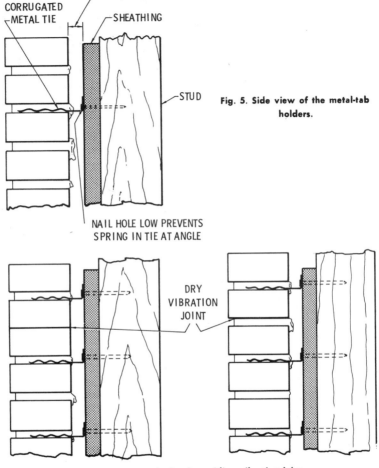

Fig. 5. Side view of the metal-tab holders.

Fig. 6. Two methods of providing vibration joins.

the brick, to allow any moisture that may be collected to run down toward the front and away from the sheathing.

Extremely important to the use of a brick veneer facing on a frame is the sturdiness of the frame structure, with the least possible give to the pressures of wind or snow load. There is little elasticity to brick and any pressure from a change in position of the frame can cause serious cracks in the mortar. If there is any suspi-

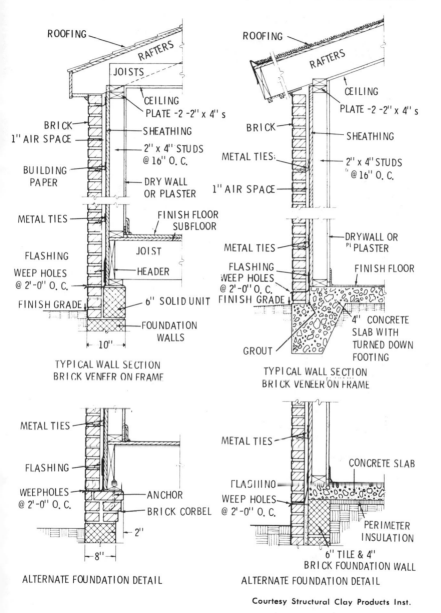

**ROOFING**

**RAFTERS**

**JOISTS**

**CEILING**

**PLATE -2 -2" x 4" s**

**BRICK**
**1" AIR SPACE**

**SHEATHING**

**2" x 4" STUDS @ 16" O. C.**

**BUILDING PAPER**

**DRY WALL OR PLASTER**

**FINISH FLOOR**
**SUBFLOOR**

**METAL TIES**

**JOIST**

**FLASHING**

**HEADER**

**WEEP HOLES @ 2'-0" O. C.**

**FINISH GRADE**

**6" SOLID UNIT**

**FOUNDATION WALLS**

**10"**

**TYPICAL WALL SECTION BRICK VENEER ON FRAME**

**ROOFING**

**RAFTERS**

**CEILING**

**PLATE -2 -2" x 4" s**

**BRICK**

**METAL TIES**

**SHEATHING**

**2" x 4" STUDS @ 16" O. C.**

**1" AIR SPACE**

**DRYWALL OR PLASTER**

**METAL TIES**

**FINISH FLOOR**

**FLASHING**
**WEEP HOLES @ 2'-0" O. C.**

**FINISH GRADE**

**4" CONCRETE SLAB WITH TURNED DOWN FOOTING**

**GROUT**

**TYPICAL WALL SECTION BRICK VENEER ON FRAME**

**METAL TIES**

**FLASHING**

**WEEPHOLES @ 2'-0" O. C.**

**ANCHOR**

**BRICK CORBEL**

**2"**

**8"**

**ALTERNATE FOUNDATION DETAIL**

**METAL TIES**

**CONCRETE SLAB**

**FLASHING**

**WEEP HOLES @ 2'-0" O. C.**

**PERIMETER INSULATION**

**6" TILE & 4" BRICK FOUNDATION WALL**

**ALTERNATE FOUNDATION DETAIL**

Courtesy Structural Clay Products Inst.

**Fig. 7. Details for employing brick veneer.**

91

Fig. 8. Weep holes at the bottom of a brick-veneer wall.

cion that there may be frame shift or vibration, sheer points should be included in the brick as it is laid up. Fig. 6 shows two methods of providing vibration joints if considered necessary. One method is to omit the mortar from one course of brick, so there is no bond between the two courses. To maintain uniform patterns, a mortar line is laid on one course and allowed to set before the next course is laid. Extra ties must be used, if this method is employed.

Fig. 7 shows two methods for handling the details in laying up a brick veneer wall. One method is for homes with raised floors—those with crawl space or basement. The other is for homes constructed on a concrete slab. Alternate foundations are also shown. A feature of brick veneer construction is the excellent barrier formed against the passage of moisture from the outside. Moisture which may get through the brick will flow down the air space, instead of passing through the frame construction. This calls for an outlet for the moisture in the form of weep holes at the bottom of the brick. Fig. 8 illustrates a typical weep hole. It consists of leaving the mortar out of the vertical joints of the bottom course about every 2 ft.

92

## SOLID BRICK WALLS

Solid brick walls are in common use in one- and two-story homes and two- and three-story apartment buildings. Floor and roof loads are borne principally by the outer walls, and to some extent by the inner room walls, usually made of 2″ × 4″ framing. Typical wall thicknesses are 8″ and 12″ and typical bonding patterns are those shown in Fig. 9. As mentioned, there has been some return to solid brick walls for multistory buildings. The best known example is a 20-story apartment building in Denver, Colorado.

8″ FLEMISH BOND            12″ ENGLISH BOND

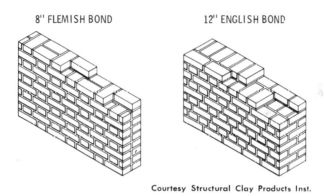

Courtesy Structural Clay Products Inst.

**Fig. 9. Typical bonding patterns for 8″ and 12″ walls.**

The thickness of walls for a multistory building will depend on the load they must bear. This will vary not only by the number of stories in the building but by the intended use. For example, industrial buildings may include floors for heavy machinery. The design of walls for heavy loads is quite involved and is determined by engineers and architects. The engineering involved is beyond the scope of this book but it is important that the apprentice bricklayer knows about the patterns used in laying thick walls since he may be called upon to construct them.

SCPI, as an engineering and educational institute, is recommending the following for standardizing on codes for structures with brick walls:

**Wall Thickness**—The minimum requirements, in building codes, for wall thickness, height, and length, are based on results of tests

93

and the performance of existing structures. The requirements will give satisfactory performance under average conditions of exposure and loading. These requirements are very lengthy and detailed, since they must establish relationships between wall thicknesses and loads, heights, degree of lateral support, bonds and the many wall types ranging from solid to veneered. Again, for purposes of demonstration only, typical building code sections for masonry walls have been quoted.

> **General:** The minimum thickness of all masonry bearing or non-bearing walls shall be sufficient to resist or withstand all vertical or horizontal loads and the fire resistance requirement of any local code.
>
> **Thickness of Bearing Walls:** The minimum thickness of masonry bearing walls shall be at least 12" in thickness for the uppermost 35 ft. of their height and shall be increased 4" in thickness for each successive 35 ft. or fraction thereof measured downward from the top of the wall.
>
> **Exceptions:**
>
> 1. Stiffened Walls: Where solid masonry bearing walls are stiffened at distances not greater than 12 ft. apart by masonry cross walls or by reinforced concrete floors, they may be of 12" thickness for the uppermost 70 ft. measured downward from the top of the wall, and shall be increased 4" in thickness for each successive 70 ft. or fraction thereof.
> 2. Top-Story Walls: The top-story bearing wall of a building not exceeding 35 ft. in height may be of 8" thickness, provided it is not over 12 ft. in height and the roof construction imparts no lateral thrust to the walls.
> 3. One-Story Walls: The walls of a one-story building may be not less than 6" in thickness, provided the masonry units meet the minimum compressive strength requirement of 2500 psi for the gross area and that the masonry be laid in Type M, S or N mortar.
> 4. Walls of Residence Buildings: In residence buildings not more than three stories in height, walls, other than coursed or rough or random rubble stone walls, may be of 8" thickness when not over 35 ft. in height. Such walls in one-story residence buildings or private garages may conform to exception 3.
> 5. Penthouses and Roof Structures: Masonry walls above roof level, 12 ft. or less in height, enclosing stairways, machinery rooms, shafts or penthouses, may be of 8" thickness and may be considered as neither increasing the height nor requir-

ing any increase in the thickness of the wall below.

6. **Walls of Plain Concrete:** Plain concrete walls may be 2" less in thickness than required otherwise in this section, but not less than 8", except that they may be 6" in thickness when meeting the provisions of exception 3.

7. **Cavity Walls:** Cavity walls and hollow walls of masonry units shall not exceed 35 ft. in height, except that 10" cavity walls shall not exceed 25 ft. in height above the supports of such walls. The facing and backing of cavity walls shall each have a nominal thickness of at least 4" and the cavity shall be not less than 2" (actual) nor more than 3" in width.

8. **Composite or Faced Walls:** Neither the height of faced (composite) walls nor the distance between lateral supports shall exceed that prescribed for the masonry of either of the types forming the facing or the backing.

**Thickness of Non-Bearing Walls:**

1. **Exterior Non-Bearing Walls:** Non-bearing exterior masonry walls may be 4" less in thickness than required for bearing walls, but the thickness shall not be less than 8", except where 6" walls are specifically permitted.

2. **Exterior Panel, Apron, or Spandrel Walls:** Panel, apron, or spandrel walls that do not exceed 13 ft. in height above their support shall not be limited in thickness, provided they meet the first resistive requirements of the code and are so anchored to the structural frame as to insure adequate lateral support and resistance to wind or other lateral forces.

Fig. 10 shows wall thicknesses based on number of brick lengths or widths. The thing to note is how the wall thicknesses fit the 4" module system. Fig. 1 shows the various combinations of brick that may be used to make these thicknesses.

Mason contractors for residential dwellings should be acquainted with the building codes in their city. Minimum wall requirements vary somewhat from city to city. The approximate requirements are about as follows:

**Eight Inch Walls**—It is claimed that a thickness of 8" for brick walls of the usual home is ample yet there are numerous cities which do not allow walls under 12" thick. Some cities allow an 8" wall for both stories of a two-story house and many thousands of dwellings have been constructed in these cities with 8" walls. Further, no city that has adopted the 8" wall has changed back to the 12" walls.

THICKNESS MULTIPLE OF 4

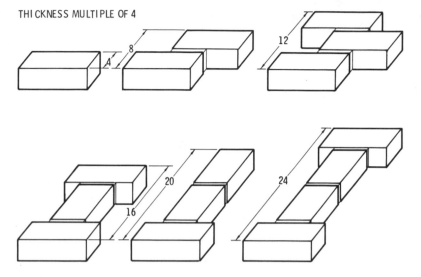

Fig. 10. Illustrating wall thickness based on 4" module system of brick sizes.

The discriminating, however, who wish first class construction will insist on 12" walls. Some cities require 16" walls. The brick arrangement for 8" walls in the various bonds is shown in Fig. 12.

**Twelve-Inch Walls**—For ordinary dwellings, an objection to 12" walls is the extra space taken up as compared with 8" walls; the excess thickness reduces the area of the rooms in the house, which, in cities where land is very valuable must be taken into consideration. For a house 20 ft. × 30 ft., approximately 31 sq. ft. of area is lost on each story, an area equal to a small bathroom or several good closets.

The extra thickness of the 12" walls, however, insulates a house better against cold or heat resulting in a warmer house in the winter and a cooler house in the summer. See Fig. 13 for brick arrangements in the various bonds.

**Sixteen Inch to Twenty-four Inch Walls**—For heavy duty, as in factory construction where the walls have to carry heavy loads of machinery and are subjected to more or less vibration, the walls may be 16" to 24" or more in thickness depending on conditions.

96

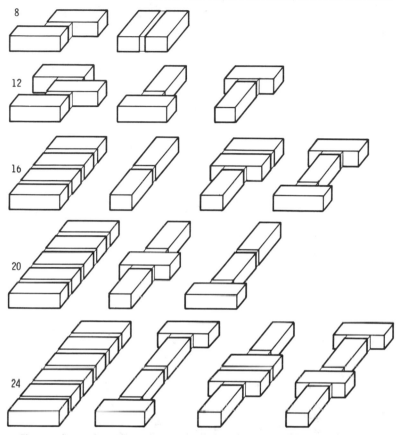

**Fig. 11.** The combination in which brick may be laid for various wall thicknesses.

The arrangement of the brick is more complicated for these thick walls and the accompanying illustrations have been prepared with progressively extended courses like steps so that the brick arrangement in each course can be clearly seen. These details for 16″ to 24″ walls are shown in Figs. 14, 15, and 16.

The widest use of brick for interior walls has been in industrial plants. Brick has low heat conduction and high fire resistance, making it ideal for fire walls. Industrial fire walls of brick are partions and usually are not load-bearing. A 4″ thick wall is considered ample and construction is ½-lap running bond. They are not

97

left free-standing but are bonded at the ends to adjacent perpendicular walls and to the ceiling above.

Partition walls of brick have many other applications, as well. They may be load-bearing, sharing in the load of floors above. They may be needed for reducing sound transfer from one work area to another. Where interior walls may be subjected to bumping by heavy equipment, the strength of a thick solid brick wall cannot be equalled.

Hollow clay tile is frequently used for interior walls. They may even be combined with solid brick. Although larger in size than brick, they follow the 4″ module size system. See Chapter 10 for details on structural clay tile. Brick or clay tile may be left unfinished or may be plastered.

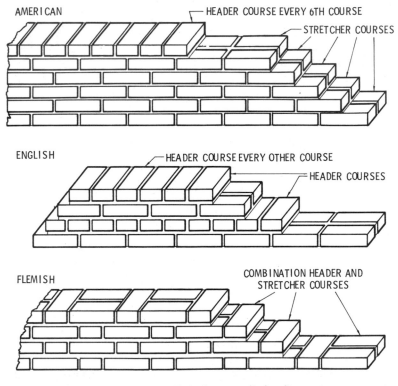

Fig. 12. Illustrating 8″ walls in three popular bonding patterns.

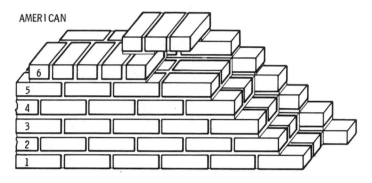

AMERICAN

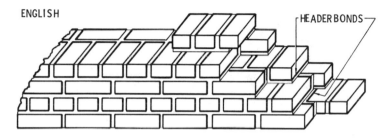

ENGLISH

HEADER BONDS

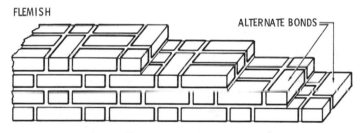

FLEMISH

ALTERNATE BONDS

Fig. 13. Illustrating 12" wall-bonding patterns.

Fig. 17 illustrates a number of typical interior brick and clay tile walls.

## CAVITY WALLS

Brick walls are not entirely impervious to the seepage of water. The need to protect against water entrance through a wall becomes

99

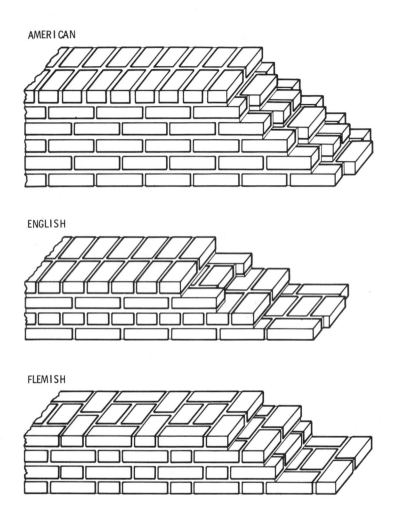

Fig. 14. A 16" wall-bonding pattern.

important in areas of high wind, coupled with heavy rainfalls. The two maps in Fig. 18 show the possible wind velocities and annual rainfall in various areas of the United States. The need to protect against water seepage through brick walls becomes greatest in those areas which combine both high winds and heavy rains, such as along the East and Gulf Coasts and nearly all of Florida.

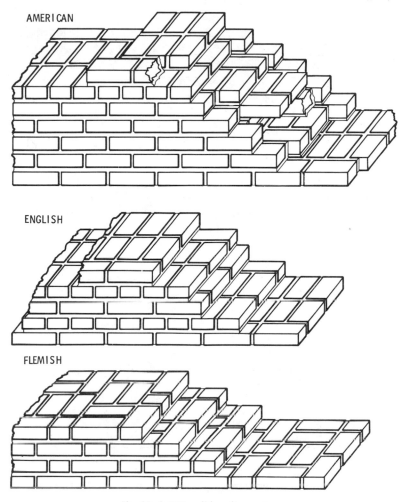

AMERICAN

ENGLISH

FLEMISH

Fig. 15. A 20" wall-bonding pattern.

The best answer to the prevention of water seepage is the use of cavity wall construction.

Cavity or dual walls are those in which *two adjacent walls are separated by an air space.* A cavity wall, therefore, is made up of two walls or tiers of masonry each nominally 4" thick with an air space between the walls or tiers for moisture resistance and thermal insulating properties.

101

Cavity-wall construction is made up entirely of masonry materials, such as brick on the outside and brick on the inside; brick on the outside and tile or concrete block on the inside; tile on the outside and tile on the inside; or any of the other masonry materials generally used for load-bearing wall construction. In each case there are two walls separated with an air space. Because there

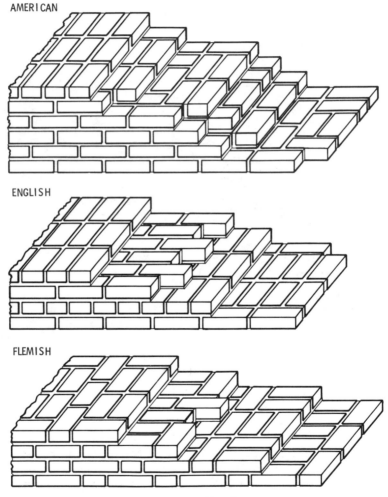

AMERICAN

ENGLISH

FLEMISH

Fig. 16. A 24" wall-bonding pattern.

are two walls, architects sometimes call cavity-wall construction dual- or barrier-wall masonry.

As illustrated in Fig. 19, the two walls are bonded or tied together with corrosion-proof, durable, and rigid metal ties. No brick headers are employed and the stretcher or running bond is generally used. Pattern bonds, such as Flemish bond, can also be used; they are, however, relatively expensive because of the cutting of bricks resulting in higher labor cost.

Cavity-wall construction has been used extensively for both commercial and residential construction in continental Europe for over a century, and more recently in the United States, where it has had an ever-increasing popularity.

### Safety Considerations

Cavity walls are generally accepted throughout the United States by local and national codes. These codes as generally recognized are for general safety purposes. Cavity walls for residences and multistory buildings are generally constructed with a 10" overall thickness. Institutional buildings like churches and schools of two-story load-bearing construction are generally 14" in overall thickness. Regardless of the thickness of the cavity wall, it is limited to a height of 35 ft. and must be supported at right angles to the wall face at intervals not exceeding 14 times the nominal wall thickness.

The 10" cavity walls are limited to not more than 25 ft. in height and must be similarly supported laterally. This lateral support can be from the roof, floors, or partitions. Many buildings of multistory design have been constructed of curtain walls having cavity-wall construction. By resting on spandrels or shelf angles they do not exceed the height limitations. Their interior treatment has varied from exposed masonry wall to plaster over lath and furring.

### Dry-Wall Construction

The cavity wall was originally erected to provide a physical separation between the outside and the inner wall. It was determined many years ago that walls that permitted water penetration were generally of a character in which the mortar did not bond properly to the brick and as a consequence wind-driven rains would penetrate through the hairline cracks created by this lack of bond. Mois-

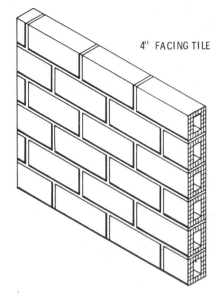

4" FACING TILE

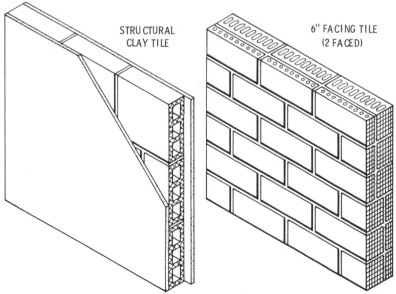

STRUCTURAL
CLAY TILE

6" FACING TILE
(2 FACED)

Fig. 17. Typical interior or partition

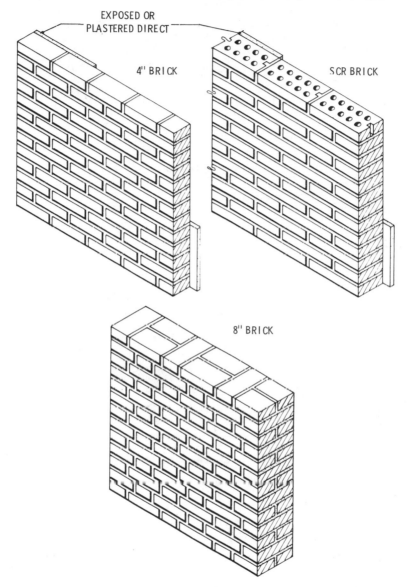

EXPOSED OR
PLASTERED DIRECT

4" BRICK

SCR BRICK

8" BRICK

**walls of brick and hollow clay tile.**

105

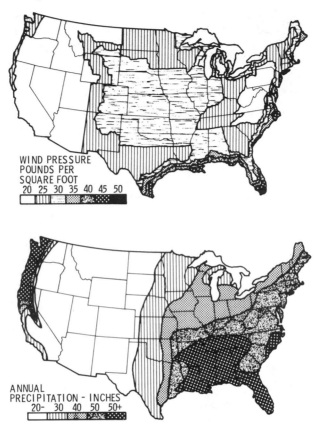

WIND PRESSURE
POUNDS PER
SQUARE FOOT
20  25  30  35  40  45  50

ANNUAL
PRECIPITATION - INCHES
20-  30  40  50  50+

Courtesy Structural Clay Products Inst.

**Fig. 18. Wind and precipitation maps.**

ture appearing on the interior surface of the wall frequently caused a distintegration of wall finishes such as plaster or wood paneling.

Building with cavity walls prevents moisture from going through the wall. As shown in Fig. 20, any moisture that may gain entrance through the exterior tier of masonry will run down the inner side or cavity to the bottom of the cavity where it drains to the outside through weep holes provided for that purpose. Drops of water that may happen to reach the metal wall ties, will drop off, before they reach the inner wall if the wall tie has the drop loop. Thus the

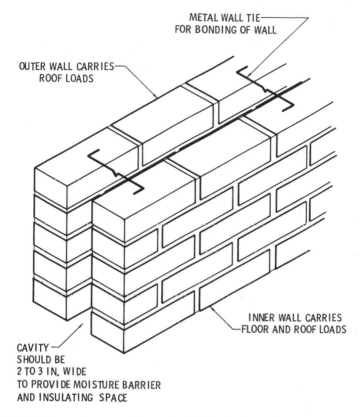

METAL WALL TIE
FOR BONDING OF WALL

OUTER WALL CARRIES
ROOF LOADS

INNER WALL CARRIES
FLOOR AND ROOF LOADS

CAVITY
SHOULD BE
2 TO 3 IN. WIDE
TO PROVIDE MOISTURE BARRIER
AND INSULATING SPACE

Fig. 19. Cavity-wall construction provides the best barrier against water seepage.

inner wall will generally remain dry. As in solid wall construction, however, the heads of windows, ventilating ducts, and other wall openings should be flashed. It is also very important to keep the cavity clean and clear of any solid material that may act as a bridge for the passage of moisture from the outer to the inner wall, since a clogged cavity or one filled with mortar does not perform well or efficiently.

## Weep Holes

Weep holes, as previously noted, are designed so that any moisture that may go through the outer wall will run down the inner side of the outer wall, as shown in Fig. 20. To drain off this mois-

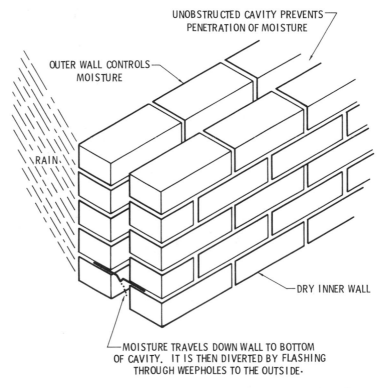

UNOBSTRUCTED CAVITY PREVENTS
PENETRATION OF MOISTURE

OUTER WALL CONTROLS
MOISTURE

RAIN.

DRY INNER WALL

MOISTURE TRAVELS DOWN WALL TO BOTTOM
OF CAVITY. IT IS THEN DIVERTED BY FLASHING
THROUGH WEEPHOLES TO THE OUTSIDE·

Fig. 20. How cavity walls prevent the penetration of moisture from the outer
wall through to the inner wall.

ture, weep holes are used, as shown in Fig. 21. As noted in the
illustration, weep holes are located in the outer wall in the vertical
joints of the bottom course, preferably two courses above grade,
and are spaced from 3 to 5 bricks apart.

Weep holes are created by various means. The simplest is the
omission of mortar from the vertical joint at predesigned intervals
in the bottom course; or, preferably, not less than two courses
above grade. Weep holes may also be made with ⅜″ oiled steel
rods, pipe, or short lengths of sash cord or rubber hose, which are
removed when the mortar sets up. Frequently, a piece of plywood
the size of the joint will be put in the vertical joint and after the
mortar sets up the plywood pieces are removed. At a later date,

108

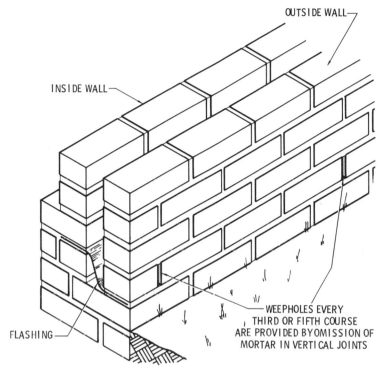

Fig. 21. Weep holes placed at various intervals which allows moisture to escape from the wall cavity.

a 2½″ × 2½″ square piece of copper screening is wrapped around the piece of plywood and inserted in the weep hole, as precaution against the entrance of bugs into the cavity. The plywood is then removed leaving the screen in place. When the holes or sash cord are used, they should extend up into the cavity and project outwards from the base of the exterior wall for easy removal. This assures a clear and clean weep hole.

Weep holes are necessary for proper drainage to keep the bottom of the cavity dry. Dirt and gravel used in landscaping should not be allowed to pile up higher than the bottom of the cavity. Such material will block the weep holes and moisture may back up in the cavity so that it gets higher than the flashing and will then penetrate the inner tier of masonry.

109

## Width of Cavity

The width of the cavity may vary considerably. The cavity in this type of wall construction is recommended to be not less than 2″ or more than 3″ wide as shown in Fig. 22. The reason for this is that a cavity of less than 2″ in width permits mortar to bridge the cavity by dripping on the wall ties as it falls down the wall.

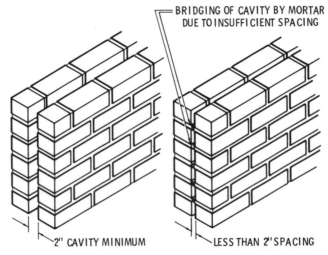

Fig. 22. Illustrating the right and wrong width for cavity walls.

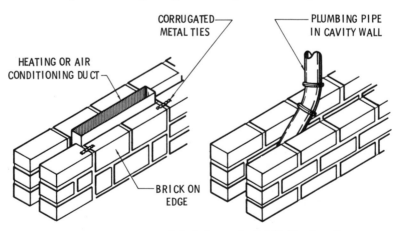

Fig. 23. Service pipes and air ducts may be installed in air cavity.

A limitation of 3″ in width on the cavity has been determined by tests made on the effective width in the cavity. Thus, it has been found that when the width of the cavity approaches 4″ the width becomes great enough to cause air coming in from the weep holes to go up the inner side of the outer wall and come down the outer side of the inner wall, taking off warmth from the inner wall, thereby defeating a purpose of the construction. The foregoing action is created by an eddying current of air which is highly undesirable in cavity-wall construction. The cavities between walls may also be used for the installation of heating and air-conditioning ducts, as well as pipes, as shown in Fig. 23.

Fig. 24 shows several methods of cavity-wall construction in addition to the cavity between two tiers (sometimes called wythes) of brick. At point (A) is the brick veneer discussed before. While the cavity is small, it is sufficient for water protection. At point (B), SCR brick is used, a type developed by the STRUCTURAL CLAY PRODUCTS INSTITUTE. Its construction and width (6″ instead of the usual 4″) makes it especially suited to prevent or reduce water penetration. The cavity wall shown at point (C) may include a tile back tier, as shown, or solid brick. The cavity may be left empty (an air cavity) or filled with water-resistant vermiculite or perlite, for added insulation. The cavity wall is the best insulator against water.

While bonding of the outer tier to the inner tier is usually done by metal straps (at point D), bonding may be accomplished by using header brick. The tiers are rowlock laid, with bricks on edge. The reduced tier thickness leaves a cavity across which a header brick can reach.

## METAL TIES

Metal ties are used in cavity-wall construction to bond the walls and to furnish the necessary rigidity between the tiers. Fig. 25 shows the various types of wall ties that have been used in cavity-wall construction and their dimensions. Metal ties should be corrosion proof, rigid and durable, and not less than 3/16″ in diameter. The most frequently used is the Z-bar in which the wire is bent to provide a hook about 2″ in length for embedment in the horizontal mortar joint of the inner and outer walls.

111

Building codes usually call for a maximum spacing of ties as one tie for each 3 sq. ft. of wall area. In standard brick work the spacing accordingly will be about 24″ on horizontal centers and each sixth course vertically. Mortar is spread on each wall section before the ties are placed, to provide a bond between the tie and the brick.

Regardless of the type of wall tie used, caution should be observed against placement with a pitch toward the inner wall. Wall ties must be placed within 12″ of all wall openings and at the bottom of joists or slabs that rest on the wall.

## EXPANSION JOINTS

No building is a perfectly rigid structure. There is always some movement, whether it is due to some settling, heavy traffic nearby, possible earth tremors, or other causes. One movement factor no

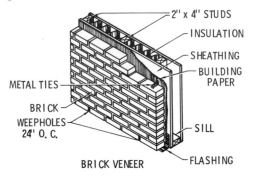

2″ x 4″ STUDS
INSULATION
SHEATHING
BUILDING PAPER
METAL TIES
BRICK
WEEPHOLES 24′ O. C.
SILL
BRICK VENEER
FLASHING

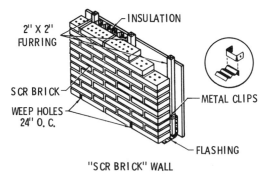

INSULATION
2″ X 2″ FURRING
SCR BRICK
WEEP HOLES 24′ O. C.
METAL CLIPS
FLASHING
"SCR BRICK" WALL

**Fig. 24. Four alternate methods**

building can avoid is that due to expansion and contraction resulting from temperature and moisture changes.

It takes a 100°F change in temperature to expand a 100-ft. long brick wall only ⅜″. As little as the change seems to be, it does not take much of a temperature change to cause cracks in masonry walls. For this reason, large walls must not be bonded into a rigid unit but must include joints in the wall, especially vertically, to permit expansion and contraction.

An expansion joint is a complete separation between large sections of walls. To prevent the entrance of moisture, however, some filler must be used in the joint and the installation must be correctly made. Preformed copper sheeting with overlapping seams have been used for years. Now available are other types, such as premolded compressible and elastic fillers of rubber, neoprene, and

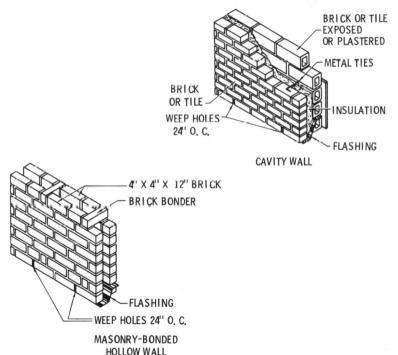

BRICK OR TILE EXPOSED OR PLASTERED

METAL TIES

BRICK OR TILE

WEEP HOLES 24′ O. C.

INSULATION

FLASHING

CAVITY WALL

4′ X 4″ X 12″ BRICK

BRICK BONDER

FLASHING

WEEP HOLES 24″ O. C.

MASONRY-BONDED HOLLOW WALL (UTILITY WALL)

Courtesy Structural Clay Products Inst.

**of producing cavities in walls.**

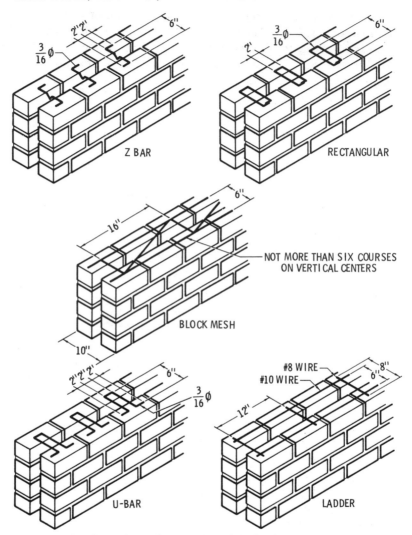

**Fig. 25. Popular reinforcing rods used for bonding cavity walls.**

other plastics. The old system of using fiberboard is not recommended, since fiberboard does not compress easily, and once compressed it does not return to its original size. Fig. 26 shows some of the newer acceptable types of expansion joints.

114

The illustrations of Fig. 27 show the treatment of a number of wall structures. Note that it is important to use metal ties around the expansion joint. The most important thing for the brickmason to keep in mind is the importance of a good job in the installation of expansion joints. If anything in the joint prevents free movement, the effectiveness of the expansion joint is completely ruined. Mortar or pieces of broken brick must not be allowed to fall into the joints. The full length of the joint must be kept free of dirt or any type of rubble. If it is necessary to use ties across the joint, they must be of the flexible type, and the ties must not be bridged with mortar.

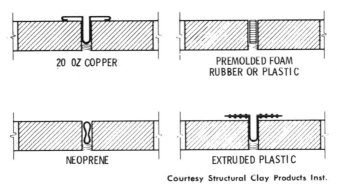

Courtesy Structural Clay Products Inst.

**Fig. 26. Expansion-joint material in common use today.**

## FOUNDATIONS

A necessity for laying up a wall with horizontal courses, and to provide long life with a minimum of settling, is to begin on a good foundation. While brick may be used as the foundation, modern practice is to pour a concrete footing.

The depth of the foundation must be at least below the frost line and the width should be twice the width of the wall. A trench dug with straight sides into which reinforcing steel rods have been placed is often a sufficient form. Wood forms may be placed if the earth is not solid enough to develop straight sides. It is important that the top surface of the foundation be as horizontal as possible. Adjustment can be made at the time of placing a mortar line and the first course of brick.

115

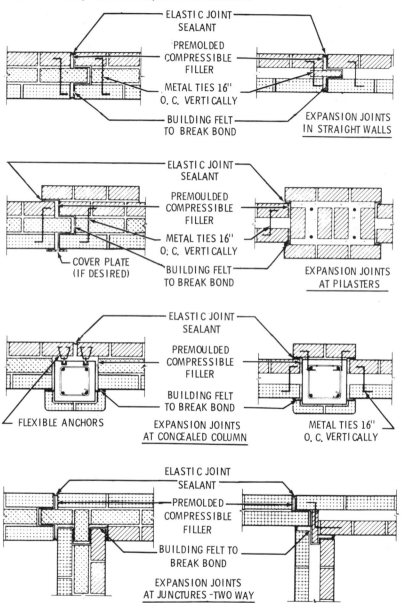

ELASTIC JOINT SEALANT

PREMOLDED COMPRESSIBLE FILLER

METAL TIES 16" O. C. VERTICALLY

BUILDING FELT TO BREAK BOND

EXPANSION JOINTS IN STRAIGHT WALLS

ELASTIC JOINT SEALANT

PREMOULDED COMPRESSIBLE FILLER

METAL TIES 16" O. C. VERTICALLY

COVER PLATE (IF DESIRED)

BUILDING FELT TO BREAK BOND

EXPANSION JOINTS AT PILASTERS

ELASTIC JOINT SEALANT

PREMOULDED COMPRESSIBLE FILLER

BUILDING FELT TO BREAK BOND

FLEXIBLE ANCHORS

EXPANSION JOINTS AT CONCEALED COLUMN

METAL TIES 16" O. C. VERTICALLY

ELASTIC JOINT SEALANT

PREMOLDED COMPRESSIBLE FILLER

BUILDING FELT TO BREAK BOND

EXPANSION JOINTS AT JUNCTURES - TWO WAY

Fig. 27. Examples of placement of

116

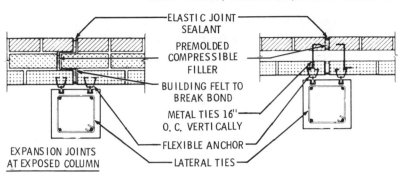

ELASTIC JOINT SEALANT

PREMOLDED COMPRESSIBLE FILLER

BUILDING FELT TO BREAK BOND

METAL TIES 16" O. C. VERTICALLY

FLEXIBLE ANCHOR

LATERAL TIES

EXPANSION JOINTS AT EXPOSED COLUMN

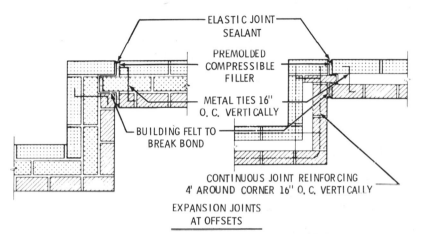

ELASTIC JOINT SEALANT

PREMOLDED COMPRESSIBLE FILLER

METAL TIES 16" O. C. VERTICALLY

BUILDING FELT TO BREAK BOND

CONTINUOUS JOINT REINFORCING 4' AROUND CORNER 16" O. C. VERTICALLY

EXPANSION JOINTS AT OFFSETS

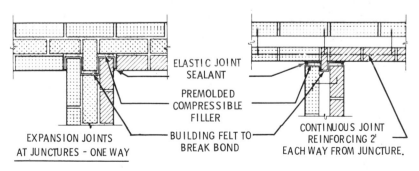

ELASTIC JOINT SEALANT

PREMOLDED COMPRESSIBLE FILLER

BUILDING FELT TO BREAK BOND

CONTINUOUS JOINT REINFORCING 2' EACH WAY FROM JUNCTURE.

EXPANSION JOINTS AT JUNCTURES - ONE WAY

Courtesy Structural Clay Products Inst.

expansion joints in various wall structures.

117

## Table 1. Recommended Water-Cement Ratio for Different Applications and Conditions

| Exposure | Water-cement ratio, U.S. gal. per sack[1] | | |
|---|---|---|---|
| Class of structure | Reinforced piles, thin walls, light structural members, exterior columns and beams in buildings | Reinforced reservoirs, water tanks, pressure pipes, sewers, canal linings, dams of thin sections | Heavy walls, piers, foundations, dams of heavy sections |
| Extreme: 1. In severe climates like in northern U. S., exposure to rain and snow and drying, freezing and thawing, as at the water line in hydraulic structures. 2. Exposure to sea and strong sulphate waters in both severe and moderate climates. | 5½ | 5½ | 6 |
| Severe: 3. In severe climates like in northern U. S., exposure to rain and snow and freezing and thawing, but not continuously in contact with water. 4. In moderate climates like southern U. S., exposure to alternate wetting and drying, as at water line in hydraulic structures. | 6 | 6 | 6¾ |
| Moderate: 5. In climates like southern U. S. exposure to ordinary weather, but not continuously in contact with water. 6. Concrete completely submerged, but protected from freezing. | 6¾ | 6 | 7½ |
| Protected: 7. Ordinary inclosed structural members; concrete below the ground and not subject to action of corrosive groundwaters or freezing and thawing. | 7½ | 6 | 8¼ |

[1]Surface water or moisture carried by the aggregate must be included as part of the mixing water.

Detailed information on concrete foundations appears in the Volume on Concrete, dealing exclusively with all aspects of concrete. The following is a summary of that information, included here for convenience.

**Foundation materials**—Foundations, due to the availability of material, are almost exclusively built of concrete. The materials necessary for making concrete are cement, sand, aggregate, water and in some instances reinforcement. It has, however, become customary to refer to concrete as having only three ingredients, namely, cement, sand, and aggregate, the combination of which is expressed as a mixture by volume in the order referred to. Thus, for example, a concrete mixture referred to as 1:2:4 actually means that the mixture contains 1 part of *cement*, 2 parts of *sand*, and 4 parts of *aggregate*, each proportioned by volume.

The general practice of omitting water from the ratio does not necessarily mean that the amount of water used in the mixture is less important but is omitted partly to simplify the formula and also because the amount of water used involves a consideration of both the degree of exposure and strength requirements of the complete structure.

**Cement Ratio**—Table 1 gives recommended water-cement ratios on the basis of a definite minimum curing condition for concrete to meet different degrees of exposure in different classes of structures.

In determining the proportions of materials, it is desirable to arrive at those proportions which will give the most economical results consistent with proper placing. The relative proportions of fine and coarse aggregates and the total amount of aggregate that can be used with fixed amounts of cement and water will depend not only on the consistency of concrete required but also on the grading of each aggregate. A combination of aggregates made up largely of coarse particles presents less total surface to be coated with cement paste than aggregate of fine particles and is therefore more economical. For this reason it is desirable to use the lowest proportion of fine aggregate which will properly fill the "void" spaces in the coarse aggregate.

Aggregates that are graded so that they contain many sizes are more economical than aggregates in which one or two sizes predominate because the former contain fewer voids. The small particles fill the spaces between the larger particles which otherwise must be filled with cement paste. A properly proportioned combination of well-graded fine and coarse aggregates contains all sizes between the smallest and the largest without an excessive amount of any one size. The best grading, however, is not necessarily one consisting of equal amounts of the various sizes because such a grading is seldom practicable. Satisfactory mixtures can usually be obtained with the commercial aggregates by proper combination of fine and coarse aggregates.

Increasing the proportion of coarse aggregate up to a certain point reduces the cement factor. Beyond this point the saving in cement is very slight, while the deficiency in mortar increases the labor cost of placing and finishing. Because coarser gradings are more economical, there has been a tendency to use mixtures that were undersanded and harsh. Harshness has been the principal cause for over-wet mixtures, resulting almost invariably in honeycombing in the finished work. While increasing the proportion of fine materials makes for smoother working mixes, excessive proportions of fine material present greater surface areas to be coated and more voids to be filled with cement paste. Under such conditions, the total amount of aggregate which can be used with fixed amounts of cement and water is greatly reduced.

The total amount of aggregate that can be used with given amounts of cement and water will depend on the consistency required by the conditions of the job. A stiffer mix permits more aggregates to be crowded into the cement paste and thus gives a larger volume of concrete. Stiffer mixes cost less for materials than the more fluid mixes but the cost of handling and placing increases when excessively dry mixes are used. On the other hand, mixes that are over-wet require high cement factors and cannot be placed without segregation of the materials. Such mixes are uneconomical in material and are seldom required for the conditions of placing. In many instances, where correct proportions of sand are used, it will be found practicable to use somewhat stiffer mixtures than have been the practice in the past, without adding materially to the cost of handling or placing.

120

Because of the restrictions imposed by limiting the amount of water for each sack of cement, experienced foremen can generally be depended upon to obtain a proper balance between the various factors, with the result that the concrete will be neither harsh nor honeycombed on the one hand nor porous and over-wet on the other.

One of the important advantages to the contractor of the water-cement ratio method is that the materials may be proportioned to facilitate handling and placing, thereby reducing the cost of these items. With some latitude open in the matter of workability and proportions, he will be quick to select those mixes which give him the necessary workability at the lowest cost. At the same time such a mixture will thoroughly fill the forms and reduce the cost of patching honeycomb spots to a minimum. Where the surfaces are to be given a special treatment, the process is invariably made easier.

The quantities of materials in a concrete mixture may be determined accurately by making use of the fact that the volume of concrete produced by any combination of materials, so long as the concrete is plastic, is equal to the sum of the absolute volume of the cement plus the absolute volume of the aggregate plus the volume of water. The absolute volume of a loose material is the actual total volume of solid matter in all the particles. This can be computed from the weight per unit volume and the apparent specific gravity as follows:

$$\text{Absolute Vol.} = \frac{\text{unit weight}}{\text{apparent specific gravity} \times \text{unit wt. of water}}$$
(62.5 lb. per cu. ft.)

in which the unit weight is based on surface dry aggregate.

The method can best be illustrated by an example. Suppose the concrete batch consists of 1 sack of cement (94 lb.), 2.2 cu. ft. of dry fine aggregate weighing 110 lb. per cu. ft., and 3.6 cu. ft. of dry coarse aggregate weighing 100 lb. per cu. ft. which is to be mixed with a water-cement ratio of 7 gallons per sack. The apparent specific gravity of the cement is usually about 3.1 and of the more common aggregates about 2.65. The volume of concrete produced by the above mix is calculated as follows:

$$\text{Cement} = \quad 1 \text{ cu. ft. at } \frac{94}{3.1 \times 62.5} = \quad .49 \text{ cu. ft. abs. vol.}$$

$$\frac{\text{Fine}}{\text{Aggregate}} = 2.2 \text{ cu. ft. at } \frac{110}{2.65 \times 62.5} = 1.46 \text{ cu. ft. abs. vol.}$$

$$\frac{\text{Coarse}}{\text{Aggregate}} = 3.6 \text{ cu. ft. at } \frac{100}{2.65 \times 62.5} = 2.18 \text{ cu. ft. abs. vol.}$$

$$\frac{\text{Volume of}}{\text{Water}} = \quad \frac{7.0}{7.5} = \quad .93 \text{ cu. ft. abs. vol.}$$

Total Volume of Concrete Produced $\quad = 5.06$ cu. ft.

Thus 1 sack of cement produces 5.06 cu. ft., neglecting absorption or losses in manipulation. The cement required for 1 cu. yd. of concrete is, therefore,

$$\frac{27}{5.06} = 5.34 \text{ sacks}$$

The quantities of fine and coarse aggregate required can be found from a simple computation based on the number of cubic feet used with each sack of cement; thus,
for fine aggregate

$$\frac{5.34 \times 2.2}{27} = .43 \text{ cu. yd.}$$

for the course aggregate

$$\frac{5.34 \times 3.6}{27} = .71 \text{ cu. yd.}$$

**Placing of Concrete**—No element in the whole cycle of concrete production requires more care than the final operation of placing concrete at the ultimate point of deposit. Before placing concrete, all debris and foreign matter should be removed from the places to be occupied by the concrete, and the forms, if used, should be thoroughly wetted or oiled. Temporary openings should be provided where necessary to facilitate cleaning and inspection immediately before depositing concrete. These should be placed so that excess water used in flushing the forms may be drained away.

**Prevention of Segregation**—With a well-designed mixture delivered with proper consistency and without segregation, placing of concrete is simplified; but even in this case care must be exercised to further prevent segregation and to see that the material flows properly into corners and angles of forms and around the reinforcement.

Constant supervision is essential to ensure such complete filling of the form and to prevent the rather common practice of depositing continuously at one point, allowing the material to flow to distant points.

Flowing over long distances will cause segregation, especially of the water and cement from the rest of the mass. An excessive amount of tamping or puddling in the forms will also cause the material to separate. When the concrete is properly proportioned, the entrained air will escape and the mass will be thoroughly consolidated with very little puddling. Light spading of the concrete next to the forms will prevent honeycombing and make surface finishing easier.

## REINFORCED BRICK MASONRY

Reinforced brick masonry is sometimes called by its intitials, RBM. Brick has tremendous compressive strength (as in the case of concrete) but the tensile or lateral strength depends on the bond between bricks. In areas where heavy winds or earth tremors are frequent, it may be necessary to increase the bond between bricks for greater lateral strength. This is done with steel reinforcing rods.

The actual number, size, and where they are placed becomes an engineering problem. It is important for the brick mason to know how to install them, to assure best bond of the rod to the brick structure. For example, it is important that a full layer of mortar be placed on the brick faces holding the rods. The rods must be imbedded in as much mortar as possible. Furthermore, there must be mortar on all sides of the rods—the rods must be suspended in the center of the mortar thickness. The mortar bed must be at least ⅛" thicker than the rods, so there is a 1/16" thickness of mortar on each side of the rods. Where large diameter

123

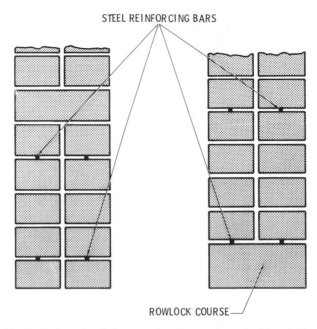

STEEL REINFORCING BARS

ROWLOCK COURSE

Fig. 28. Horizontal rods for extra bonding are shown in this end view.

rods are used, this may call for a thicker mortar joint. All joints must have the greater thickness to maintain a uniform pattern.

Fig. 28 is an example of steel rods laid the length of an 8″ wall. A transverse rod bridging the two tiers of a cavity wall is shown in Fig. 29. One of the most important applications of reinforcing rods in brick construction is in the erection of columns and pillars made of brick. Fig. 30 is an example.

It is common practice to include horizontal reinforcing rods in the concrete poured as a footing for brick walls. Often this includes vertical-rod members placed every few feet along the footing. These rods are gauged to protrude into the open space of a cavity brick wall. Concrete is poured into the cavity for a couple of feet in height, to bond to the vertical rods. This results in a solid structural mass between the concrete footing and the brick wall. The remaining height may leave the air space in the cavity for bleeding water, as explained before. Weep-holes must be included, of course. The

124

Courtesy Structural Clay Products Inst.

**Fig. 29. Transverse rods used to bond tiers of brick in a cavity wall.**

illustration in Fig. 31 shows a mason pouring concrete into the cavity, using vertical-rod reinforcing.

## USE OF ANCHORS

The metal ties for securing one tier of brick to another and the reinforcing rods mentioned above are called anchors. However, special heavy-duty forms of anchors are used:

1. To reinforce corners of brickwork.
2. To tie joists and roof plates to the brickwork.

The anchors are made in a multiplicity of shapes to meet the requirements of the service for which they are needed.

### Anchoring Walls at Angles

An important feature in brickwork is that the walls should be anchored where they meet at corners; that is, the front and rear

125

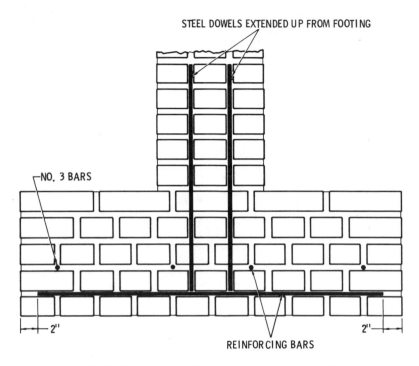

Fig. 30. A column of brick using vertical reinforcing rods.

walls should be securely anchored as well as bonded to the side, partition, or partition walls. Fig. 32 shows some forms of the rods commonly used.

The provision for tying consists of an anchor placed at the center of a 4″ recess or blocking. The T or pin anchor should be built into the center of the recess which should occur every thirteen courses. The anchor should project so as to give not less than 8″ of holding on the wall to be tied. These anchors should never be omitted when one wall is coursed up before the wall to be tied is built.

Fig. 33 shows an anchor in an 8″ wall. It will secure this wall to the adjoining one when the next wall is laid up. In Fig. 34, anchors in a 12″ wall are shown. An intersecting wall is tied to an outside wall with a nut and washer anchor in Fig. 35.

126

Fig. 31. Vertical rods extending from the footing tie the bricks to the footing

## Anchoring Floor Joints

In brickwork the courses can easily be adjusted so that the courses supporting joists will be at the exact height required. No "shims" or blocking under the joists are needed or should be allowed.

Joists and timbers should be set directly on the brick unless their bearing surface is so small that they transmit a load over the safe bearing capacity of the wall, which occurs very seldom but which would require bearing plates. These two conditions are shown in Fig. 36.

In the better class of residence work, floor joists are anchored to the walls. Some cities require this by ordinance. In the great majority of residence work outside of such cities, however, anchors are not used. Anchors are spaced approximately 6 ft. apart for both floor joists and roof plate. Great care should be exercised in placing these anchors as near the bottom of the joists as possible, in order to lessen the strain on the brick wall, in case a fire causes the

127

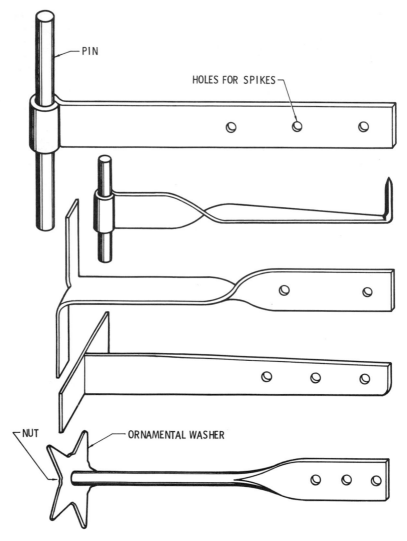

Fig. 32. Various forms of heavy anchor rods used in brick work.

joists to drop. Fig. 37 shows the right and wrong placement of joist anchors in solid walls, and Fig. 38 shows the correct placement in hollow walls.

128

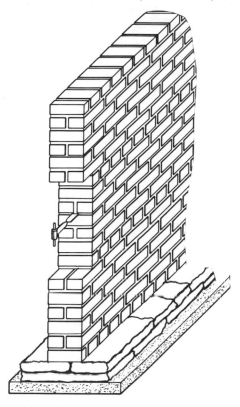

Fig. 33. A T-anchor in an 8″ wall which will tie into a perpendicular wall.

In constructing the walls, the brickwork should be stopped at the point where the first floor joists are to rest on it. Care should be taken to have the top course perfectly level, so that the joists may be set without wedging or blocking. After the joists are placed, the brickwork is continued up leaving a small "breathing" space around the joist to prevent dry rot. The same method of joisting is followed at the upper floors. On anchor joists the anchors are attached to the joists with spikes driven through the holes seen in the illustrations of anchors.

The ends of all joists are beveled whether they are anchor joists or intermediate joists so that in case of fire they will readily fall without injury to the wall.

129

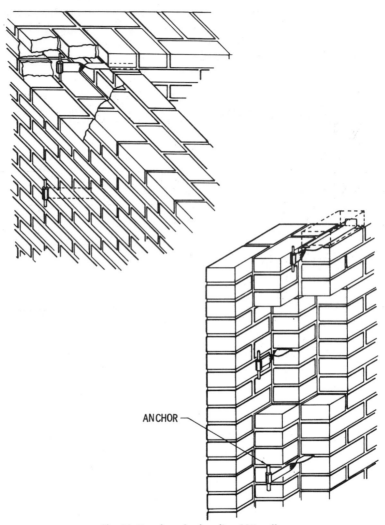

Fig. 34. T-anchors for bonding 12" walls.

## Anchoring the Roof Plate

Before the top of the wall is reached, the anchors for bolting down the roof plate should be placed and the brickwork carried up around them as shown in Fig. 39. The bolts should be ½" in

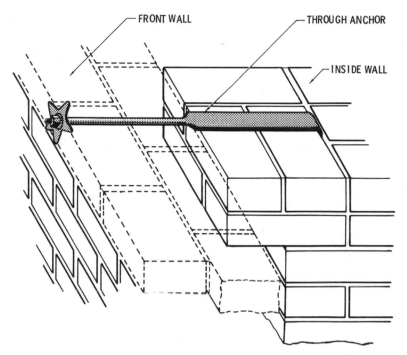

Fig. 35. A through anchor with nut and washer for intersecting walls.

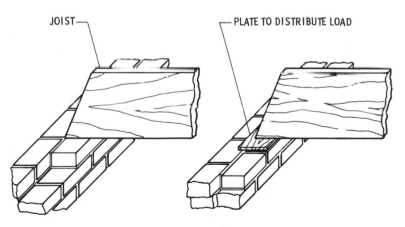

Fig. 36. A metal plate placed under floor joist in some instances, to distribute weight.

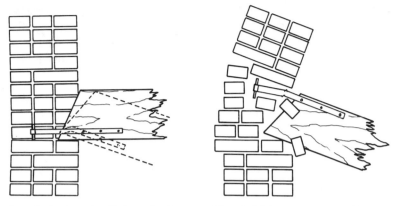

Fig. 37. Anchors installed to the bottom of beveled joist to prevent pulling out of bricks in case of joist breakage.

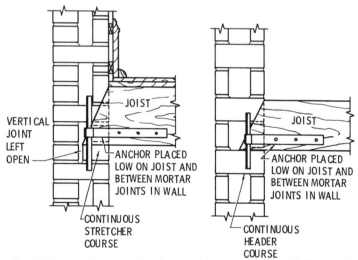

Fig. 38. Correct placement of anchors on joists in two types of hollow wall construction.

diameter and at least 12" long, with a tee or washer at the bottom and a nut and washer at the top, and should be set approximately every 6 ft. along the wall. After the carpenter has placed the roof plate and before it is bolted down, the mason should place a bed of mortar under the plate.

132

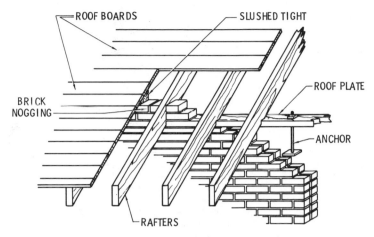

**Fig. 39. Anchoring roof plate to brick wall.**

When the wall is finally carried to the top and the roof rafters set, but before the roof boarding is in place, the mason should fill in between the roof rafters with one tier of brick as shown. This is called nogging. Its purpose is to effectively block the openings between the roof rafters and to prevent the wind from entering the walls and attic. This adds greatly to the comfort of the house in cold weather. In warm climates, nogging will not be necessary.

## CHAPTER 7

# Corners, Openings, and Arches

As distinguished from each other, a corner is *the meeting of the ends of two converging walls,* whereas, an intersection is *the meeting of one wall with another wall at some intermediate point.* In the case of intersections, one wall may end at the point of intersection, or continue. These distinctions are shown in Fig. 1.

## CORNERS

The corner, which is the beginning or end of a wall, is the point where the bond starts; it is here that means must be provided so that the courses may be shifted the amount required by the bond employed. This is obtained by the proper arrangement of the brick at the corner and by the use of special brick if necessary.

The various kinds of corners encountered may be classed:

1. With respect to the angle of the walls, as:
    a. Square (90°).
    b. Obtuse.
    c. Acute.
2. With respect to the direction of angle, as:
    a. Outside.
    b. Inside.

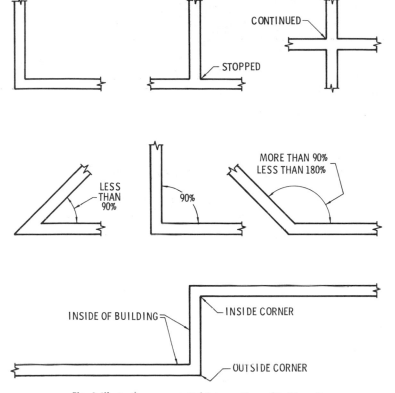

Fig. 1 Illustrating corners and Intersections of brick walls.

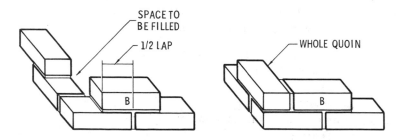

Fig. 2. How ½-lap corners are started. Whole bricks are used.

135

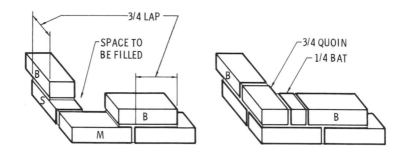

Fig. 3. In ¾-lap bonding, ¼-lap and ¾-quoin sizes are needed.

## Starting the Bond at 90° Corners

To start the bond in two walls, diverging from a corner, some special arrangement of the brick is necessary otherwise the courses would not have the required shift resulting in incorrect lap. The brick used for this purpose are:

1. Quoins.
2. Closers.
3. Bats.

With these forms, various spacings may be obtained so as to obtain the proper lap in starting the bonds. The numerous spacing combinations that can be made are illustrated fully in Chapter 4. The following rule should not be violated. This rule states: *a course should be started with a quoin, never a ¼ closer.* That is, the end brick should never be less than 4″ in width. Sometimes ¼ closers are used but this is a very bad practice and cannot be too strongly condemned.

In starting a bond at the corner, the requirements of both walls must be considered so that proper quoins and closers may be selected. The examples which follow illustrate the method of solving the problem:

*Example*—Determine the brick arrangement at a corner for stretcher bond 4″ wall, ½ lap; ¾ lap.

Case 1, ½ lap—This is the simplest case. In Fig. 2, the bond starts with brick B, leaving ½ of the brick to be covered to the

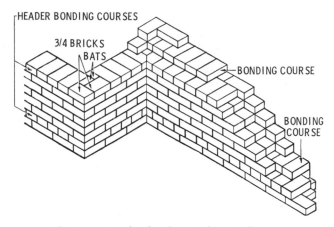

Fig. 4. American bond with 8" and 12" wall corners.

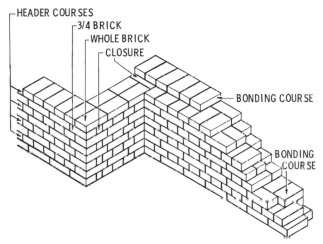

Fig. 5. English bond with 8" and 12" wall corners.

edge and requiring a whole brick length on the other wall. Hence, a whole quoin or end brick will fill the space.

Case 2, ¾ lap—The first bond brick B, Fig. 3, will have a ¼ lap on the end stretcher M, leaving ¾ of brick M to be covered. On the other wall ¼ of brick S is to be covered or ¾ each way. Hence, a ¾ quoin and a ¼-bat closer is required to fill the space as shown.

137

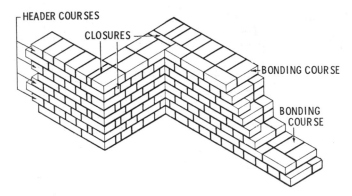

HEADER COURSES

CLOSURES

BONDING COURSE

BONDING COURSE

Fig. 6. English cross or Dutch bond corners for 8″ and 12″ walls.

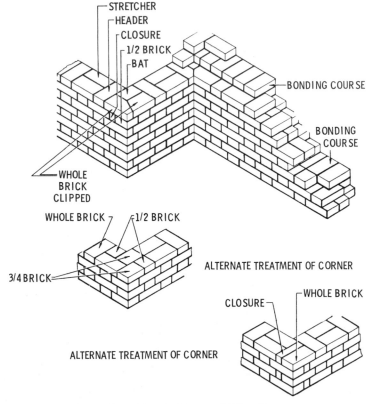

STRETCHER
HEADER
CLOSURE
1/2 BRICK
BAT

BONDING COURSE

BONDING COURSE

WHOLE BRICK CLIPPED

WHOLE BRICK   1/2 BRICK

3/4 BRICK

ALTERNATE TREATMENT OF CORNER

CLOSURE   WHOLE BRICK

ALTERNATE TREATMENT OF CORNER

Fig. 7. Flemish bond with 8″ and 12″ wall corners.

138

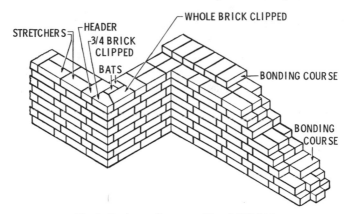

Fig. 8. Garden-wall corners 8″ and 12″ thick.

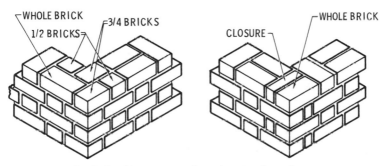

Fig. 9. Outside corners made with and without closers.

Fig. 10. English cross and Dutch bond corners can be started without closers.

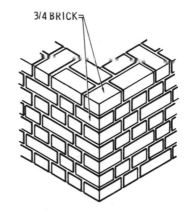

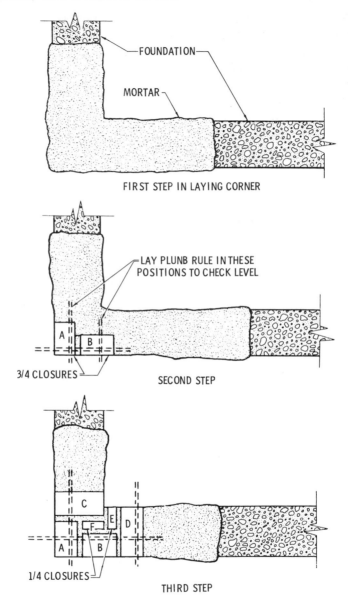

FIRST STEP IN LAYING CORNER

LAY PLUNB RULE IN THESE
POSITIONS TO CHECK LEVEL

3/4 CLOSURES

SECOND STEP

1/4 CLOSURES

THIRD STEP

Fig. 11. Five steps in laying

The above examples together with the explanations given in Chapter 4 should be ample to show how the brick may be arranged to meet various conditions. Both outside and inside corners for the various bonds for walls of various thickness are shown in Figs. 4 through 10.

The most frequently encountered wall construction is that of an 8″ wall. The best way to start is with a first course, over the foun-

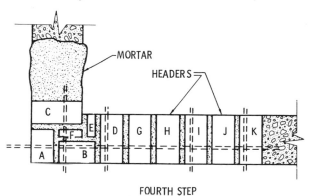

FOURTH STEP

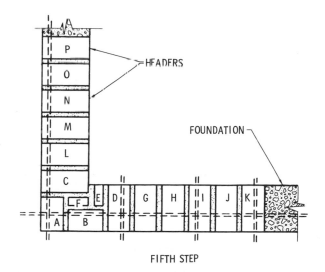

FIFTH STEP

a first course of all headers.

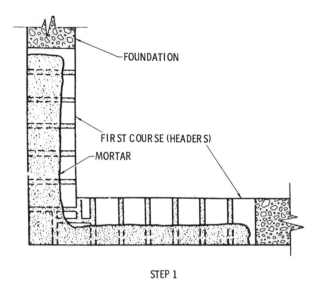

STEP 1

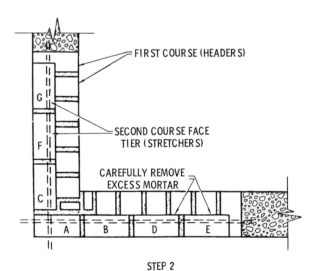

STEP 2

Fig. 12. Succeeding courses are common ½-lap bond up to from five to seven courses.

dation, of all header brick. Fig. 11 shows, step-by-step, how to begin the course. This is the first course and the most important in making the correct start. The dashed lines are the positions of the level. Note the frequency with which it is used. The letters show the alphabetical order in which the brick is laid.

The second step illustrated in Fig. 12 shows the position of the second and succeeding course, up to about the fifth to the seventh, at which time another course of headers is placed for bonding. Fig. 13 shows how the outside of the corner will look with the first course all headers, five courses of stretchers, and the start of the sixth course for headers.

Fig. 14 is a view of the inside of the same corner. As mentioned previously, it is important that a measurement from corner to corner is accurately made and that the level is used frequently to be sure it is vertical on both sides and that all courses are horizontal. With two corners laid up, the rest of the brick is laid between them by the use of the taut line.

### Obtuse Angle Corners

If the angle of turn is 30°, 45°, or 60°, specially shaped brick made for the purpose and called *splay* or *octagon* brick may be obtained from dealers and manufacturers. If for any reason these special shapes are not available, the angles may be formed by the use of standard size brick. There are two methods of using standard brick for outside corners as shown in Fig. 15; both are objectionable as can be seen from the illustrations.

Fig. 16 shows outside and inside obtuse angle turns with standard brick in an 8″ wall. This arrangement results in a minimum amount of brick cutting. Fig. 17 shows a 12″ wall with minimum brick cutting. Fig. 18 shows special brick for making standard turns of 30°, 45°, and 60°.

### Acute Angle Corners

In the less expensive class of work, to save time the "pigeon hole" method of making an acute turn is employed. In this method the wall is built out almost to a sharp edge; the brick is laid up with vacant indented spaces, or pigeon holes, on each side, as shown in Fig. 19.

143

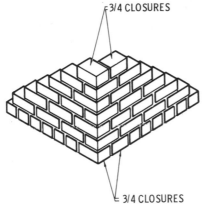

3/4 CLOSURES

3/4 CLOSURES

Fig. 13. The start of an American bond corner.

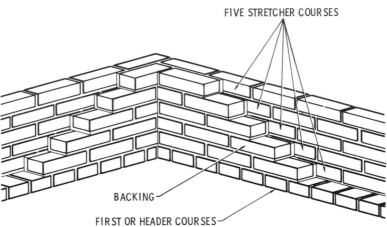

FIVE STRETCHER COURSES

BACKING

FIRST OR HEADER COURSES

Fig. 14. Inside tier of corner.

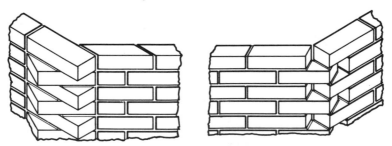

Fig. 15. Methods of making obtuse angles with standard brick without cutting. Neither are recommended.

144

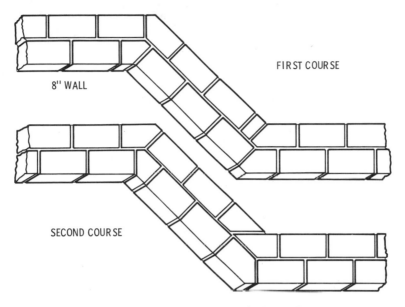

FIRST COURSE

8" WALL

SECOND COURSE

Fig. 16. Standard brick should be cut to make better obtuse corners.

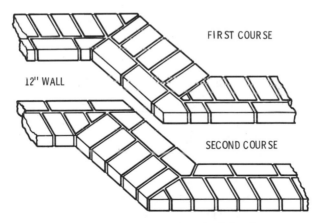

FIRST COURSE

12" WALL

SECOND COURSE

Fig. 17. English bond 12" wall with cut brick for obtuse corner.

The pigeonholes are the result of laying the brick with square ends instead of using special brick or chipping to shape. The pigeonholes form spaces for the accumulation of dirt, water, snow, etc.,

145

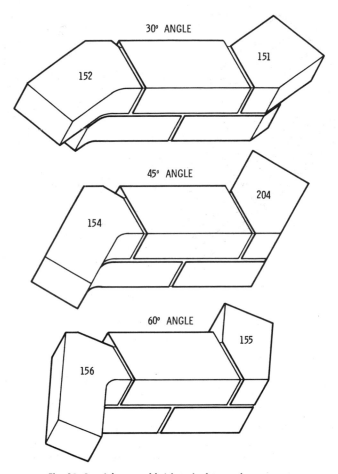

30° ANGLE

152     151

45° ANGLE

154     204

60° ANGLE

156     155

**Fig. 18. Special pressed brick make better obtuse corners.**

with the result that the brickwork rapidly deteriorates and, moreover, is unsightly. A better method of making an acute angle corner is shown in Fig. 20. Here the sharp edge and pigeonholes are avoided, thus, improving the appearance and leaving no spaces for the lodging of dirt, etc.

There are two types of wall intersections:

1. Stopped or L shape.
2. Continued or cross shaped.

Fig. 19. "Pigeon hole" corners are developed when uncut bricks are used to construct an obtuse corner.

These intersections are usually at right angles. The brick is arranged in various ways at these intersections depending on the wall thickness and kind of bond. The object is to bond the two walls together at the same time preserving the bond in each wall.

*Stopped Intersections*—This is the simple case of intersections, as illustrated in the intersection of a partition wall with the outer wall. In arranging the brick at the intersection, the aim should be to get the maximum amount of bonding. Fig. 21 shows the first and second courses of an 8″ wall.

*Continued Intersections*—Frequently, an intersecting wall continues past the intersected wall forming a cross-shaped figure. The same general principles apply as for stopped intersections, the aim being:

1. To get as much bond area as possible.
2. To preserve the bond in both walls.
3. To avoid chipped brick when possible.

147

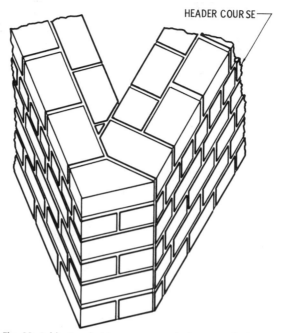

HEADER COURSE

Fig. 20. A blunt end obtuse corner made from standard brick.

The methods of brick arrangement for 8″ and 12″ walls, common or American bond, are shown in Figs. 23 and 24. A study of these illustrations will show the general scheme to be followed. The student should practice by applying the principles illustrated to the other bonds for walls of various thicknesses.

## OPENINGS

Window and floor frames are available in standardized sizes to permit placement in brick openings without the need for cutting brick to fit. This applies to the height, which allows for a whole number of courses, and to the width to allow for a whole number of bricks for the width of the needed opening.

For years windows were of wood sash frames and were called double-hung (both lower and upper windows movable). Newer

148

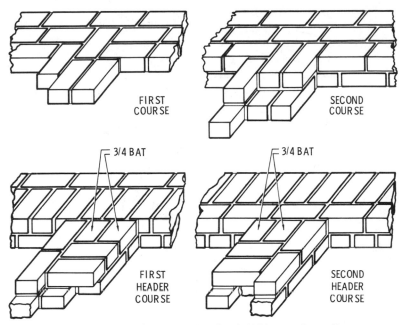

FIRST
COURSE

SECOND
COURSE

3/4 BAT

3/4 BAT

FIRST
HEADER
COURSE

SECOND
HEADER
COURSE

Fig. 21. Courses for an American bond, 12" intersecting wall.

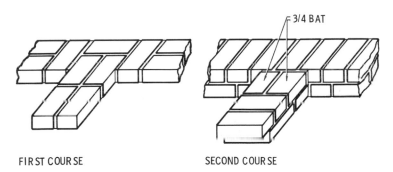

3/4 BAT

FIRST COURSE

SECOND COURSE

Fig. 22. English bond, 8" intersecting wall.

home construction has turned to aluminum and steel sash windows, with the lower window counterbalanced on springs for raising. The upper window is generally fixed. Metal sash windows include the narrow vertically hinged windows that swing inward allowing for the use of screens on the outside.

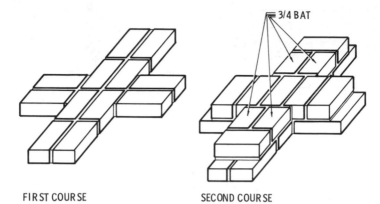

FIRST COURSE          SECOND COURSE

Fig. 23. Continued intersecting 8" American bond wall.

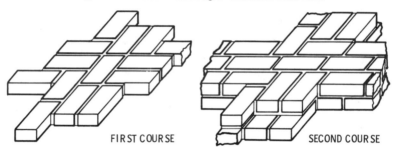

FIRST COURSE          SECOND COURSE

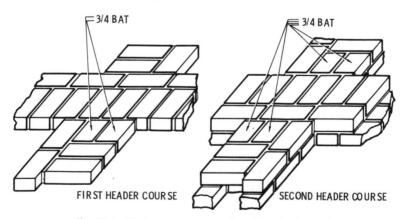

FIRST HEADER COURSE          SECOND HEADER COURSE

Fig. 24. A 12" American bond continued intersecting wall.

Fig. 25. Brick sill used at a window opening.

Door frames for homes are still principally of wood. The large doors on office and industrial buildings are often of metal. The bottom sill of a door is usually precast concrete. The sill of a window may be precast concrete or brick (Fig. 25). At the top is a lintel, usually steel, to support the weight of the brick over the openings.

In bricklaying, the problem of discontinuing the bond or stopping the brickwork for openings is not a difficult one when once understood. The bond should be worked out by the architect in designing the building so that the sizes and spacing of the openings will permit stopping the bond without irregular lap conditions. The brick linear dimensions should, wherever possible, be calculated so as to reduce cutting to a minimum. The competent architect will attend to this.

## Window Openings

Window sills in brick buildings should be of brick or stone. Concrete unless it is precast is not well adapted for this purpose. Brick window sills are preferable to stone. Brick sills add to the appearance of the building and are inexpensive since they are of the same material as the wall and placed by the same workmen who lay up the wall, thus, eliminating the necessity of additional labor to place the heavy stone. Brick for sills should be laid on edge, rowlock style, and pitched approximately at an incline of 1″ in 6″ to shed the water.

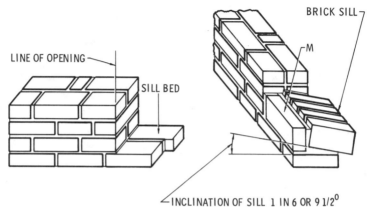

Fig. 26. The construction of a brick window sill.

Fig. 26 shows how an opening for a window is started and the inclined brick on edge which holds the window frame. The illustration shown is for an 8″ wall. A better finish is secured by the use of special sill brick. Some of these special shaped bricks and the method of laying are shown in Fig. 27.

To obtain the best effect, brick sills should be "slip sills" not wider than the actual masonry opening. Brick sills laid horizontally with a pitch formed with concrete are not satisfactory, since the action of the weather may cause the concrete to loosen. In general, brick is the most satisfactory material for window sills, although it may be made to form attractive combinations with other materials. Where brick is used throughout, however, no material has to be specially ordered. An appearance of great solidity may be gained by sloping the brick window sills very sharply, thus, increasing the depth of the reveal of the windows.

Windows should begin a whole number of courses above the floor level or the beginning of the brick wall. Use the 4″ module system, but remember it takes three brick courses to equal 8″,

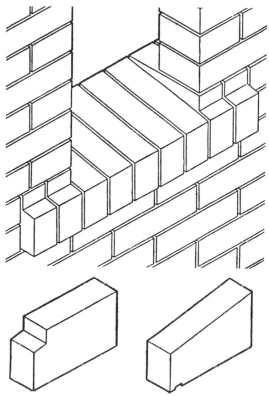

Fig. 27. Specially formed brick is available for window sills.

or two 4" module dimensions. At sill height, lay the sloped row lock course to occupy the height of two normal courses. Fig. 28 shows a cross section of a sill for a wood window frame and back sill. As soon as the mortar is set, put the window frame in place and brace it with boards to be sure it holds its vertical and horizontal position (Fig. 29). The boards should be left in place for several days. The rest of the wall is then built up to the height of the top of the window frame. If the top course does not come out at least ¼" from the top, the difference can be adjusted with mortar.

Wood window frames must be prepainted with a prime coat before they are set into place. Stock sizes ordered from the supplier will usually be applied with a prime coat. Complete wind and

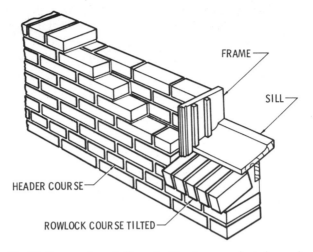

FRAME

SILL

HEADER COURSE

ROWLOCK COURSE TILTED

Fig. 28. Cross section of sill construction for a wood window sash.

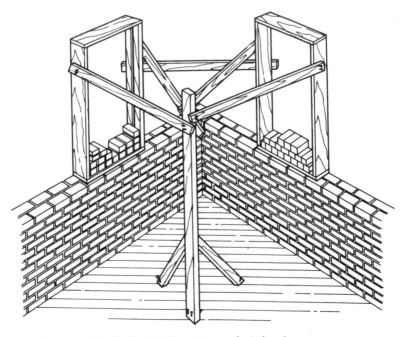

Fig. 29. Method of bracing wood window frames.

rainproofing is done at the time of installation by a thin layer of mortar. Steel frames may be plated or painted to prevent rust. Aluminum frames are nearly always anodized, a process that gives it a hard coat and also prevents oxidation. Anodizing can be ordered in a variety of colors.

## Door Openings

The treatment of door openings is the same as for window openings, except that they begin at the bottom. A precast concrete sill is laid on the foundation, the same as the first course of brick. To assure a firm hold onto the sides of the brick wall, pieces of wood the same size as a half-bat brick are mortared into the side opening

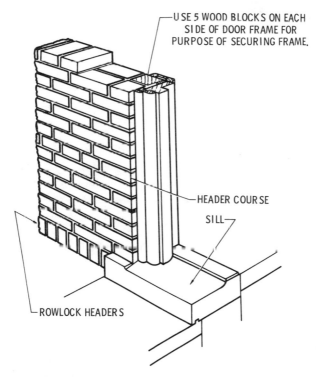

Fig. 30. Precast concrete door sill. Wood blocks mortared to the brick will later hold the door frame.

the same as though they were brick. Screws are used later to secure the door frame. This is indicated in Fig. 30. Precast concrete is the most satisfactory material for door sills.

## LINTELS

The support over window or other openings is formed by lintels or by arches. The treatment of arches is explained later. A lintel is

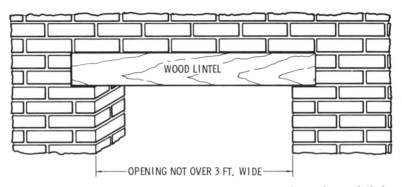

WOOD LINTEL

OPENING NOT OVER 3 FT. WIDE

Fig. 31. A lintel supports the brick over an opening. Wood may be used if the opening is not over 3 ft. wide.

the horizontal top piece of a window or doorway opening serving to support the brickwork as in Fig. 31. It should be understood that the lintel is not a part of the window (or door) frame but serves to support the brickwork so that no undue stress will be brought on the frame tending to distort it.

A wooden lintel is all the support required for brickwork over openings 3 ft. wide and less. When the mortar is set, brickwork will support itself over spans of this width, even though the wood lintel should burn or decay. However, since brick should never be required to support its own weight over an opening, it is preferable to use steel, precast reinforced concrete, or reinforced brick (RBM).

Fig. 32 is a cutaway view of a steel lintel. It consists of two angle irons, ¼" thick and back-to-back. Fig. 33 shows the use of this type of lintel over a door opening. The ends of the lintel should extend 4" to 8" into the brick work, for support. The depth of the

156

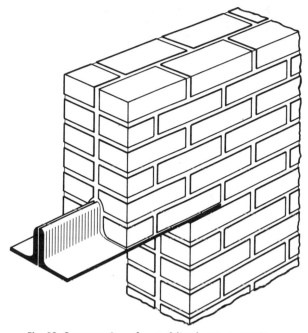

Fig. 32. Cutaway view of a steel lintel over an opening.

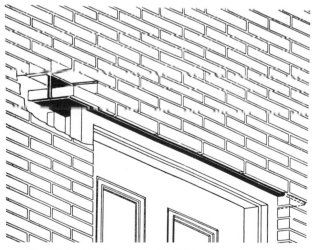

Fig. 33. Another type of steel lintel used over an opening.

157

lintel into the brick work depends on the length of the span and should be deeper for longer spans. Table 1 shows the lintel sizes recommended for two wall thicknesses and several span lengths.

### Table 1. Lintel Sizes Recommended for Two Wall Thicknesses and Several Span Lengths

| Wall thickness | 3 feet | | 4 feet* steel angles | 5 feet* steel angles | 6 feet* steel angles | 7 feet* steel angles | 8 feet* steel angles |
|---|---|---|---|---|---|---|---|
| | Steel angles | Wood | | | | | |
| 8" - - - - - - | 2-3x3x¼ | 2x8 2-2x4 | 2-3x3x¼ | 2-3x3x¼ | 2-3½x3½x¼ | 2-3½x3½x¼ | 2-3½x3½x¼ |
| 12" - - - - - - | 2-3x3x¼ | 2x12 2-2x6 | 2-3x3x¼ | 2-3½x3½x¼ | 2-3½x3½x¼ | 2-4x4x¼ | 2-4x4x4¼ |

*Wood lintels should not be used for spans over 3 ft. since they burn out in case of fire and allow the brick to fall.

Reinforcing rods in brickwork (Fig. 34) will handle moderate loads and are economical.

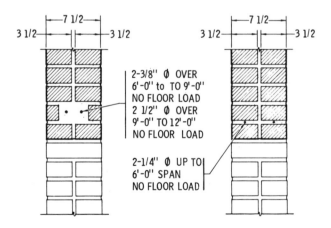

Fig. 34. Cutaway view of reinforcing rods to strengthen openings.

## ARCHES

Properly constructed, an arch of brick is capable of supporting very heavy loads. Arches were used even in ancient times, before

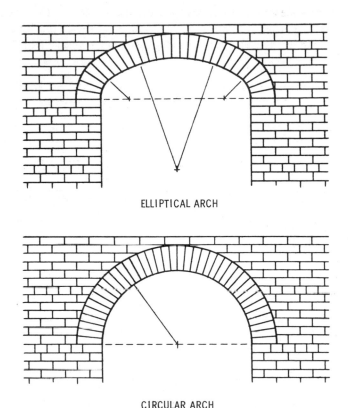

ELLIPTICAL ARCH

CIRCULAR ARCH

**Fig. 35. The two most common arches used.**

the discovery of concrete or mortar for a bonding agent. Arches hewn from stone were able to support aqueducts and roads over rivers, just by their shape and careful placement. While circular and elliptical (Fig. 35) are the most common shapes given to arches, others are jack and segmental as shown in Fig. 36.

The construction of an arch should be left only to the most experienced mason. It involves a great amount of brick cutting, for careful fitting of the horizontal courses to the edge of the arch, and careful application of mortar to the arch bricks. Mortar should not be less than ¼ " in thickness. Because of the form of the arch, the outer edges of the brick will be farther apart and will require

159

JACK ARCHES

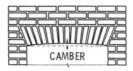

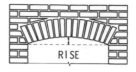

NOTE:
CAMBER 1/8" PER FOOT OF SPAN

NOTE:
MIN. RISE 1" PER FOOT OF SPAN

SEGMENTAL ARCHES

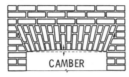

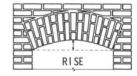

Courtesy Structural Clay Products Inst.

**Fig. 36. Other popular arch contours.**

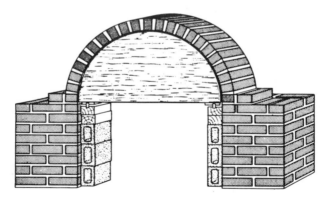

**Fig. 37. A plywood template is used to support the brick while mortar is curing.**

progressively thicker mortar joints from the inner edge to the outer edge.

Arches of brick can be successfully placed and temporarily supported with templates or wood forms (Fig. 37). After carefully determining their size, two pieces of plywood are cut and fastened together with two pieces of 2" × 4" between. This gives two edges

Fig. 38. A double arch used in a Spanish designed wall.

Fig. 39. A fireplace opening with a brick arch.

161

for the support of the brick. When the wall is built up to the beginning of the arch, the template is put into place supported on wood posts, brick, or concrete block, as shown in Fig. 37. Brick is placed on edge over the arch to determine the number of bricks needed. If possible there should be an uneven number of bricks, so the middle brick is at the center of the arch. This will be the closer brick and is the last one to be buttered with mortar and placed.

Once the number of bricks is determined, start work from both ends, buttering and placing. In a good job the arch sections will meet in the center, for placing the closer brick. Also, all mortar thicknesses will be alike. The wood form should be left in place while the rest of the courses continue up the wall, around the arch. After several days, the mortar will have taken a good set and the arch will be self-supporting.

Arches continue to be favored in architectural design, especially in Spanish style homes in the Southwest. They are used for both exterior and interior design.

The illustration in Fig. 38 shows a double arch in a Spanish style wall. In Fig. 39, a brick arch is used for a fireplace opening.

## CHAPTER 8

# Brick Surfaces and Patterns

Brick is not only an excellent material structurally for homes and buildings, because of its high compressive strength, but with today's patterns and colors it is used almost as much for its aesthetic value. The home in Fig. 1 is a stucco and brick veneer home. On three sides it is stuccoed (a 1″ thick layer of concrete) over frame, which provides a sturdy and well-insulated home. The front side, however, is a single tier of brick (brick veneer), purely for its decorative value.

Fig. 1. Brick veneer adds beauty to a home.

163

Fig. 2 is a closeup look at the brick used in this home. It carries the name "white bark." Its outer texture is like the bark of a tree and its color is a buff white, rather than pure white. Standard mortar, with no color added, seems to blend well with the color of the brick.

Fig. 2. Appearance of the texture in the brick used in the home in Fig. 1.

As mentioned in Chapter 1, color is altered in brick by chemicals added, and by the amount of heat and the length of time used in the kiln. Texture is the result of the processing. Figs. 3, 4, and 5 show a few of the variations and textures available in one small local brickyard. They may or may not be available in other brickyards. When planning a new home or building, one should review the brick colors and textures he can obtain locally. A large brick processor will produce a large variety of brick. If he is located at some distance from your city, expect to pay more for the brick, because of the high cost of transportation of such heavy material.

Brick probably offers the greatest flexibility in decorative variations, at a reasonable cost, than any other building material of comparable strength. Because brick is available in such a variety

Fig. 3. Illustrating common brick with different amounts of oxide added to produce different colors.

Fig. 4. Deep vertical scoring in brick can alter apparent dimensions of a wall.

Fig. 5. Brick can be made to look like natural stone.

of colors, it lends itself easily to the formation of patterns with endless variations.

## HOW TO MAKE PATTERNED WALLS

Chapter 4 described the standard patterns resulting from bonding in a number of traditional forms. Included were garden walls (Fig. 6) representing variations of the standard patterns. By the use of the imagination, and artistic genius, an almost infinite variety of patterns become possible, without loss of good bonding.

A great variety of ornamental figures may be obtained by the use of light and dark brick or brick of various shades, and by the combination of headers and stretchers in each course variously arranged.

### Stretcher Bond Patterns

With alternate light and dark brick, various effects may be produced depending on:

1. Lap.
2. Shift.

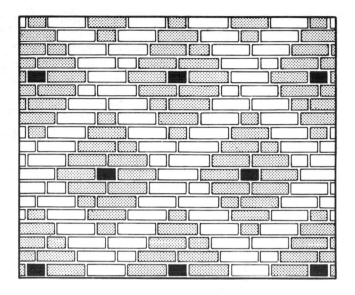

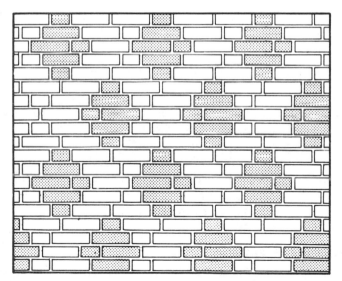

Fig. 6. Diagonal lines and dovetail patterns form a garden-wall pattern with the help of brick color variations.

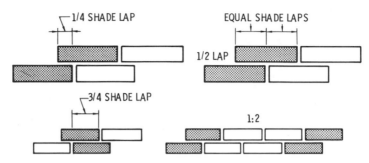

Fig. 7. Various diagonal patterns may be formed by altering the lap.

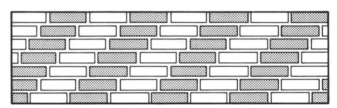

Fig. 8. A diagonal pattern in a wall using ¼ lap.

3. Relative position of shades in adjacent courses as shown in Fig. 7.

A variation consists of laying two light bricks to one dark brick, thus, further separating the dark diagonals. Various other combinations of the two shades may be made, securing additional effects.

### Header Bond Patterns

Similar two-shade effects may be obtained in header courses but only with ¼ lap. The general appearance of a wall laid with two-shade headers alternating is indicated in Fig. 9.

### Reversal of Shift

The monotony of long "dark diagonals" may be broken by the simple device of reversing the shift as indicated in Fig. 10. The appearance of a wall laid in header bond with reversal of shift is shown in Fig. 11.

168

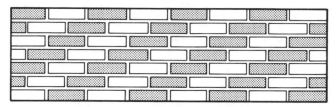

Fig. 9. Appearance of a wall laid with header bond, two-shade, ¼ lap.

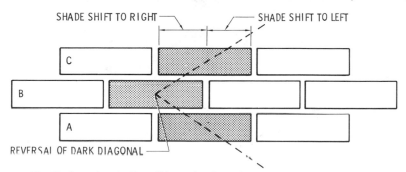

Fig. 10. Reversing the line shift can break up the monotony of a continuous diagonal line.

Various patterns may be obtained by the use of dark brick for:

1. Headers.
2. Stretchers.
3. Both headers and stretchers in combination with various shade shifts, reversal of shifts, etc.

Effects may be obtained in this combination of stretcher and header bonds in various ways. Thus, dark horizontals at uniform intervals are obtained with dark headers, also "V's" and even diamonds are made by proper placing of dark brick.

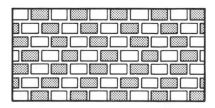

Fig. 11. Appearance of a wall with reverse shift of shading.

A multiplicity of patterns are obtainable in Flemish bond (single and double) using the bonds just described, dark headers, dark stretchers, or combination of both in groups. The Flemish bond with dark headers gives dark uprights and dark diagonals combined as shown in Fig. 12. It also illustrates the single and double form of bonding.

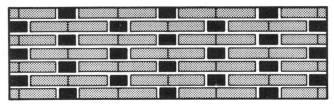

Fig. 12. Flemish bond with shaded headers.

## Garden-Wall Bond Patterns

Due to the increased number of stretchers used in this bond, the patterns obtained are more extended than in the other bonds. Fig. 13 shows appearance of the three-stretcher form with dark headers the latter centered over stretchers. A three-shade effect with garden-wall courses alternating with stretcher courses is shown in Fig. 14.

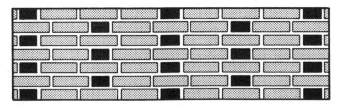

Fig. 13. A three stretcher garden wall with dark headers.

## Diamond Unit Patterns

The accompanying illustrations in Fig. 15 show the unit system. The diamond shapes formed by various combinations of headers and stretchers represent the various units or "eyes" upon which all diagonal bonds are based.

Beginning with unit 1, which is composed of a stretcher with a header centered above and below it, each succeeding unit is formed by extending every course of the preceding unit the width of a header, always centering the courses on the middle course regarded as the horizontal axis of the unit, and terminating the whole above and below by a header. As a result, no matter how far they may be carried out, they always present exact mathematical proportions and bear a definite relationship to each other.

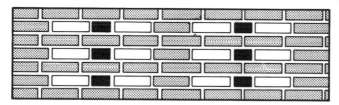

Fig. 14. A garden wall with bricks of three different shades.

It is interesting to note that the units may also be recognized by their horizontal axes which in odd-numbered units are always composed entirely of stretchers, while in even-numbered units they always carry one, and only one, header, set as near their center as possible. The number of an even-numbered unit is double the number of stretchers in its axis, while that of an odd-numbered unit is one less than double the number of its axial stretchers. Thus, if we see a unit with a horizontal axis of 4 stretchers only, we may be sure that it is the odd-numbered unit 7; but if it has 4 stretchers and a header, we know that it is the even-numbered unit 8.

With unit 4 (Fig. 15), there begins to appear units within units. While the header, crossed by vertical stretcher joints which appears at the center of unit 4, is not strictly a unit in our sense of the term, it is nevertheless the primary unit of all, as the smallest normal element in brickwork. Unit 1 clearly comes to view as the center of

171

Fig. 15. Diamond pattern of various sizes may be developed by a unit system.

unit 5; unit 2 appears in 6; unit 3 in 7; and so on. It is by the treatment of these units, each of which in itself is a bond pattern, that various patterns may be worked out on the surface of the wall by the proper handling of the shades and textures in the brick, or of the mortar joints.

172

The units may be made to join, or butt, each other vertically and horizontally; or they may be separated by introducing between them one or more courses above and below, or variously arranged rows of brick in a general vertical direction on the side, as may be seen in the accompanying diagrams. When separated, the units are said to be surrounded by horizontal and vertical borders. Much of the artistic value of the pattern will depend on the skill and taste with which these borders are worked out.

The designer in brickwork is urged to remember that the use of pattern bonds obligates him to pay the strictest and most thoughtful attention to the beginning and ending of the pattern, at either the bottom or top of the structure or on piers as they occur separately or between windows. He must first decide on a unit which is suitable to the size of the panel to be covered, and then exactly center it on the panel, so that his pattern may end in a symmetrical manner, both laterally and vertically. In order to secure vertical symmetry, the panel must always have an odd number of courses, that is, an even number on each side of the median line.

## Treatment of the Units

The accompanying illustrations in Fig. 15 show the appearance of the units in a wall pattern and indicate the way to treat the shades and textures of brick in designing patterns. The illustrations are by no means intended to dictate what may or may not be the best shade combinations in any given bond, or the blendings of light and shade or the contrasts of color and texture in brickwork, but merely as suggestions for pattern design.

At the same time, an underlying principle is involved in what has been pictured. It will be readily understood that the smaller units which are worked into patterns of finer texture and quieter shadings, are most appropriate for walls of limited area, while the bolder outlines and heightened contrasts of the larger figures are more suitable for larger sweeping wall surfaces.

## Brick Pattern Diagrams

To assist the bricklayer in laying out pattern designs, a diagram or drawing of the brick units in the wall surface may be made.

The brick manufacturers usually employ specially designed cross section paper which is ruled with spaces equal in length to a stretcher and a mortar joint.

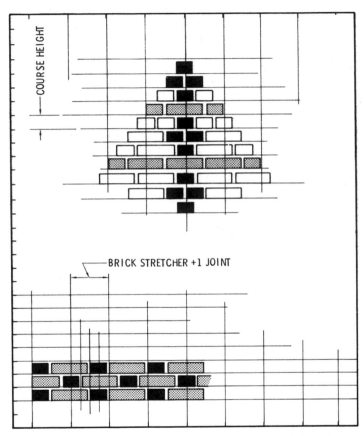

Fig. 16. Cross-section paper is an aid to developing patterns before the start of actual brick work.

This sectional paper is laid out in such a way that the actual dimensions have been reduced to $\frac{1}{16}$ of the original. The length is also divided into four equal parts, so that the overlapping of the brick into the various courses may be properly located. The

174

course heights are laid out by using the depth or thickness of a brick and the width of a mortar joint.

Fig. 16 represents a drawing on which the stretchers and course heights of brick are indicated by definite units of measurement. A diagonal pattern, designed in the upper part of the diagram, is laid out from a center line so that the bond pattern is symmetrical on each side of the center.

In addition to laying out the pattern bond on paper, the bricklayer should compute the length of courses in feet and inches and the total height of various pattern bonds with varying widths of mortar joints in feet and inches.

This distance can be determined in a wall laid up in running bond by multiplying the unit length of a brick and mortar joint by the number of brick in the course. In other types of bonds such as the Flemish, where the courses are made up of stretcher and header the problem is not quite so simple.

Tables, scales, and bricklayer's rules however, have been devised to assist the bricklayer in determining the number of brick in a course of a certain length and the number of courses in a definite height.

## MORTAR JOINTS

In addition to variations in brick, mortar joints may also be treated in a number of ways to produce different artistic effects.

The following is quoted from technical notes published by the STRUCTURAL CLAY PRODUCTS INSTITUTE.

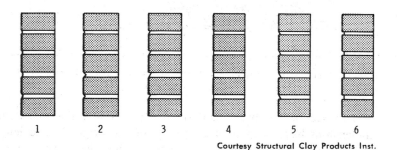

1    2    3    4    5    6

Courtesy Structural Clay Products Inst.

Fig. 17. Mortar joint treatment must be considered in brick masonry appearance.

Mortar joint finishes fall into two classes: troweled and tooled joints. In the troweled joint, the excess mortar is simply cut off (struck) with a trowel and finished with the trowel. For the tooled joint, a special tool, other than the trowel is used to compress and shape the mortar in the joint. Fig. 17 shows a cross section of typical mortar joints used in good brickwork.

*Concave Joint (1) and V-Shaped Joint (2)*—These joints are normally kept quite small and are formed by the use of a steel jointing tool. These joints are very effective in resisting rain penetration and are recommended for use in areas subjected to heavy rains and high winds.

*Weathered Joint (3)*—This joint requires care as it must be worked from below. However, it is the best of the troweled joints as it is compacted and sheds water readily.

*Rough Cut or Flush Joint (4)*—This is the simplest joint for the mason, since it is made by holding the edge of the trowel flat against the brick and cutting in any direction. This produces an uncompacted joint with a small hairline crack where the mortar is pulled away from the brick by the cutting action. This joint is not always watertight.

*Struck Joint (5)*—This is a common joint in ordinary brickwork. Since the mason usually works from the inside of the wall, this is an easy joint to strike with a trowel. Some compaction occurs, but the small ledge does not shed water readily, resulting in a less permeable joint than some of the previous.

*Raked Joint (6)*—This is made by removing the surface of the mortar, while it is still soft, with a square-edged tool. While the joint may be compacted it is difficult to make weathertight and is not recommended where rains, high winds, or freezing are likely to occur. This joint produces marked shadows and tends to darken the overall appearance of the wall.

Colored mortars may be successfully used to enhance the patterns in masonry. Two methods are commonly used: First, the entire mortar joint may be colored; second, where a tooled joint is used, tuck pointing is the best method. In this technique, the entire wall is completed with a 1″ deep raked joint and the colored mortar is carefully filled in later.

176

## CHAPTER 9

# Chimneys and Fireplaces

The term chimney generally includes both the chimney proper and (in house construction) the fireplace. There is no part of a house that is more likely to be a source of trouble than a chimney that is improperly constructed. Accordingly, it should be so built that it will be mechanically strong and properly shaped and proportioned to give adequate draught.

For strength, chimneys should be built of solid brickwork and should have no openings except those required for the heating apparatus. If a chimney fire occurs, considerable heat may be engendered in the chimney, and the safety of the house will then depend on the integrity of the flue wall. A little intelligent care in the construction of fireplaces and chimneys will prove to be the best insurance. As a first precaution, all wood framing of floor and roof must be kept at least 2″ away from the chimney and no other woodwork of any kind should be projected into the brickwork surrounding the flues (Fig. 1).

When it is understood that the only motive power available to produce a natural draught in a chimney is that due to the small difference in weight of the column of hot gases in the chimney and of a similar column of cold air outside, the necessity of properly constructing the chimney so that the flow of gases will encounter the least resistance must be apparent.

The intensity of chimney draught is measured in inches of a water column sustained by the pressure produced and depends on:

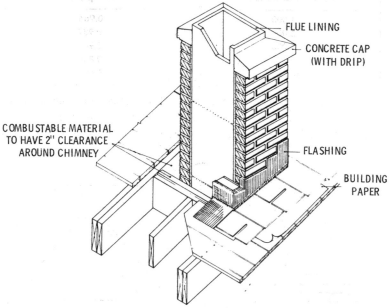

FLUE LINING

CONCRETE CAP
(WITH DRIP)

COMBUSTABLE MATERIAL
TO HAVE 2'' CLEARANCE
AROUND CHIMNEY

FLASHING

BUILDING
PAPER

**Fig. 1. Chimney construction above the roof.**

1. The difference in temperature inside and outside the chimney.

2. The height of the chimney.

Theoretical draft in inches of water at sea level is as follows: let,

$D$ = Theoretical draft,
$H$ = Distance from top of chimney to grates,
$T$ = Temperature of air outside of chimney,
$T_1$ = Temperature of gases in the chimney.

then,

$$D = 7.00 \, H \left( \frac{1}{461 + T} - \frac{1}{461 + T_1} \right)$$

The results obtained represent the theoretical draft at sea level.

For higher altitudes the calculations are subject to correction as follows:

178

| For altitudes (in feet) of | Multiply by |
|:---:|:---:|
| 1,000 | 0.966 |
| 2,000 | 0.932 |
| 3,000 | 0.900 |
| 5,000 | 0.840 |
| 10,000 | 0.694 |

A frequent cause of poor draught in house chimneys is that the peak of the roof extends higher than the chimney. In such case the wind sweeping across or against the roof will form eddy

BAD DRAUGHT

Fig. 2. Illustrating how a roof peak higher than the top of the chimney can cause down drafts.

179

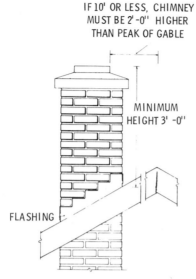

IF 10' OR LESS, CHIMNEY
MUST BE 2'-0" HIGHER
THAN PEAK OF GABLE

MINIMUM
HEIGHT 3'-0"

FLASHING

Fig. 3. Ample clearance is needed between peak of roof and top of chimney.

Courtesy Structural Clay Products Inst.

currents that drive down the chimney or check the natural rise of the gases as shown in Fig. 2. To avoid this, the chimney should be extended at least 2 ft. higher than the roof, as shown in Fig. 3.

In order to reduce to a minimum the resistance or friction due to the chimney walls the chimney should run as near straight as possible from bottom to top. This not only gives better draught but facilitates cleaning. If, however, offsets are necessary from one story to another, they should be very gradual. The offset should never be displaced so much that the center of gravity of the upper portion falls outside the area of the lower portion. In other words, the center of gravity must fall within the width and thickness of the chimney below the offset.

## FLUES

A chimney serving two or more floors should have a separate flue for every fireplace. The flues should always be lined with some fireproof material. In fact, the building laws of large cities provide for this. The least expensive way to build these is to make the walls 4" thick lined with burned clay flue lining. With walls of this thickness, never omit the lining and never replace the lining with plaster. The expansion and contraction of the chimney would cause the plaster to crack and an opening from the interior of the flue would be formed. See that all joints are completely filled with mortar.

### Table 1. Standard Sizes of Modular Clay Flue Linings

| Minimum Net inside Area (sq. in.) | Nominal[1] Dimensions (in.) | Outside[2] Dimensions (in.) | Minimum Wall Thickness (in.) | Approximate Maximum Outside Corner Radius (in.) |
|---|---|---|---|---|
| 15 | 4x 8 | 3.5x 7.5 | 0.5 | 1 |
| 20 | 4x12 | 3.5x11.5 | 0.625 | 1 |
| 27 | 4x16 | 3.5x15.5 | 0.75 | 1 |
| 35 | 8x 8 | 7.5x 7.5 | 0.625 | 2 |
| 57 | 8x12 | 7.5x11.5 | 0.75 | 2 |
| 74 | 8x16 | 7.5x15.5 | 0.875 | 2 |
| 87 | 12x12 | 11.5x11.5 | 0.875 | 3 |
| 120 | 12x16 | 11.5x15.5 | 1.0 | 3 |
| 162 | 16x16 | 15.5x15.5 | 1.125 | 4 |
| 208 | 16x20 | 15.5x19.5 | 1.25 | 4 |
| 262 | 20x20 | 19.5x19.5 | 1.375 | 5 |
| 320 | 20x24 | 19.5x23.5 | 1.5 | 5 |
| 385 | 24x24 | 23.5x23.5 | 1.625 | 6 |

[1]Cross section of flue lining shall fit within rectangle of dimension corresponding to nominal size.

[2]Length in each case shall be 24 ± 0.5 in.

## Flue Lining

Walls 8" or more in thickness may be used without a flue lining. However, walls under 8" must have a lining of fired clay. With the increased use of gas furnaces in homes, fired-clay linings are recommended for all chimneys because of chemical action of gas residue on common brick.

Clay lining for flues also follows the modular system of sizes. Table 1 lists currently available common sizes. The flue lining should extend the entire height of the chimney, projecting about

4″ above the cap and a slope formed of cement to within 2″ of the top of the lining as shown in Fig. 3. This helps to give an upward direction to the wind currents at the top of the flue and tends to prevent rain and snow from being blown down inside the chimney.

The information given here is intended primarily for chimneys on residential homes. They will usually carry temperatures under 600°F. Larger chimneys, used for schools and other larger buildings, have a temperature range between 600°F and 800°F. Industrial chimneys with temperatures above 800°F often are very high and require special engineering for their planning and execution. High-temperature brick chimneys must include steel reinforcing rods to prevent cracking due to expansion and contraction from the changes in temperature.

## CHIMNEY CONSTRUCTION

Every possible thought must be given to providing good draft, leak-proof mortaring, and protection from heat transfer to combustible material. Good draft means a chimney flue without obstructions. The flue must be straight from the source to the outlet. Metal pipes from the furnace into the flue must end flush with the inside of the chimney and not protrude into the flue, as shown in Fig. 4. The flue must be straight from the source to the outlet, without any bends, if at all possible. When two sources, such as a furnace and a fireplace feed the one chimney, they each must have separate flues.

To prevent leakage of smoke and gas fumes from the chimney into the house, and to improve the draft, a special job of careful mortaring must be observed. The layer of mortar on each course of brick must be even and completely cover the bricks. End buttering must be complete. However, it is best to mortar the flue lining lightly between the lining and the brick. Use just enough to hold the lining securely. The air space that is left acts as additional air insulation between the lining and the brick and reduces the transfer of heat.

No combustible material, such as the wood of roof rafters or floor joists, must abut the chimney itself. There should be at least

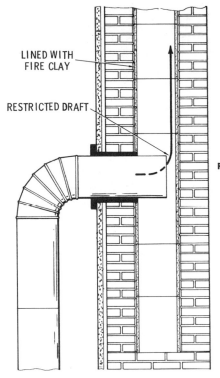

LINED WITH
FIRE CLAY

RESTRICTED DRAFT

Fig. 4. Furnace pipes must not project
into the flue of a chimney.

a 2" space between the wood and the brick of the chimney, as shown in Fig. 1. Brick and flue lining are built up together. The lining clay is placed first and the bricks built up around it. Another section of lining is placed and brick built up, etc.

Chimneys carrying away the exhaust of oil- and coal-burning furnaces, where still used, need a cleanout trap. An air-tight cast iron door is installed at a point below the entrance of the furnace smoke pipe.

Because of the heavier weight of the brick in a chimney, the base must be built to carry the load. A foundation for a residential chimney should be about 4" thick. If a fireplace is included, the foundation thickness should be increased to about 8".

After the chimney has been completed, it should be tested for leaks. Build a smudge fire in the bottom and wait for smoke to

183

come out of the top. Cover the top and carefully inspect the rest of the chimney for leaks. If there are any, add mortar at the points of leakage.

Builders should become acquainted with local codes for the construction of chimneys. They should also check the National Building Code recommendations as set up by the AMERICAN INSURANCE ASSOCIATION.

## FIREPLACES

With modern-day home heating systems, a fireplace contributes very little toward heating the home. But there is nothing like the flickering flames of a wood-burning fireplace to add cheer to the hearts of those sitting around it. Most new construction for single-family homes includes a fireplace when the house is built. A fireplace can be added to just about any home not so equipped.

There was a time when the fireplace, or an open fire, was the sole source for cooking and heating. In a few areas of the United States, where the winter climates are too mild for a heating system, the fireplace is still the only source of heat to take the chill off a cool evening.

The fireplace dates back to the earliest history of man. The first home fires, forerunners to the modern fireplace, were those kindled on the earth or on a conveniently placed slab stone around which the family gathered to prepare its food. In just what period in our history fires were first used will perhaps never be known. We have evidence that primitive man made use of caves in his first temporary dwelling and built fires at the mouth of these caves not only to prepare food but also to protect his family from enemies.

Later, when dwellings were constructed outside of caves, family life centered in one large room in the middle of which a wood fire was lighted. Here, the smoke was allowed to escape as best it could through a hole in the roof or crevices in the wall. This use of fire for heating and cooking was adopted even by the nomads, who built fires in the center of their tents and allowed the smoke to escape through a prepared opening at the top.

As more permanent and larger habitations were built and balconies or second floors were used for sleeping quarters, the hearthstone was moved to the corner of the room and an opening made in the wall to allow the smoke to escape. Later a stone hood which sloped back against the wall was added to aid in carrying the smoke out of the building.

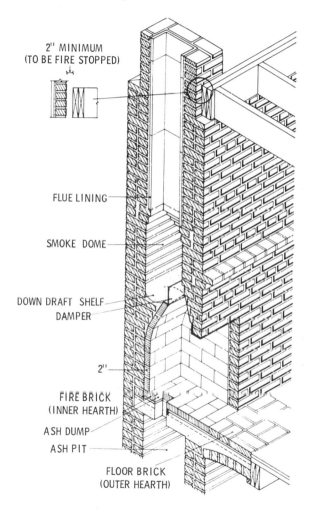

2" MINIMUM
(TO BE FIRE STOPPED)

FLUE LINING

SMOKE DOME

DOWN DRAFT SHELF
DAMPER

2"

FIRE BRICK
(INNER HEARTH)

ASH DUMP

ASH PIT

FLOOR BRICK
(OUTER HEARTH)

Courtesy Structural Clay Products Inst.

**Fig. 5. Cross section of a typical fireplace and chimney of modern design.**

185

## Table 2. Recommended Sizes of Fireplace Openings

| Opening | | Depth, d | Minimum back (horizontal) c | Vertical back wall, a | Inclined back wall, b | Outside dimensions of standard rectangular flue lining | Inside diameter of standard round flue lining |
|---|---|---|---|---|---|---|---|
| Width, w | Height, h | | | | | | |
| Inches | Inches | Inches | Inches | Inches | Inches | Inches | Inches |
| 24 | 24 | 16—18 | 14 | 14 | 16 | 8½ by 8½ | 10 |
| 28 | 24 | 16—18 | 14 | 14 | 16 | 8½ by 8½ | 10 |
| 24 | 28 | 16—18 | 14 | 14 | 20 | 8½ by 8½ | 10 |
| 30 | 28 | 16—18 | 16 | 14 | 20 | 8½ by 13 | 10 |
| 36 | 28 | 16—18 | 22 | 14 | 20 | 8½ by 13 | 12 |
| 42 | 28 | 16—18 | 28 | 14 | 20 | 8½ by 18 | 12 |
| 36 | 32 | 18—20 | 20 | 14 | 24 | 8½ by 18 | 12 |
| 42 | 32 | 18—20 | 26 | 14 | 24 | 13 by 13 | 12 |
| 48 | 32 | 18—20 | 32 | 14 | 24 | 13 by 13 | 15 |
| 42 | 36 | 18—20 | 26 | 14 | 28 | 13 by 13 | 15 |
| 48 | 36 | 18—20 | 32 | 14 | 28 | 13 by 18 | 15 |
| 54 | 36 | 18—20 | 38 | 14 | 28 | 13 by 18 | 15 |
| 60 | 36 | 18—20 | 44 | 14 | 28 | 13 by 18 | 15 |
| 42 | 40 | 20—22 | 24 | 17 | 29 | 13 by 13 | 15 |
| 48 | 40 | 20—22 | 30 | 17 | 29 | 13 by 18 | 15 |
| 54 | 40 | 20—22 | 36 | 17 | 29 | 13 by 18 | 15 |
| 60 | 40 | 20—22 | 42 | 17 | 29 | 18 by 18 | 18 |
| 66 | 40 | 20—22 | 48 | 17 | 29 | 18 by 18 | 18 |
| 72 | 40 | 22—28 | 51 | 17 | 29 | 18 by 18 | 18 |

Gradually the efficiency of the open fire was increased and eventually the fireplace was constructed in a recess in the center of one of the walls, with its own hood and enclosed flue, leading up to a chimney on top of the wall. As time passed, more consideration was given to the comforts of living. The fireplace was not only improved, but became the central decorative feature of the home.

The value of fireplaces was appreciated in England as early as the latter part of the fourteenth century, when they became an ornamental feature in the better homes. Count Rumford, an English scientist who published a series of essays on chimneys and fireplaces in 1796, is the one to whom we are most indebted for the improvement in fireplace design and for the rules governing the openings and flues. He spent a great deal of time studying the errors of fireplace construction and the principles governing the circulation of gases and combustion.

Probably in no other country have so many types and styles of fireplaces been constructed as in the United States. Although the ornamental mantel facings of fireplaces may be of other materials than brick, the chimney and its foundation are invariably of masonry construction. Fig. 5 shows a cross section of a fireplace and chimney stack suitable for the average home.

Fig. 6. A modern all-brick fireplace of ample size for burning good-sized logs.

187

Fireplaces are generally built in the living room or den. Newer homes have a den, in addition to the living room, and they are frequently wood paneled. The location of the fireplace should allow the maximum of heat to be radiated into the room, with consideration given to making it the center of a conversation area. At one time its location was dictated by the location of the furnace, to make use of a common chimney. In modern construction, with heating systems of the compact gas-fired type, the chimney is often a metal pipe from the furnace flue, straight through to the roof, not of the brick construction type. The brick fireplace chimney can then be placed to suit the best fireplace location in the home and room.

Fig. 7. A small corner fireplace made of brick and stucco.

Fireplace styles vary considerably from a rather large one with a wide opening (Fig. 6) to a smaller corner fireplace. The one shown in Fig. 6 is Spanish style. The larger fireplace is capable of burning larger size wood. Fireplace decorative finishes vary to suit the taste of the owner or the style of the home. Good heat insulation permits the use of wood trim or mantels. Often natural

188

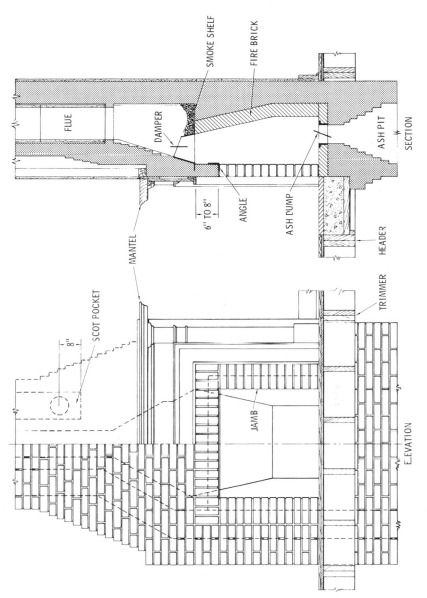

Fig. 8. Sketch of a basic fireplace. Letters refer to sizes recommended in Table 2.

rock is set in concrete. The smaller fireplace of Fig. 7 is all-brick construction, with a 1″ thick stucco finish.

Although large pieces of wood can be burned in the larger fireplaces, regardless of size, experience has indicated certain ratios of height, width, depth, etc., should be maintained for best flow of air under and around the burning wood. Recommended dimensions are shown in Table 2 which are related to the sketches in Fig. 8.

## FIREPLACE CONSTRUCTION

Brick masonry is nearly always used for fireplace construction. Sometimes brick masonry is used around a metal form frequently given the name heatilator. While any type of brick may be used for the outside of the fireplace, the fire pit must be lined with a high-temperature fire clay or fire brick.

The pit is nearly always sloped back and generally sloped on the sides. This is to reflect forward as much of the heat as possible. The more surface exposure that is given to the hot gases given off by the fire, the more heat will be radiated into the room. Fig. 5 is a cutaway view of an all-brick fireplace for a home with a basement. The only non-brick item is the adjustable damper. A basement makes possible a very large ash storage before cleanout is necessary. The ash dump opens into the basement cavity. A cleanout door at the bottom opens inward into the basement.

Fig. 9 is a side cutaway view of a typical fireplace for a home built on a concrete slab. It uses the metal form mentioned. The ash pit is a small metal box which can be lifted out, as shown in Fig. 10. In some slab home construction, the ash pit is a cavity formed in the concrete foundation with an opening for cleanout at the rear of the house. A metal grate over the opening prevents large pieces of wood from dropping into the ash pit as shown in Fig. 11.

### Importance of a Hearth

Every fireplace should include a brick area in front of it where hot wood embers may fall with safety. The plan view of Fig. 12 shows a brick hearth built 16″ out from the fireplace itself. This

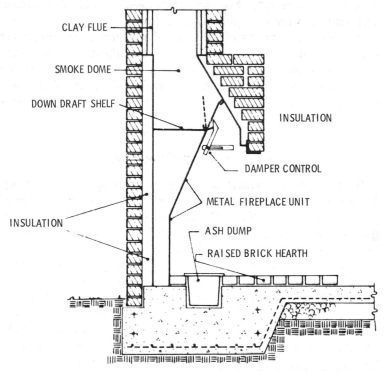

CLAY FLUE

SMOKE DOME

DOWN DRAFT SHELF

INSULATION

DAMPER CONTROL

METAL FIREPLACE UNIT

INSULATION

ASH DUMP

RAISED BRICK HEARTH

Courtesy Structural Clay Products Inst.

Fig. 9. Fireplace built on a concrete slab.

should be about the minimum distance. Most often the hearth is raised several inches above the floor level. This raises the fireplace itself, all of which makes for easier tending of the fire.

In addition to the protection of the floor by means of a hearth, every wood burning fireplace should have a screen, to prevent flying sparks from being thrown beyond the hearth distance and onto a carpeted or plastic tile floor.

## Ready-Built Fireplace Forms

There are a number of metal forms available, which make fireplace construction much easier. They make an ideal starting point for the handy homeowner who can build his own fireplace addition

Fig. 10. Metal lift-out ash box used in many fireplaces built on a concrete slab.

Fig. 11. A cast iron grate over the ash box to keep large pieces of burning wood from falling into the ash box.

192

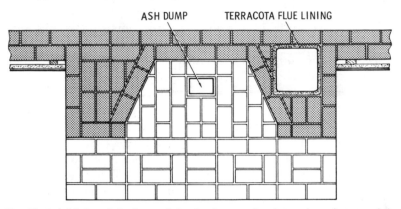

**Fig. 12. A brick hearth in front of the fireplace catches hot embers that may fall out of the fire.**

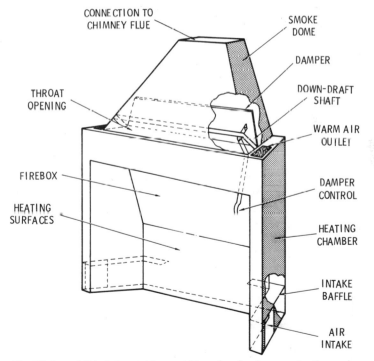

**Fig. 13. A prefabricated metal form which makes fireplace construction easier.**

to his home. They may be called by several names—heatilator or modified forms (Fig. 13).

These units are built of heavy metal or boiler plate steel and designed to be set into place and concealed by the usual brickwork, or other construction, so that no practical change in the fireplace mantel design is required by their use. One claimed advantage for modified fireplace units is that the correctly designed and proportioned fire box manufactured with throat, damper, smoke shelf, and chamber provides a form for the masonry, thus reducing the risk of failure and assuring a smokeless fireplace.

There is, however, no excuse for using incorrect proportions; and the desirability of using a foolproof form, as provided by the modified unit, is not necessary merely to obtain good proportions. Each fireplace should be designed to suit individual requirements and if correct dimensions are adhered to, a satisfactory fireplace will be obtained.

Prior to selecting and erecting a fireplace, several suitable designs should be considered and a careful estimate of the cost should be made; and it should also be borne in mind that even though the unit of a modified fireplace is well designed, it will not operate properly if the chimney is inadequate. Therefore, for satisfactory operation, the chimney must be made in accordance with the rules for correct construction to give satisfactory operation with the modified unit as well as with the ordinary fireplace.

Manufacturers of modified units also claim that labor and materials saved tend to offset the purchase price of the unit and that the saving in fuel tends to offset the increase in first cost. A minimum life of 20 years is usually claimed for the type and thickness of metal commonly used in these units.

As illustrated in Figs. 14 and 15, and sketches of Figs. 16 and 17, show how the brick work is built up around a metal fireplace form. The back view of Fig. 14 shows a layer of asbestos between the metal form and brick. The layer of fireproof asbestos wool battan or cementitious asbestos should be about 1″ thick. Note the ash door, which gives access to the ash pit for removal from the outside of the house.

Fig. 15 shows a partially built front view. By leaving a large air cavity on each side of the metal form and constructing the brick

Fig. 14. Brick work around the back of a fireplace form.

Fig. 15. Front view of the brick work around a metal fireplace form.

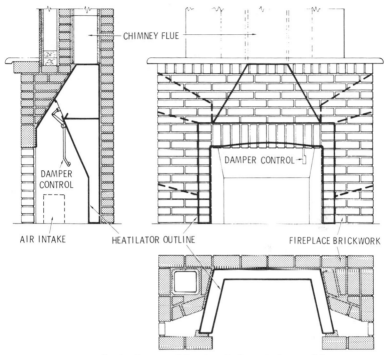

CHIMNEY FLUE

DAMPER CONTROL

DAMPER CONTROL

AIR INTAKE          HEATILATOR OUTLINE          FIREPLACE BRICKWORK

Fig. 16. Sketch of a typical fireplace built around a metal form

work with vents, some of the heat passing through the metal sides will be returned to the room. The rowlock stacked brick with no mortar, but an air space, permits cool air to enter below and warmed air to come out into the room from the upper outlet.

The front of the form includes a lintel for holding the course of brick just over the opening. A built-in damper is part of the form. Even with the use of a form, a good foundation is necessary for proper support as there is still quite a bit of brick weight. Chimney construction, following the illustrations and descriptions previously given, is still necessary.

## Other Fireplace Styles

The increasing popularity of fireplaces has produced a number of completely new styles and forms. One is the hooded type which

197

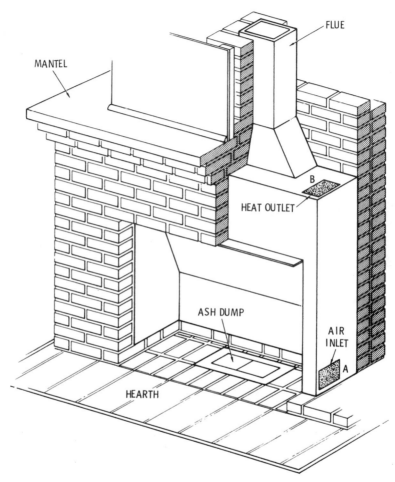

Fig. 17. Cutaway sketch of fireplace using a metal form.

permits the construction of the fireplace out into the room, rather than into the wall (Fig. 18).

Another, now shown in catalogs of the large mail-order companies, is completely free-standing and quite modern in appearance design. They stand away from the wall about 3 or 4 ft., on legs which require only a small tile base, and are vented with a simple

198

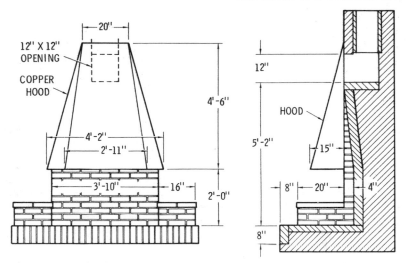

Fig. 18. A hood projecting out from the wall carries flue gasses up through chimney.

metal flue going through the ceiling, much like a space heater. They handle only very small-sized firewood.

A fireplace style being used in increasing numbers is a two-sided fireplace similar to that shown in the sketch of Fig. 19. It is ideal for building into a semi-divider type wall such as between a living area and a dining area. Thus, the burning logs may be enjoyed from either room, or both at once, and what heat is given off is divided between the two areas.

Important to successful wood burning is good circulation of air under and around the sides. A heavy metal grate which lifts the burning logs above the floor of the fireplace is essential (Fig. 20).

## SMOKY FIREPLACES

When a fireplace smokes, it should be examined to make certain that the essential requirements of construction as previously outlined, have been fulfilled. If the chimney has not been stopped up with fallen brick and the mortar joints are in good condition, a survey should be made to ascertain that nearby trees or tall buildings do not cause eddy currents down the flue.

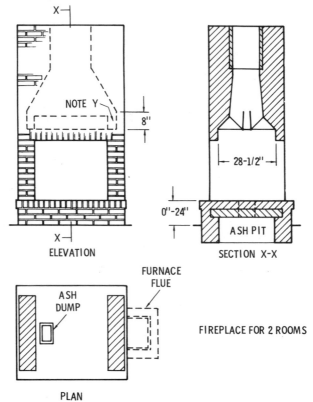

ELEVATION

SECTION X-X

FURNACE FLUE

ASH DUMP

FIREPLACE FOR 2 ROOMS

PLAN

Fig. 19. A two-sided fireplace which is ideal for a room divider.

To determine whether the fireplace opening is in correct proportion to the flue area, hold a piece of sheet metal across the top of the fireplace opening and then gradually lower it, making the opening smaller until smoke does not come into the room. Mark the lower edge of the metal on the sides of the fireplace.

The opening may then be reduced by building in a metal shield or hood across the top of the fireplace so that its lower edge is at the marks made during the test. Trouble with smoky fireplaces can also usually be remedied by increasing the height of the flue.

Uncemented flue-lining joints cause smoke to penetrate the flue joints and descend out of the fireplace. The best remedy is to tear out the chimney and join linings properly. When this is impractical,

200

Fig. 20. A grate is used to hold logs above the base allowing air to move under and through the burning wood.

try the alternate method described in the following paragraph.

Where flue joints are uncemented and mortar in surrounding brick work disintegrated, there is often a leakage of air in the chimney causing poor draft. This prevents the stack from exerting the draft possibilities which its height would normally ensure.

Another cause of poor draft is wind being deflected down the chimney. The surroundings of a home may have a marked bearing on fireplace performance. Thus, for example, if the home is located at the foot of a bluff or hill or if there are high trees close at hand the result may be to deflect wind down the chimney in heavy gusts. A most common and efficient method of dealing with this type of difficulty is to provide a hood on the chimney top.

Carrying the flue lining a few inches above the brickwork with a bevel of cement around it can also be used as a means of promoting a clean exit of smoke from the chimney flue. This will effectively prevent wind eddies. The cement bevel also causes moisture to drain from the top and prevents frost troubles between lining and masonry.

201

## CHAPTER 10

# Hollow Tile and Glass Block

Hollow tile, usually referred to as structural clay tile, is made of burned clay or shale, the same as brick. However, it is made in much larger sizes, with hollow cores of considerable size, and thus is lighter per sq. ft. of wall area.

Hollow tile is made by forcing clay through special dies then cutting it to various lengths. The hollow spaces are called cells and the outside is called the shell. The inside partitions between hollow sections are called the web. The shell is at least ¾" thick and the web is ½" thick. Structural clay tile is available in two basic strengths, two basic quality classes, and a number of facing finishes.

Load-bearing tile can be a direct substitute for load-bearing brick construction. Load-bearing tile is available in two qualities: Grade LB for masonry construction, not exposed to the weather, and requiring an outside coating at least 3" thick. Facing may be plaster, stucco, or a tier of regular brick. Grade LBX may be exposed to weathering, without any facing layer. Load-bearing tile is used for backing up load-bearing brick walls or for interior partition walls. It is light in weight and has good sound- and heat-insulation qualities. When laid vertically, it may carry utility services, such as electrical conduit, gas and water pipes, telephone wires and even heat and air-conditioning ducts. The outer scoring permits plastering directly to the tile, without the need for furring.

Structural clay tile, where not exposed, may be scored on all four sides. Where they are to be exposed, they are available in several surface finishes. Tile with one side smooth has the general appearance of brick, inasmuch as they are made of the same material, and fired in the same way. Type FTX is defect-free and has a smooth surface that is easy to clean. It is also called special-duty tile. Type FTS is inferior in surface quality but good for general-purpose use. Structural glazed facing tile has a hard glazed appearance. It may be ceramic-glazed, salt-glazed, or clay coated. It is stain-proof, very easily cleaned, and available in many colors.

## PHYSICAL CHARACTERISTICS OF TILE

Structural clay tile comes in various sizes and shapes as shown in Fig. 1. The sizes shown are nominal, based on the 4″ module system, the same as brick. Actual sizes are slightly smaller, to allow for mortar thickness.

The compressive strength of tile depends on the material used and the method of manufacture. It is also a function of the shell and web thickness. The tensile strength, of course, is much less, probably less than 10% of the compressive strength.

Heat insulation of tile is better than solid masonry because of the air spaces of the cores. The resistance to fire is somewhat less, however. Typically, a 6″ thick partition wall of tile will resist a fire of 1700°F for about one hour.

### Table 1. Nominal Modular Sizes of Structural Load-Bearing Tile

| Backup Tile | | |
|---|---|---|
| Thickness, in. | Face Dimension in Wall | |
| | Height, in. | Length, in. |
| 4 | 2⅔ | 8 or 12 |
| 4 | 5⅓ | 12[2] |
| 4 | 8 | 8 or 12 |
| 4 | 10⅔ | 12 |
| 6 | 5⅓ | 12 |
| 6 | 8 | 12[2] |
| 6 | 10⅔ | 12 |
| 8 | 5⅓ | 12 |
| 8 | 8 | 8 or 12[2] |
| 8 | 10⅔ | 12 |

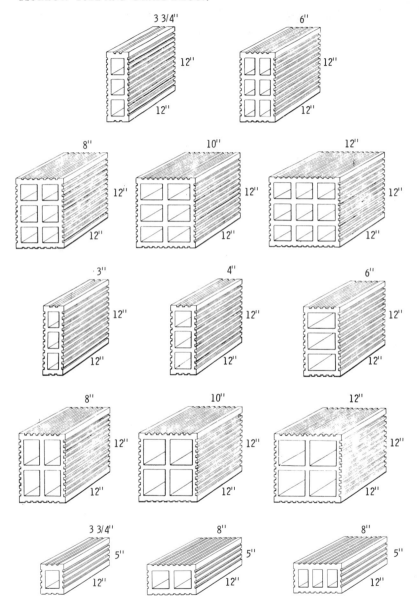

Fig. 1. Most popular shapes and sizes of structural clay tile. The sizes shown are nominal and include the mortar thickness.

## Table 1. Nominal Modular Sizes of Structural Load-Bearing Tile (cont'd.)

### Wall Tile

| Thickness, in. | Height, in. | Length, in. |
|---|---|---|
| 4 | 5⅓ | 12 |
| 4 | 8 | 8 or 12 |
| 4 | 12 | 12 |
| 6 | 5⅓ | 12 |
| 6 | 12 | 12 |
| 8 | 5⅓ | 12 |
| 8 | 6 | 12 |
| 8 | 8 | 8, 12 or 16 |
| 8 | 12 | 12 |
| 10 | 8 | 12 |
| 10 | 12 | 12 |
| 12 | 12 | 12 |

(1) Nominal sizes include the thickness of the standard mortar joint for all dimensions.

(2) Includes header and stretcher units.　　Courtesy Structural Clay Products Inst.

## Table 2. Materials Used for Hollow Clay Tile Walls

| Wall thickness—tile size—wall area, sq. ft. | 4 inches—4 x 5x 12 | | 8 inches—8 x 5 x 12 | |
|---|---|---|---|---|
| | Number of tile | Cu. ft. mortar | Number of tile | Cu. ft. mortar |
| 1 | 2.1 | 0.045 | 2.1 | 0.09 |
| 10 | 21 | .45 | 21 | .9 |
| 100 | 210 | 4.5 | 210 | 9.0 |
| 200 | 420 | 9.0 | 420 | 18 |
| 300 | 630 | 13.5 | 630 | 27 |
| 400 | 840 | 18.0 | 840 | 36 |
| 500 | 1050 | 22.5 | 1050 | 45 |
| 600 | 1260 | 27.0 | 1260 | 54 |
| 700 | 1470 | 31.5 | 1470 | 63 |
| 800 | 1680 | 36.0 | 1680 | 72 |
| 900 | 1890 | 40.5 | 1890 | 81 |
| 1000 | 2100 | 45.0 | 2100 | 90 |

Quantities are based on ½-inch thick mortar joint.

### Table 3. Materials Needed for End Construction Using Hollow Tile

| Wall thickness.... | 4 inches | | 6 inches | | 8 inches | | 10 inches | |
|---|---|---|---|---|---|---|---|---|
| Tile size............. | 4 x 12 x 12 | | 6 x 12 x 12 | | 8 x 12 x 12 | | 10 x 12 x 12 | |
| Wall area, sq. ft. | Number of tile | Cu. ft. mortar | Number of tile | Cu. ft. mortar | Number of tile | Cu. ft. mortar | Number of tile | Cu. ft. mortar |
| 1.......................... | 0.93 | 0.025 | 0.93 | 0.036 | 0.93 | 0.049 | 0.93 | 0.06 |
| 10....................... | 9.3 | .25 | 9.3 | .36 | 9.3 | .49 | 9.3 | .4 |
| 100........................ | 93 | 2.5 | 93 | 3.6 | 93 | 4.9 | 93 | 6 |
| 200........................ | 186 | 5.0 | 186 | 7.2 | 186 | 9.8 | 186 | 12 |
| 300........................ | 279 | 7.5 | 279 | 10.8 | 279 | 14.7 | 279 | 18 |
| 400........................ | 372 | 10.0 | 372 | 14.4 | 372 | 19.6 | 372 | 24 |
| 500........................ | 465 | 12.5 | 465 | 18.0 | 465 | 24.5 | 465 | 30 |
| 600........................ | 558 | 15.0 | 558 | 21.6 | 558 | 29.4 | 558 | 36 |
| 700........................ | 651 | 17.5 | 651 | 25.2 | 651 | 34.3 | 651 | 42 |
| 800........................ | 837 | 22.5 | 837 | 32.4 | 837 | 44.1 | 837 | 54 |
| 900........................ | 744 | 20.0 | 744 | 28.8 | 744 | 39.2 | 744 | 48 |
| 1000....................... | 930 | 25.0 | 930 | 36.0 | 930 | 49.0 | 930 | 60 |

Quantities are based on ½-inch thick mortar joint.

The greatest feature of clay tile is its saving in weight. A solid brick wall weighs about 125 lbs. per sq. ft. A 6″ hollow tile wall is about 30 lbs. per sq. ft. and a 12″ wall about 45 lbs. per sq. ft.

## SIZES AND SHAPES OF CLAY TILE

Local suppliers attempt to comply with a universally accepted range of nominal sizes, as shown in Fig. 1. But suppliers do vary and their catalogs should be consulted before designing a structure using hollow clay tile. In addition to normal rectangular sizes, a number of special shapes are available. These provide for jambs for openings and have cutaways for accepting a header brick from a tier of regular brick, or have special shapes for other purposes (Fig. 2). For example, hollow clay tile is often used around steel girders to fireproof them. Special shapes may be obtained which fit around the I-beam shape of a girder.

Table 1 lists common nominal sizes which may be purchased. Note the number of 5⅓″ tiles, which make a perfect match to a tier of regular brick. With this size, three courses build up to a 16″ height.

# Hollow Tile and Glass Block

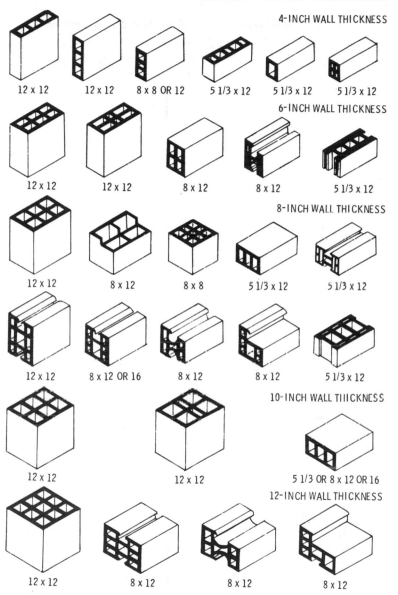

Fig. 2. Showing some of the various shapes of clay tile.

207

## BUILDING WITH HOLLOW CLAY TILE

Table 2 shows the number of hollow clay tiles needed for 4″ thick walls using 4″ × 5″ × 12″ tiles. Table 3 shows the number for 4″, 6″, 8″, and 10″ thick walls. Shown are the tiles needed for various wall areas and the amount of mortar for a ½″ mortar thickness. Mortar is the same as that used on brick, since the material of hollow clay tile is the same as brick. See Chapter 2 for details on mortar.

Hollow tile may be laid horizontally or vertically. There is no real structural difference between the two styles. Laying them with the hollow cores horizontal is a little easier. Laid vertically, the hollow cores may be used for piping in the wall. In either case, the tiles of each course should be staggered, or overlap the course below and above for best bonding, as for brick.

Fig. 3. How a corner is started with hollow tile.

Fig. 3 shows the beginning corner using tile with overlapping bond. The letters in the sketch indicate the order in which they should be laid. The first course must be laid on a level foundation

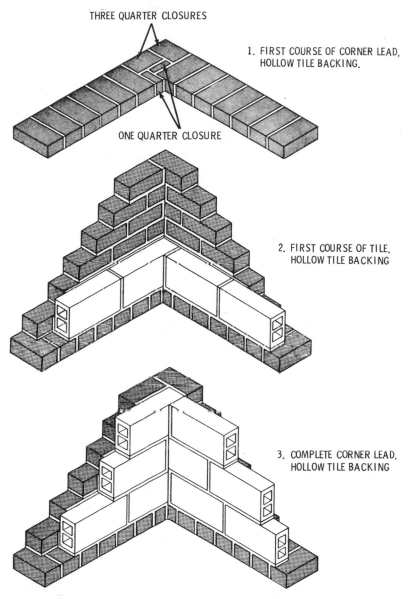

THREE QUARTER CLOSURES

1. FIRST COURSE OF CORNER LEAD, HOLLOW TILE BACKING.

ONE QUARTER CLOSURE

2. FIRST COURSE OF TILE, HOLLOW TILE BACKING

3. COMPLETE CORNER LEAD, HOLLOW TILE BACKING

Fig. 4. Steps in the construction of a tile wall with a brick facing.

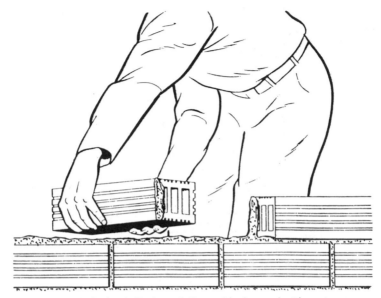

Fig. 5. Only the shell edges of tile need be buttered with mortar.

of concrete and with a 1″ thick mortar bed. Use a spirit level frequently to be sure the first course is perfectly horizontal.

Fig. 4 shows three steps in laying tile with a brick facing. The first course, on the foundation, consists of all header brick. The facing tier of brick follows the standard procedure described in earlier chapters. These sketches clearly indicate how many fewer pieces of tile need to be handled, when the larger sizes are used, as compared to a solid brick wall.

Hollow tile need not be covered completely with mortar. A layer along the facing edges is sufficient. Only the shell edges are buttered, not the inner web edges. This is illustrated in Fig. 5 Vertically laid tile is shown in Fig. 6. In overlap bonding, it can be recognized that web edges may not match the next tile below or above, so buttering them does not add to the strength.

There are two methods for bonding a face brick tier to a backing of hollow tile. Where rectangular tile is used exclusively, the bond between the brick and tile is accomplished with metal ties. This is shown In Fig. 7. Odd-shaped hollow tile of special design per-

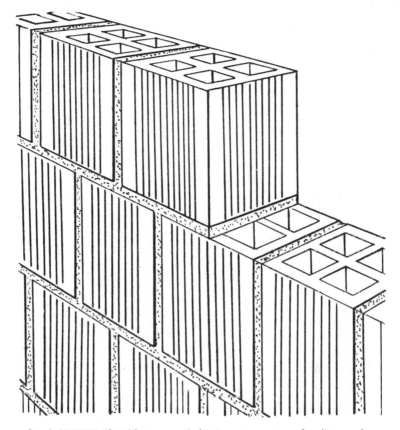

Fig. 6. In laying tile with cores vertical it is necessary to use bonding overlap.

mits the use of header brick for the tie between tiers. This is illustrated in Fig. 8. In Fig. 9, open air cavities are left for running pipes and ducts. This method may be necessary where large size pipes are needed (soil pipes, for example) and larger duct work than provided by the cores of the tiles.

Fig. 10 shows two other applications of tile. In the top sketch, a combination of tile and brick is used for the construction of the chimney. The bottom sketch shows a fireplace using hollow tile for the main wall and fire brick facing for the hearth.

211

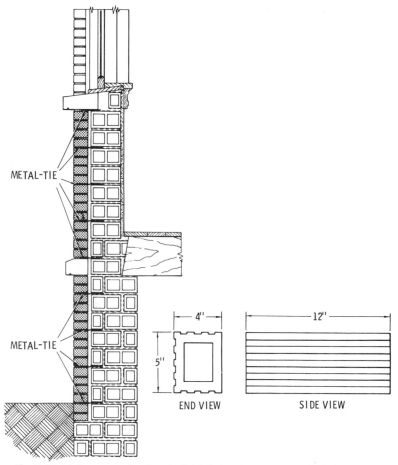

METAL-TIE

METAL-TIE

4"

5"

12"

END VIEW

SIDE VIEW

Fig. 7. Metal ties are used to bond a brick facing tier to rectangular hollow tile.

## Table 4. Mortar Material Needed for Glass Block

|  | 5¾ In. Blocks | 7¾ In. Blocks | 11¾ In. Blocks |
|---|---|---|---|
| **Number of Blocks** | 400 | 225 | 100 |
| **Volume of Mortar in Cubic Feet** | 4.3 | 3.2 | 2.2 |

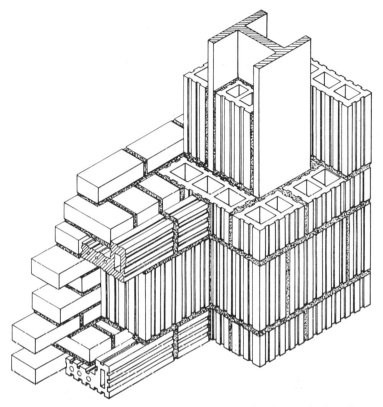

Fig. 8. Showing odd shaped tile used to bond brick headers in a brick wall

## GLASS BLOCK

Glass blocks are hollow glass structures made of pressed glass from which part of the air has been evacuated. These blocks are hermetically sealed at the time of manufacture, leaving a sealed-in dead air space. The edges of the blocks are of a gritty texture, making them mortar-binding. Some types of blocks on the market have a flanged "key-lock" edge; others have a corrugated type edge which is in contact with the mortar.

Glass blocks are available in a variety of shapes, sizes, and designs. There are squares, radials, and corners. The designs

213

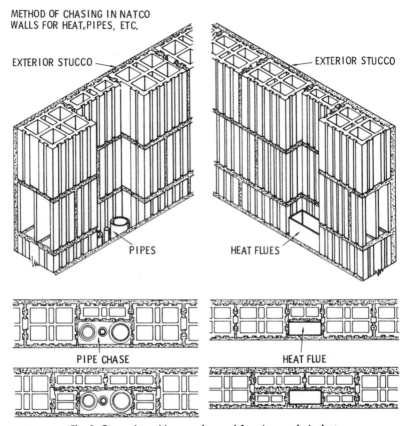

METHOD OF CHASING IN NATCO
WALLS FOR HEAT, PIPES, ETC.

EXTERIOR STUCCO

EXTERIOR STUCCO

PIPES

HEAT FLUES

PIPE CHASE

HEAT FLUE

Fig. 9. Open air cavities may be used for pipes and air ducts.

include convex and concave ribs or flutes, arranged vertically, horizontally or both. The ribs may be on the interior or the exterior of the block. There are also clear, smooth, transparent types, which permit full view through them. The most widely used types are the square blocks which are 5¾″, 7¾″ and 11¾″ on 2 of their dimensions and 3⅞″ thick (Fig. 11).

The advantages of glass blocks are of course dependent on their unique construction. Among the outstanding advantages are:

1. Excellent temperature control because of the sealed-in dead air space.

214

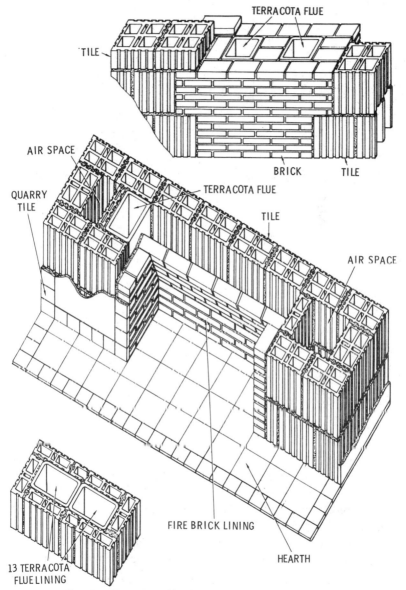

Fig. 10. Hollow tile and brick are used for chimney construction.

215

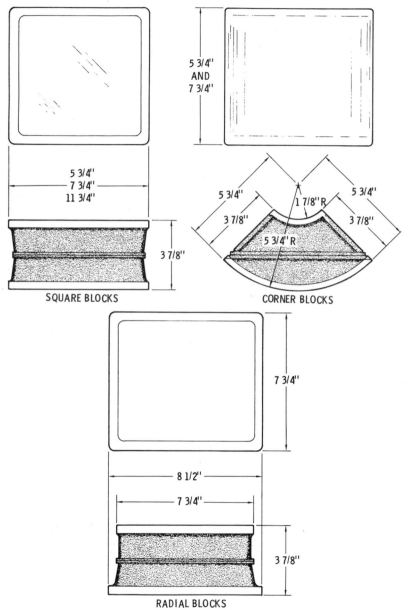

SQUARE BLOCKS

CORNER BLOCKS

RADIAL BLOCKS

Fig. 11. Popular sizes and shapes of glass block.

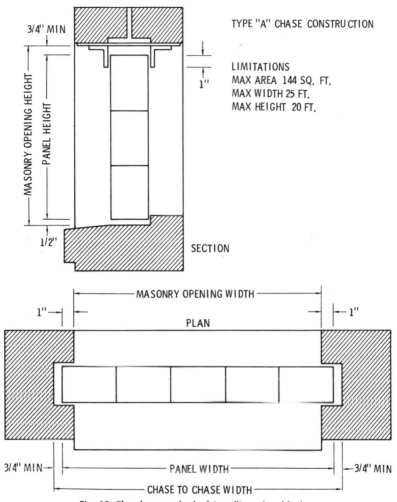

TYPE "A" CHASE CONSTRUCTION

LIMITATIONS
MAX AREA 144 SQ. FT.
MAX WIDTH 25 FT.
MAX HEIGHT 20 FT.

Fig. 12. The chase method of installing glass block.

2. Low condensation on the surfaces compared to glass windows—therefore regulating humidity.
3. They transmit light, therefore, making it possible to daylight interiors which would otherwise be dark or artificially illuminated. They can also be used to control the direction of light transmission.

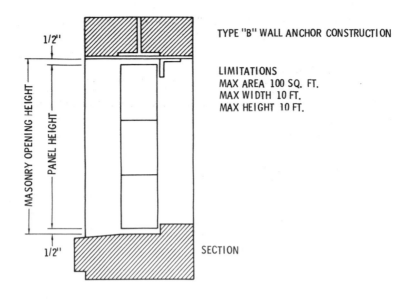

TYPE "B" WALL ANCHOR CONSTRUCTION

LIMITATIONS
MAX AREA 100 SQ. FT.
MAX WIDTH 10 FT.
MAX HEIGHT 10 FT.

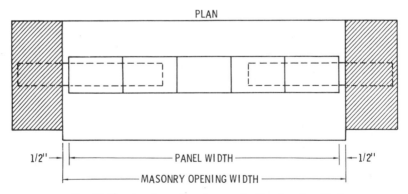

Fig. 13. Showing the wall-anchor construction for glass block.

4. They are easy to maintain and easy to replace.
5. They provide privacy.
6. They reduce sound transmission.

These advantages dictate the use of glass block in industrial and office buildings which are completely air-controlled both in summer and winter. Where open windows are never required, glass block windows and walls allow light to enter, yet provide excellent insulation against heat transmission. In homes, glass block is favored for use in stairwells and alcoves, where daylight illumination is desired but open windows are not necessary.

Glass blocks may be set as panels in masonry, concrete, steel frames and wood frames, both interior and exterior, using mortar joints. Ventilation units in the form of windows or louvers may be installed in the panels. Construction in masonry usually employs the chase method. Where this is not practicable, wall-anchor construction may be employed.

The chase method is shown in Fig. 12. Indents in the masonry lock the edges of the glass block panel in place. Where the chase method is not practical, anchors are used as shown in Fig. 13. The most economical size and the most widely used type of block is the 7¾" square. The smaller and the large type squares are chosen when they will make a better working scale possible.

In selecting the design, it is well to keep in mind the purpose for which the installation is being made. The most important considerations will be the appearance and the type of light transmission required. Where the type of light transmission is not important, the design selected will be guided by the choice of the consumer or contractor.

Blocks which do not control the direction of light are the so-called "general purpose" blocks which are widely used. Where it is important to direct the light either upward or downward, or through the glass, the "functional" block is to be used. This type has its design arranged so as to direct the light properly. These vary in their effects and their selection is best made by consulting the descriptions and recommendations in the catalogs of the manufacturers.

Mortar mix used for the setting of glass blocks should have the following composition by dry volume: 1 part portland cement, 1 part lime, 4 to 6 parts sand. Mix the materials to a consistency as stiff as will permit good working. These materials should be drier than for ordinary clay brickwork. A metallic-stearate waterproofer is recommended by some manufacturers. The sand must be free from silt, clay, and loam in excess of 3% by weight as determined by decantations. Not more than 5% by weight shall pass a No. 100 mesh sieve and 100% shall pass through a No. 8 mesh sieve.

Mortar thickness is generally only ¼". Thus 5¾", 7¾", and 11¾" square glass blocks are considered to have nominal sizes of 6", 8", and 12" square. Table 4 shows the approximate amount of mortar needed for glass blocks of different sizes and in different quantities. Mortar must be spread completely across all edge surfaces of the glass blocks to assure watertightness and weathertightness. Carefully tool mortar joints and completely clean excess mortar off the glass.

## CHAPTER 11

# Brick Terraces, Walks and Floors

Because of its weathering qualities, hard, well-burned brick was once used for roadways. Because of high labor cost in laying brick roads and the development of high-speed automatic road-building equipment, brick has been replaced by asphalt and concrete. Because of its aesthetic values, brick is still used for many terraces, and walks.

In contemporary home design an attempt is made to match the interior with the exterior. This is especially true for families who believe in indoor-outdoor living. An example of this is shown in the sketch of Fig. 1, in which the terrace, the garden wall, and even planters extend into the house.

Because of the variety of brick available, there is no limit to the tasteful architectural designs and uses to which brick may be used. Patterned walls go well with brick terraces (see Chapter 8 on various surfaces and patterns). Brick makes excellent enclosures for trash cans (Fig. 2) or to conceal the condenser of a central air-conditioning system (Fig. 3). Planters of brick (Fig. 4) make waist-high gardening easy. Improving the exterior with brick is easy to do, even for the homeowner, whether it is a simple grass edge for guiding the mower (Fig. 5) or the more elaborate jobs.

A sloping area can cause erosion of the top soil from a prized tree. A brick retaining wall is easily put in place to straighten out

221

Courtesy Structural Clay Products Inst.

Fig. 1. Brick terrace, walls, and garden extend into the house to give that indoor-outdoor living look.

the soil around the tree (Fig. 6). Brick terracing goes well with concrete open grill block. Brick also fits well with various styling such as Early American and Spanish. Historic Georgetown is probably the best example of the early use of brick at the beginning of American history. "Old Town" in Albuquerque, New Mexico (Figs. 7, 8, and 9) was originally settled in 1706. By this time most of the brick walks have been replaced. But the original design was maintained.

Brick is available in a variety of colors and textures some of which are described in Chapter 8. Brick can be laid in many patterns, to make overall style choices very large indeed. Fig. 10 shows some of the patterns that can be formed with brick. Such choices make a brick terrace or walk preferable to the monotony of poured concrete.

222

Courtesy Structural Clay Products Inst.

Fig. 2. The proper design of a trash-can enclosure made with brick can add to, rather than detract, from the garden architecture.

## TYPE OF BRICK FOR WALKS

Since walks and terraces must bear human traffic, it is wise not to select brick with too rough a texture. A smooth texture is preferable, particularly if rolling equipment such as a mower

223

Courtesy Structural Clay Products Inst.

**Fig. 3. An enclosure for an outdoor central air-conditioning condenser. Open wall pattern on the front brick wall permits good air circulation.**

or wheelbarrow is to be used occasionally. Brick must stand up against the elements of the area. Use only very hard well-burned brick if weather is severe. Avoid rough seconds or textures which can collect drops of water which may freeze and cause cracking.

For laying any pattern other than the stacked pattern (lower right corner of Fig. 10) the brick size to order depends on whether you intend to mortar the joints or lay the bricks edge-to-edge. Nominal sizes of brick, as used for laying up a wall, allow for a ½" mortar thickness between bricks; however, brick is also available in actual sizes which follow the 4" module system. In actual

Courtesy Structural Clay Products Inst.

**Fig. 4. Properly designed brick walls make good earth retainers and planter boxes.**

sizes, the patterns shown can be laid without mortar joints. This is obvious when you note how many patterns require laying the 4" widths against the 8" lengths. Brick cannot be laid dry and tight unless the width is actually ½ the length. When laying with mortar, the same brick as used on walls will give the ratio of two half-widths to one length, as the mortar makes up the difference. Some "pavers" can be bought, which have actual dimensions of 4" × 8" and are from 1½" to 2¼" thick. Also available are larger square-shaped fired-clay brick.

## INTERIOR BRICK FLOORS

Brick is frequently used in some residential and other structures for floors, where they fit the decor of the building style. Brick flooring for the den and some other rooms (sometimes all the rooms) fits well with ranch, Spanish, and adobe styling.

225

Fig. 5. A brick edging for grass is a simple job to do even for the homeowner.

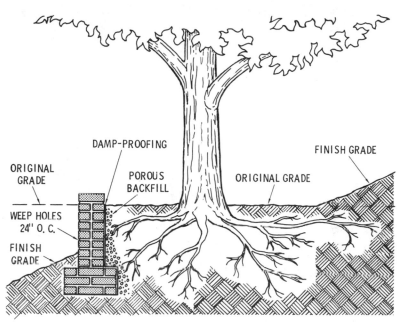

ORIGINAL GRADE

DAMP-PROOFING

POROUS BACKFILL

ORIGINAL GRADE

FINISH GRADE

WEEP HOLES 24" O. C.

FINISH GRADE

Courtesy Structural Clay Products Inst.

Fig. 6. A brick retaining wall is used here to level the soil around tree and to prevent erosion.

While not faced with the need to stand up under severe weather, interior brick should be smooth and hard and should be carefully laid to form a perfectly level floor. Solid colors predominate but patterns and variations in color are frequently appropriate. Textured brick is not recommended. In both interior floors and exterior walks, brick may be laid with mortar joints or mortarless. Mortarless floors are less expensive to place and faster to complete.

Altogether, three layers are involved in laying interior brick floors:

1. The *base*—the principal support. It may be a concrete slab or well-tamped earth.
2. The *cushion*—a layer of sand about 2" thick to facilitate leveling and placing of the brick.
3. The *brick*.

227

Fig. 7. New brick replaces old in sidewalks built in 1706.

Fig. 8. New brick replacing old steps. Old brick in upper portion of illustration was not mortared in place, notice signs of shifting.

Fig. 9. A very old brick walk laid without mortar. Notice the joint separation in some areas.

The best base is a concrete slab poured as part of the footing at the time the home is built. All requirements of good slab construction apply, as described in the volume on Concrete. Leveling the surface of the concrete is not as as important as when used for a direct tile or carpeted floor, since the sand cushion can be adjusted to compensate for any unevenness. The slab should include reinforcing rods and, in cold climates, a layer of insulation between the slab and the earth support.

In mild climate areas, and if the base earth is hard when dry and has little or no organic material, the base may be the earth itself. It must be heavily tamped with the blunt end of a 4 × 4 or a tamping tool. The cushion of sand must be treated to reduce air spaces between sand granules. This is done by floating with water or tamping. Draw a straight board across in all directions to obtain a perfectly level surface. Any unevenness resulting from walking on it while laying the brick can be adjusted by hand at the time the brick is laid.

229

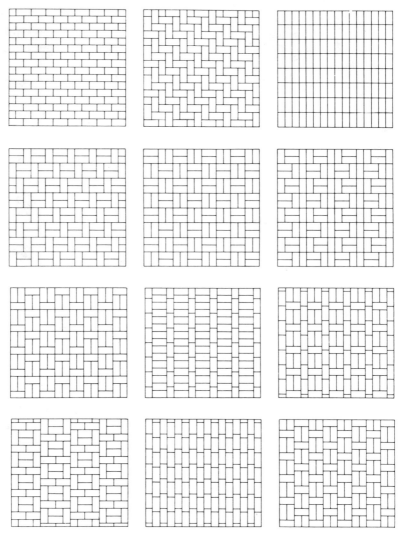

Fig. 10. A sample of the variety of patterns possible with the use of brick.

When considering a pattern with brick, keep in mind there is less shifting if a herringbone or overlapping bond pattern is used, as against the straight stack pattern. Mortarless brick is laid edge-to-edge with the least possible space between bricks. As mentioned before be sure actual dimensions of 4″ × 8″ brick is used. After the brick is laid, sweep very fine sand over the brick surface to fill any possible cracks.

If a mortared brick floor is used, the cushion should also be of mortar. However, the cushion is not poured all at one time. It is placed as a mortar bed for the brick as each brick is laid along with the edge mortar. The mortar cushion can be over a concrete base or an earth base. If over an earth base, it is wise to add strength by reinforcing the brick and the cushion with ¼″ steel rods.

Carefully wipe off any excess mortar from the surface of the brick as you work. Strike mortar joints flush. Use a rough rag for wiping. To increase the density of the mortar joints, they should be tooled. The height of the mortar should be the height of the brick.

## EXTERIOR WALKS AND TERRACES

Because exterior walks and terraces are exposed to moisture and weathering, it is important that the brick selected have low absorption qualities and be extra hard and well-burned. They should meet the requirements for grade SW of ASTM standards for facing brick. A good grade of hard brick naturally has the qualities for long life and good weathering, and is an excellent choice for walk material where the style is appropriate.

Basically, exterior walks and terraces follow the same construction as for interior floors, requiring a base, a cushion and the final brick layer, but with a few other considerations for weathering. The base is well-tamped earth or a concrete slab. The cushion is a layer of sand for mortarless brick or a thin bed of mortar for mortared brick. The sketch of Fig. 11 shows both in a cutaway view.

The edging shown in the sketches of Fig. 11 is a most important part of walk construction, if a care-free walk is to be achieved. If the earth is used as a base, dig a trench along both edges of the walk and pour concrete for a footing. Lay a row of rowlock brick on edge after you pour the concrete. Of course, it will be necessary to accurately measure the distance between edges to be sure the

231

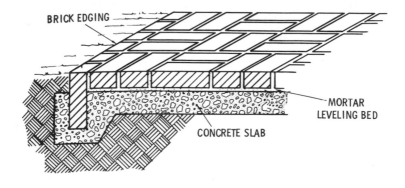

BRICK EDGING

MORTAR LEVELING BED

CONCRETE SLAB

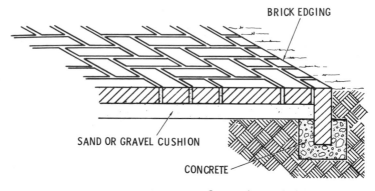

BRICK EDGING

SAND OR GRAVEL CUSHION

CONCRETE

Courtesy Structural Clay Products Inst.

Fig. 11. Mortared brick walk with earth base and with concrete base.

width will accept the desired pattern and that the bricks will come out even. With a concrete base, a deeper footing is dug for the edges of the slab and a row of brick are placed on edge. The walk in Fig. 9 shows a poor job of edging, with evidence of the edging breaking away and a shifting of the brick.

Good drainage is very important to any kind of work laid on the ground and particularly so for bricks. In cold climates, water collecting between bricks can freeze and crack the edges or push bricks out of place. In areas of high humidity and/or with a high water table, water can accumulate for long periods of time and cause the growth of fungi and molds. Walks should be sloped or a slight crown provided to permit water runoff. A slope of ⅛" to ¼" per ft. is adequate. For good drainage from underneath, sandy soil will provide the necessary treatment. Where the soil is hard, dig away approximately 2 ft. and replace it with gravel. However, where gravel is used, the sand cushion layer for mortarless laying should be omitted, otherwise the sand will work its way down into the gravel and lose its value.

Construction follows the directions given before for interior floors: Tamp the soil well (this is the base). Use a bed of well-leveled sand for the cushion for mortarless brick and for mortared brick the cushion is mortar.

If the base is sandy, and a good leveling job can be done, the sand cushion may be omitted for a mortarless layer of brick. To reduce labor, the mortar bed may be omitted. While the durability of the final job is less, the reduction is not in proportion to the reduction in labor. Type S mortar should be used when there is a concrete base. This consists of 1 part portland cement, ½ part lime, and 4½ parts sand. On an earth base, use Type M mortar consisting of 1 part portland cement, ¼ part lime, and 3 parts sand. Portland masonry cement with the proper amount of lime already added may be purchased.

Mortaring can be done by hand, of course. Two methods which reduce the amount of labor are frequently used. These are the dry-mix method and the pourable-grout method. In the dry-mix method, place the brick into position, leaving a ½" space between each brick. Make a dry mix of one part portland cement and 3 or 4 parts of fine dry sand. Sweep the dry mix into the spaces between the bricks. Spray with a fine mist of water until the walk is damp. The water will seep into the mix and start hydration. Keep the walk damp for 2 or 3 days for good curing strength. It is important that the mix be swept into the cracks and completely off the top surface of the brick. Otherwise, the brick may stain when the cement is watered.

The other method is to make a pourable grout of cement, sand, and water. Use slightly higher amounts of sand than the dry-mix mentioned. Add water to make a soft and loose grout which can be poured into the spaces between the brick, from the lip of a bucket, or the spout of a large watering can.

233

## REINFORCED BRICK

When a walk must span a culvert or small ditch, the brick should be reinforced or it will soon break down under the weight of traffic. It must be supported on a reinforced concrete foundation. Wood and sheet steel spans can be used, if the brick is reinforced. Fig. 12 shows three methods of reinforcement, depending on the thickness

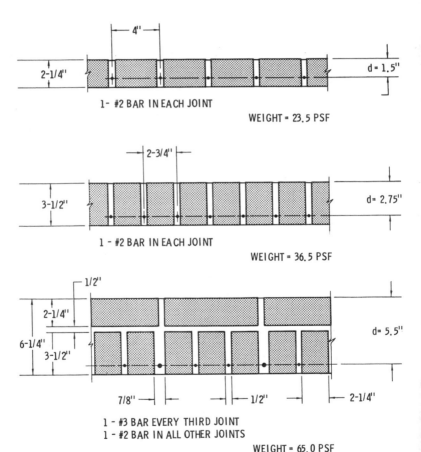

1- #2 BAR IN EACH JOINT

WEIGHT = 23.5 PSF

1 - #2 BAR IN EACH JOINT

WEIGHT = 36.5 PSF

1 - #3 BAR EVERY THIRD JOINT
1 - #2 BAR IN ALL OTHER JOINTS

WEIGHT = 65.0 PSF

Courtesy Structural Clay Products Inst.

**Fig. 12. Reinforced brick may be necessary over culverts or ditches or where there is no firm base.**

234

of the brick. The joints should be well tooled to make sure they are dense and that the mortar fully surrounds the reinforcing rods.

## STEPS

Where the path of a walk runs into a rise or drop in the earth, the best way to handle the change in elevation is by means of steps.

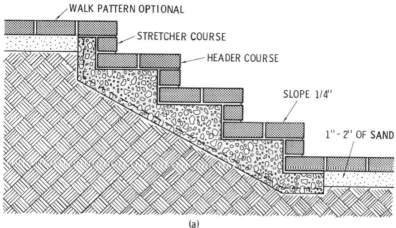

(a)

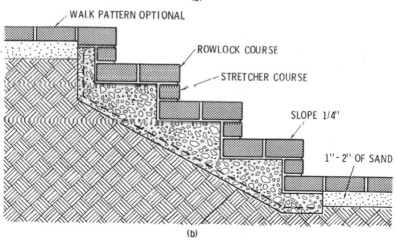

(b)

Courtesy Structural Clay Products Inst.

Fig. 13. For good step support pour the concrete step base first. Note how brick can be laid to change the degree of rise.

Steps of brick will match the rest of the walk and can be adjusted to fit the slope. Fig. 13 shows how the same number of steps can handle two different angles of slope, by the way in which the brick is laid. In Fig. 13A, a smaller angle of rise uses brick on its face. At Fig. 13B, setting the brick on edge, rowlock style, increases the rise angle.

Because an earth base and sand cushion can be too easily affected by traffic and erosion in heavy rains, it is best to make the base of poured concrete to maintain a firm set. After determining tread and riser dimensions from brick sizes, make wooden forms for the poured concrete. Include reinforcing rods, which are indicated by the dotted lines in the sketch of Fig. 13.

## RETAINING WALLS

Brick walls make excellent retaining walls, whether for holding dirt for planting or for terracing a sloping garden. Construction is similar to that of a wall for structures, with a few precautions added.

An earth retaining wall is subject to lateral pressures from the earth it is holding. It is also exposed to a considerable amount of All joints must be well mortared over the entire surface of the moisture. Depending on the amount of earth fill the wall is to hold, extra care is needed to make sure the wall has high lateral strength. bricks. If a large amount of earth fill is to be retained by the wall, add steel reinforcing rods.

Because stains and efflorescence can develop on brick when exposed to moisture over long periods of time, care must be used to prevent the moisture of the earth from penetrating the brick. Fig. 14 shows the details of a retaining wall. Weep holes in the wall, made by leaving the mortar out of some vertical joints, allows moisture to drain through the wall to the outside, and reduces the absorption of water by the brick. Fig. 16 shows how this wall is used to correct a sloping grade around a tree.

Fig. 15 is an example of a brick planter of typical construction. Coarse gravel below and above the foundation, connected by a pipe through the foundation, drains away moisture settling at the bottom of the planter. In addition tar paper between the dirt and brick wall prevents seepage into the brick.

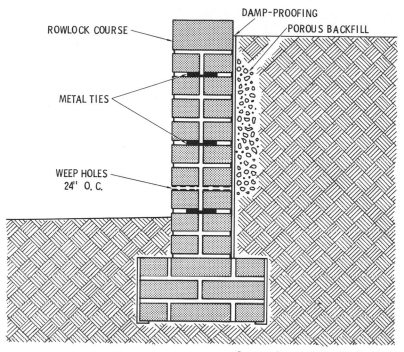

DAMP-PROOFING

POROUS BACKFILL

ROWLOCK COURSE

METAL TIES

WEEP HOLES
24" O. C.

Courtesy Structural Clay Products Inst.

Fig. 14. Details of retaining wall illustrated in Fig. 6. Tar paper, rock backfill, and weep holes are precautions against moisture absorption by the brick.

## CLEANING UP

If a mortared brick floor or walk is laid, it is almost impossible to prevent mortar droppings from falling onto the face of the brick. It is essential to work with care, to reduce these droppings to a minimum. Most of it can be cleaned off by wiping the brick with a burlap cloth but this must be done while the mortar is still damp.

Once cement has hardened it cannot be removed with water. There is only one solution that dissolves dried cement and that is muriatic acid (commercial grade hydrochloric acid). But acid is not the easy solution. Acid is extremely harmful to skin, clothing, and especially dangerous to the eyes. Acid, and the fumes from acid, can corrode metals such as aluminum and galvanized steel. It is injurious to plant life. It should be handled only by the most

237

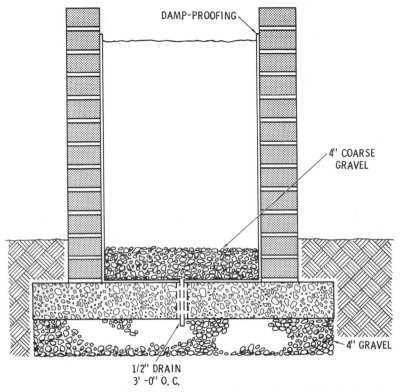

DAMP-PROOFING

4" COARSE
GRAVEL

4" GRAVEL

1/2" DRAIN
3' -0" O. C.

Courtesy Structural Clay Products Inst.

Fig. 15. Brick planter with tar paper, gravel, and drain pipe at bottom to reduce
moisture absorption.

experienced mason and using rubber gloves, goggles, and plenty
of ventilation.

There are some brand-name cleaning solutions which frequently
are inhibited acids or are self-neutralized. These are less harmful than muriatic acid but more costly. Before applying acid, a fine
spray of water should be applied to the brick. The layer of water
reduces the absorption of acid into the brick and especially into
the mortar joints reducing the possibility of "acid burn" on the
brick. Scrub the acid onto the brick using a stiff brush and working
only a small area at a time. Thoroughly rinse off all acid afterward.

## BRICK FLOOR FINISHING

Mortared floors may be given a perfectly smooth finish by grinding with a terrazzo grinder. However, floor grinding should be anticipated before the floor is laid as certain requirements are essential in advance. Brick to be ground should be of the high-density type hard burned and nonporous. On softer brick, the grinding will merely expose the less dense clay under the surface which may have small air bubbles that can absorb water. In addition, the sand used for the mortar should be extra fine. Coarse sand granules will be dislodged by the grinder and tend to scratch the brick surface.

Brick should be allowed to set for a few days to make sure the mortar has begun to hydrate well. Otherwise, the grinder may dislodge some of the brick. A wax coating is frequently used on indoor brick floors to reduce the absorption of water from mopping. Wax should not be used on outdoor walks because it may tend to hold water under the wax, which can freeze on cold days.

One of the better treatments for brick is a silicone coating. Silicone has a long life and is a good sealer against water. Use masonry silicone sealer available in two types: solvent-based, and water-based. The solvent-based dries quicker and waxing, if desired, may be applied sooner.

## CHAPTER 12

# Brick Repairs and Maintenance

The need for repairs and cleaning on new brick masonry is reduced when the original construction is done in a careful manner and certain precautions are observed. The bricklayer craftsman should take pride in the work he is doing. A clean job with well-tooled and clean joints in the first place means less cleanup afterward and is less costly in the long run.

Piles of brick waiting for use should be stacked off of the ground on plattens or rows of $2'' \times 4''$ lumber. This will keep the lower layer of brick from absorbing moisture from the ground. If the brick is not to be used immediately, it should be covered with a tarpaulin to keep off rain and dust.

As a wall is laid up, debris of mortar will naturally fall to the ground. It can be kept away from the base of the wall, by placing a layer of sand or a vinyl sheet at the base. Scaffolding should not abut the wall. Mortar droppings should be allowed to fall to the ground. At the end of the day, the walk planks near the wall should be turned back to prevent rain and wind from blowing collected dust onto the wall.

As the wall work progresses, excess mortar should be struck even with the face of the wall to prevent mortar from running down the face of the brick. Fill taut-line holes immediately after the pins are removed. Tool joints after the mortar is thumb-print dry.

Tool firmly, moving in one direction, to prevent forming air pockets. After tooling, cut off tailings and brush excess mortar from the brick.

When the wall is finished, inspect it for loose pieces of mortar. Remove them with a chisel, if dry, and brush away loose particles. Use a hose to wash off cement dust.

## CLEANING NEW BRICK

After cleaning the brick as mentioned before, some staining may appear. Stains are cleaned as follows:

Mortar stains are removed with hydrochloric acid prepared by mixing 1 part commercial muriatic acid with 9 parts water. Pour the acid into the water. Before applying the acid, soak the surface thoroughly with water to prevent the mortar stain from being drawn into the pores of the brick.

The acid solution is applied with a long handled stiff-fiber brush. Proper precautions must be taken to prevent the acid from getting on hands, arms, and clothing. Goggles are worn to protect the eyes. An area of 15 to 20 sq. ft. is scrubbed with acid and then immediately washed down with clear water. All acid must be removed before it can attack the mortar joint. Door and window frames must be protected from the acid.

### Cleaning Off Efflorescence

Efflorescence is a white deposit of soluble salts frequently appearing on the surface of brick walls. These soluble salts are contained in the brick. Water penetrating the wall dissolves out the salts and when the water evaporates the salt remains. Efflorescence cannot occur unless both water and the salts are present. The proper selection of brick and a dry wall will keep efflorescence to a minimum. It may be removed, however, with the acid solution recommended for cleaning new walls. Acid should be used only after it has been determined that scrubbing with water and stiff brushes will not remove the efflorescence.

## CLEANING OLD BRICK

Sandblasting, steam with water jets, and the use of cleaning compounds are the principal methods of cleaning old brick masonry. The process used depends on the materials used in the wall and the nature of the stain. Many cleaning compounds that have no effect on brick will damage mortar. Rough-textured brick is more difficult to clean than smooth-textured brick. Often, brick cannot be cleaned without removing part of the brick itself, thus, changing the appearance of the wall.

### Sandblasting

This method consists of blowing hard sand through a nozzle against the surface to be cleaned. Compressed air forces the sand through the nozzle. A layer of the surface is removed to the depth required to remove the stain. This is a disadvantage in that the surface is given a rough texture which can collect soot and dust. Sandblasting usually cuts deeply into the mortar joints and it is often necessary to repoint them. After the sandblasting has been completed, it is advisable to apply a transparent waterproofing paint to the surface to help prevent soiling of the wall by soot and dust. Sandblasting is never done on glazed surfaces. A canvas screen placed around the scaffold used for sandblasting will make it possible to salvage most of the sand.

### Steam With Water Jets

Cleaning by this method is accomplished by projecting a finely divided spray of steam and water at a high velocity against the surface to be cleaned. Grime is removed effectively without changing the texture of the surface, which gives it an advantage over sandblasting.

The steam may be obtained from a portable truck-mounted boiler. The pressure should be from 140 to 150 lbs. per sq. in., and about 12 boiler horsepower per cleaning nozzle is required. The velocity with which the steam and water spray hits the wall is more important than the volume of spray used.

A garden hose may be used to carry the water to the cleaning nozzle. Another garden hose supplies rinsing water. The operator experiments with the cleaning nozzle in order to determine the best angle and distance from the wall to hold the nozzle. The steam and water valves may also be regulated until the most effective spray is obtained. No more than a 2-ft. sq. area should be cleaned at one time. The cleaning should be done by passing the nozzle back and forth over the area then rinsing it immediately with clean water before moving to the next space.

Sodium carbonate, sodium bicarbonate, or trisodium phosphate may be added to the cleaning water entering the nozzle to aid in the cleaning action. The amount of salt remaining can be reduced considerably by washing the surface down with water before and after cleaning.

Hardened deposits that cannot be removed by steam cleaning should be removed with steel scrapers or wire brushes. Care must be taken not to cut into the surface. After the deposit has been removed, the surface should be washed down with water and steam cleaned.

### Cleaning Compounds

There are a number of cleaning compounds that may be used, depending on the stain to be removed. Most cleaning compounds contain material that will appear as efflorescence if allowed to penetrate the surface. This may be prevented if the surface to be cleaned is thoroughly wetted first. Whitewash, calcimine, and cold-water paints may be removed by the use of a solution of 1 part hydrochloric acid to 5 parts water. Fiber brushes are used to scrub the surface vigorously with the solution while the solution is still foaming. When the coating has been removed, the wall must be washed down with clean water until the acid is completely removed.

## PAINTING

A large selection of paint colors is available for painting brick. They are cementitious in character, having a small amount of port-land cement as part of the ingredients. To make sure of proper adhesion to the brick, it is necessary that the brick be clean from any dust. Wash down the brick with a stream of water and let dry before painting.

More recently developed (and tougher) paints are epoxy and latex. Epoxy paints have a glossy finish. Latex has a flat finish. Both dry quickly; and both have a tough finish that is impregnable to water, oil, and is also stainproof. Epoxy and latex paints must be applied to brick that has an etched finish. It will not stick to painted brick.

First, wash the brick with TSP, available everywhere. Then apply muriatic acid, diluted about 1 part to 9 parts water, using a long-handled brush. The acid is available in liquid or dry form. The latter is sometimes called "Dry Muric." Wash the acid off thoroughly with clean running water. Be sure to protect yourself with rubber gloves, old clothes, and goggles over the eyes.

## TUCK POINTING

As mortar dries, some shrinkage occurs. This forms small cracks in which water can collect. Because of the need to make mortar easily workable, the addition of lime and the ratio of water to cement results in mortar being somewhat weaker than concrete. In time, freezing and thawing action can cause deterioration and some of the mortar must be replaced. This is called tuck pointing.

Tuck pointing consists of cutting out all loose and disintegrated mortar to a depth of at least ½ " and replacing it with new. If leakage is to be stopped, all of the mortar in the affected area should be cut out and new mortar placed. Tuck pointing done as routine maintenance requires the removal of the defective mortar only.

All dust and loose material should be removed by a brush or by means of a water jet after the cutting has been completed. A chisel with a cutting edge about ½ " wide is suitable for cutting. If water is used in cleaning the joints, no further wetting is required. If not, the surface of the joint must be moistened.

### Mortar for Tuck Pointing

The mortar to be used for tuck pointing should be portland-cement-lime, prehydrated Type S mortar, or prehydrated prepared mortar made from Type II masonry cement. The prehydration of mortar greatly reduces the amount of shrinkage. The procedure for prehydrating mortar is as follows: The dry ingredients for the mortar are mixed with just enough water to produce a damp mass of such consistency that it will retain its form when compressed into a ball with the hands. The mortar should then be allowed to stand for at least 1 hour and not more than 2 hours. After this, it is mixed with the amount of water required to produce a stiff but workable consistency.

## Filling the Joint

Sufficient time should be allowed for absorption of the moisture used in preparing the joint before the joint is filled with mortar. Filling the joint with mortar is called repointing and is done with a pointing trowel. The prehydrated mortar that has been prepared as above is packed tightly into the joint in thin layers about ¼" thick and finished to a smooth concave surface with a pointing tool. To reduce the possibility of forming air pockets, the mortar is pushed into the joint with a forward motion in one direction from a starting point.

# CHAPTER 13

# Masonry Patio Projects

Building with brick is really quite easy. A number of garden projects, involving little material and time, make excellent training lessons for the apprentice brickmason or easy projects for the homeowner. This chapter describes a number of projects, easy enough to complete in one weekend, for the handyman who wants to do-it-yourself or for the beginner bricklayer to pick up a few extra dollars during his time off from his regular job.

One aspect of the projects described here that makes them "non-hurry" projects is the use of premixed concrete and mortar. Nearly all cities have one brand or another of packaged dry ingredients for the mixing of concrete or mortar. The packages include the right amount of cement and other ingredients, requiring only the addition of water to make concrete or mortar. Instructions for adding the water are given on the bag. They are available in various amounts of weights and sizes. Brand names may vary from city to city, depending on the local supplier. One national brand available almost everywhere is *Sakrete*.

## PREMIXED MATERIALS

*Packaged Concrete* as a dry mix can be purchased in three basic forms and in several sizes:

*Concrete.* The ingredients are cement, sand, and larger aggregates. This is the mixture for the base of many of the projects in this chapter. It can be obtained in 90-lb. and 25-lb. sacks.

*Sand Mix.* A mixture of sand and cement for use on shallow bases and for repairs. It can be purchased in 80-lb. and 25-lb. sacks and 11-lb. packages.

*Mortar.* A mixture of cement, lime, and sand, for use as a brick mortar. It is available in the same sizes as the sand mix.

In addition to the above, *Sakrete* makes a plaster mix in 25-lb. sacks. *Sakrete* and other prepared dry mixes will cost more per lb. than buying the separate ingredients. However, on small jobs, the time spent in gathering the separate ingredients for small quantities may cost more in time and effort than the use of packaged concrete mixes. Even contractors should consider this if called to do a small job, because, after all, time is money.

## A FLAGSTONE WALL

Flagstone is a natural rock available in many shapes and sizes, from large flat pieces for walks to smaller and thicker pieces approximately the size and shape of brick. Its naturally rough texture and size variations give it a rustic appearance, especially suited for use in garden architecture.

In the illustrations accompanying this project a flagstone wall is being built as a retaining wall after dirt has been dug away from a high-rising small hill. This will be disregarded and only the construction of the wall considered. (Note the concrete block for the first two courses, which later will be underwater.)

As is necessary for any brick wall, a firm foundation on which to build is the order of first importance. Dig out a trench about 5″ deep and 10″ to 12″ wide in areas of mild climate or down to the frost line in cold climates. The trench will be for a concrete base. If the soil is firm enough to be dug out with straight sides, concrete can be poured directly into the trench. If the soil is quite sandy, and straight sides cannot be maintained, it will be necessary to install board forms to hold the concrete.

Pour a sack of *Sakrete* (or other packaged-concrete) mix into a wheelbarrow and add the prescribed amount of water. Using a

---

Note: All of the illustrations in the projects that follow are supplied through the courtesy of *Sakrete, Inc.*

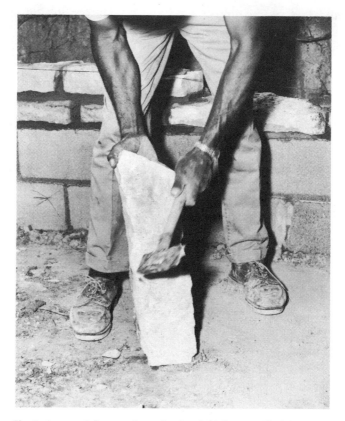

Fig. 1. A mason's hammer is used to knock high spots off of flagstone.

garden hoe, thoroughly mix the dry ingredients and water. Pour the concrete into the trench to about the half-way point. Lay a couple of ½" steel rods into the trench for reinforcing, and fill the rest of the trench with concrete. This may require mixing several wheelbarrows of concrete, depending on the length and depth of the wall. Drive wooden stakes into the ground at each end of the base. Tie a heavy string between the stakes. Use a spirit level and adjust the taut line level. With the taut line as a guide, trowel the top of the concrete until it is perfectly level, or equidistant from all parts of the line. Allow about 24 hours for the concrete to take a good set before building up the wall.

Fig. 2. Mix only as much SAKRETE mortar mix as can be handled in 2 hours.

Flagstone is quite irregular as to texture, size, and shape. To lay up a wall of flagstone with good overlap bonding, some uniformity of size is needed, and high spots should be removed. Use a mason's hammer (Fig. 1) to knock off high spots and rough edges, just enough to prevent interference with good construction.

If the wall is a one-man job, it is best to mix only 1 sack of mortar, lay up the stones with the amount mixed, then mix an-

249

Fig. 3. Reset the taut line for each course of stone. The end of the taut line is secured to the stone corners.

other sack of mortar, etc. Pour the mortar mix into a wheel barrow and add the amount of water indicated on the sack. Mix the dry ingredients with the water using a garden hoe, by a push-pull action (Fig. 2). Push the material out from the center and draw it back from the edges over into the center. A shovel may also be used, of course, but is a little less handy.

Lay a 2" thick layer of mortar across the top of the concrete base. Lay a row of flagstone in line from one end to the other, buttering one edge of each stone as you place them. Place a loose stone at each end of the wall and reset the taut line between the two stones (Fig. 3). Fasten the line to sticks held by the stones. Be sure the line ends are the same distance above the base at each end. This becomes the guide for adjusting the mortared stones to level. Tap down each stone that is above the level of the line, using the back of the trowel.

Succeeding courses of flagstone should be laid up like brick. Place about a 1″ layer of mortar on each of the corners and place the corner stones. These will support loose stones temporarily for holding the reset taut line. Work from the ends to the center (Fig. 4). Tap each stone about level with the taut line (Fig. 5). Excess mortar squeezed out may be removed with the trowel and thrown onto the bed for the next stone (Fig. 6).

Fig. 4. Laying a bed of mortar on the course just finished. The bed is generally thicker for flagstone than for brick.

For greater bonding strength, and for better appearance, try to maintain a running bond overlap, as one would with brick. Use the level frequently (Fig. 7) for horizontal positioning of each stone. Lay only about 4 or 5 stones at one time. As each course is completed, the taut line is raised to the next level. It must be rechecked each time with a level or the ends carefully measured for equal distance from the base.

The mortar in the joints between the stones must not be allowed to set hard before tooling. About one-half hour after the mortar has

Fig. 5. Tap stone into place and level to the taut guide line.

Fig. 6. Squeezed out excess mortar is struck off and thrown onto the bed ahead.

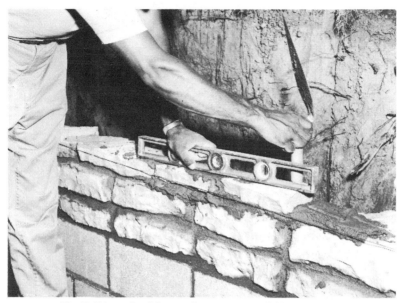

Fig. 7. Using a level frequently as stones are laid into position.

Fig. 8. A jointing tool or a rounded stick is used to tool the mortar into a dense and neat joint.

253

been placed is a good time to tool, whether the wall has been completed or not. A slow worker may be tooling only 3 or 4 courses below the one being laid. Use a jointing tool, or a rounded stick, and press it hard into the joints, pushing mortar in about ½ ″ behind the surface of the stones. Tooling increases the density of the mortar making it more watertight and improves the appearance. The tool is held at a slant as it is drawn across the mortar (Fig. 8). Push excess mortar feathers off with the tool.

As a finishing touch, brush the mortar joints with a stiff brush (Fig. 9). Use the brush to clean off small pieces of mortar from the face of the stones. If the mortar has hardened some, dampen the brush before using it.

## A BRICK WALK

Chapter 11 described brick walks and terraces, the type of best suited brick material, patterns, and construction. Shown here (Fig. 10) is the step-by-step procedure for building the small walk. The same procedure applies to a brick walk or patio of any size and

Fig. 9. A stiff brush is used to smooth the mortar after tooling.

Fig. 10. Illustrating how well a brick walk can blend with stone in a garden or patio area.

pattern. This walk was built on a 2″ sand base, plus a 1″ concrete cushion, plus mortared brick. This calls for excavating the dirt for a depth of about 5½″ from the top level of the walk. The difference is the thickness of the brick.

After digging out the dirt, place form boards along the edges of the walk (Fig. 11). Make sure the board tops are level with

255

Fig. 11. Setting form boards for sidewalks.

Fig. 12. Concrete foundation to support edging brick for walk.

Fig. 13. Mortart bed spread over concrete foundation.

Fig. 14. Placing edging brick in mortar.

the top of the walk surface and perfectly horizontal along the length of the walk. Parallel boards should be set so one is slightly lower than the other, for a slight tilt to the walk for water runoff. If the boards are to be removed later, ordinary 2″ × 4″ may be used. If they are to be left in place, as many prefer, use redwood, which does not decay with time, although it does change color.

For building up a more secure edging, as recommended in Chapter 11, dig edge trenches deeper and pour concrete until the top of the concrete is about 4″ below the top of the form boards. Mix mortar and place a ½″ layer over the concrete. This will form the bed for the edge brick (Fig. 13). Put edge bricking in place and tap to exactly match the top edge of the board (Fig. 14). The brick is placed on edge, rowlock style. Be sure to butter the edge of the brick with mortar. Tool the mortar joints smooth. Allow 24 hours for the mortar to set before proceding with the walk surface. Make up a leveling board like the one shown in Fig. 15. The bottom edge should be the right depth for the top of the sand base. Pour in sand and level it with the board.

Fig. 15. Using a board to level the sand base.

The next step is the laying of a concrete cushion. This may seem opposite to the method described in Chapter 11 but it is an alternate method, which is suggested by *Sakrete, Inc.* as a simplified method. The secret of this method is the use of dry *Sakrete* sand mix which is poured dry over the sand and levelled. This method is usable only in areas with considerable moisture in the ground,

Fig. 16. Dry SAKRETE sand mix is poured over the sand base and leveled.

since it depends on moisture seeping up through the sand base, and penetrating the concrete dry mix, to eventually hydrate and form a hard concrete cushion.

Remake the leveling board so the bottom edge is only the depth of a brick, usually 3⅝". Pour the dry *Sakrete* sand mix over the sand base (Fig. 16) and level it carefully with the leveling board (sometimes called a screed). Having established the brick pattern desired, lay the brick onto the dry mix allowing for space between each brick, from ⅜" to ½" (Fig. 17).

Mix *Sakrete* dry mortar ingredients with water but this time use about 30% more water than prescribed. The purpose is to make

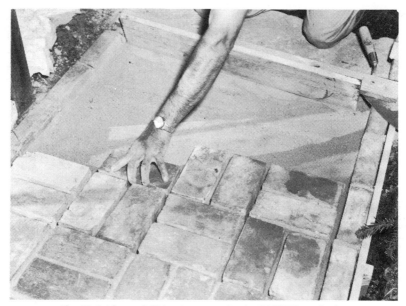

Fig. 17. Bricks are laid in place over the dry SAKRETE sand mix.

Fig. 18. Mortar is poured into the joint spaces between the bricks. A trowel is used to force mortar completely into all spaces.

260

a mortar that is quite fluid. Pour the mortar into the spaces. Where the mortar does not fill completely,use the trowel to force it down (Fig. 18). When the mortar is about "thumbprint dry," use a jointing tool and work each of the joints smoothly (Fig. 19). Brush away all the loose mortar. If, after four days, it appears some of the cement from the mortar is still on the brick, it should be re-

Fig. 19. Tool mortar joints before joints harden.

moved before it stains the brick. The only solvent for cement is about a 10% solution of muriatic acid. Rinse it off thoroughly afterwards. Use care in handling muriatic acid. The walk should be allowed to set undisturbed for 48 hours before using.

## CIRCULAR BARBECUE PIT

A barbecue pit in the center of the patio has some advantages (Fig. 20). It becomes the focal point for gatherings. Marshmallow toasters can work from any point around it. In the evening, when firewood is used, it can cast a pleasant light and provide some heat.

261

Fig. 20. A circular pit in the center of the patio can be the focal point of outdoor gatherings.

Fig. 21. The diameter of the barbecue pit in the center of the patio is 19" deep and 50" in diameter with a 2" layer of gravel in the bottom.

It will be seen from the series of illustrations to follow that the concrete for the patio was laid some time during the middle of the construction of the barbecue pit. The patio may be built, before, during, or after the pit is built. If built before, of course, the area for the pit should be left open.

The pit should be at least 50″ in diameter and dug to a depth of 19″ below the patio level (Fig. 21). Lay a 2″ bed of gravel and drive a stake into the center. The stake will be used for height and radius measurements. Mix a small amount of *Sakrete* with water and place a 2″ layer over the gravel around the edges. While this is still wet, smooth the top and scribe a circle from the stake with a string and nail. This will establish an outer diameter guide for laying the brick. (Fig. 22). This will be the base for the buildup of a circular brick wall. Allow 24 hours for the concrete to set.

The first course of brick is set on edge (soldier style) on a ¾″ to 1″ bed of mortar. The bricks should be dampened before being mortared in place. Butter the edges with mortar and follow the

Fig. 22. A 2″ thick layer of concrete in a circle will be used as the foundation for the brick barbecue pit. Notice the circle being scribed from the center stake.

263

Fig. 23. Fire brick being mortared and set on end which forms the circle for the barbecue pit.

circle around the base (Fig. 23). This course must be measured frequently with a level to make sure it is perfectly horizontal. It forms the base and guide for the remaining courses. Above the first course of rowlock brick, set another course, also rowlock style (on end). This should bring the construction level up to the level of the ground or patio surface. Two courses of brick above the patio floor should be enough. These are laid header style and with an overlapping pattern.

Lay a complete circle of brick dry. This is to establish the number of brick and the space between them. Remove about 5 of the brick and lay down a ½ " bed of mortar. Butter the ends of the brick removed and put them back in place. Be sure the joints between bricks are completely filled with mortar. It is obvious that the mortar joints will be wider at the outer edge than the inner. The illustrations in Figs. 24 through 28 show the steps. Note the straight stick in the illustration of Fig. 25 being used to adjust a newly laid brick to the level of the preceding one. Use a spirit level frequently. Use the handle of the trowel to tap bricks into position.

Allow about 15 minutes for the mortar to take a set then strike off excess mortar level with the brick (Fig. 29). This rule should be observed as you progress with the work. Do not wait until the entire job is done to smooth off excess mortar. Be sure to scrape off mortar that has fallen to the patio concrete.

Fig. 24. The top two courses of brick are laid as all headers with an overlap to improve bonding.

## GARDEN EDGING

There is probably nothing so appropriate to the landscape of a garden as edging made of brick to separate sections of a garden. Note the effect in the illustration of Fig. 30 and how one can vary the style to fit the effect desired. In the foreground is a thin edge of brick laid end-to-end. In the center the edging is brick laid face-to-face and on edge (rowlock style).

The job may be as difficult or as simple as desired, depending on how sturdy the construction is to be. The one described here is

265

Fig. 25. Lay brick on a bed of mortar, tapping them into place. A straight stick is used for alignment.

Fig. 26. Striking off excess mortar.

Fig. 27. Brick must be placed carefully to make sure the circle is even.

Fig. 28. Making sure all joints are completely filled with mortar.

Fig. 29. Strike off excess top mortar and follow up with a thorough cleanup job.

Fig. 30. Brick edging is excellent for separating garden sections.

fairly easy to construct and will provide an edging that will stand up under weathering for many years. The brick is to lay on a 1″ thickness of concrete and the concrete on a 1″ thickness of gravel for drainage. The same concrete base material will be used for mortaring the brick. A sand mix will do which, in this case, was *Sakrete* sand mix. Mortar contains lime which adds to its stiffness and allows building several courses of brick on top of each other. Since a brick edging is only one course, it is not necessary to use mixes containing lime. In fact, concrete mixes are stronger than mortar and will provide a stronger bond and longer life.

Stake out a string line to act as a guide for digging a trench. Dig a trench the thickness of the brick plus 1″ for the concrete and 1″ for the gravel. Lay a 1″ layer of gravel along the bottom of the trench. Readjust the string line near the level of the ground and adjust it for a perfect level, using a carpenter's spirit level. Mix a quantity of *Sakrete* sand mix with water and lay a 1″ bed over the gravel. Make enough to butter the joints between bricks.

Butter each brick with the concrete and lay them into place one at a time. Tap them into position, using the taut string as a guide. Allow about ⅜″ to ½″ between bricks for the joints. Trowel off excess concrete 15 minutes after laying to make the top smooth. You can add a course or two of brick above the ground level, for terracing or other effects. But if you do, the brick should be laid and jointed with mortar rather than concrete.

## BARBECUE GRILL

A barbecue grill which has many uses and is sturdily built is illustrated and fully dimensioned in sketches of Fig. 31. The top row of steel bars support cooking utensils or steaks placed directly on the bars. The lower row of bars is for firewood and allows ashes to drop to the bottom. A brick ledge accommodates a slide-in pan for holding charcoal for this method of outdoor cooking.

A heavy concrete base extends 10″ into the ground which eliminates any possibility of settling or of heaving in severe cold climates. Half-inch bars imbedded into the top section of the base will add to the strength to prevent cracking. Brick courses above the base follow the American bond pattern and, if well-mortared, will give years of service.

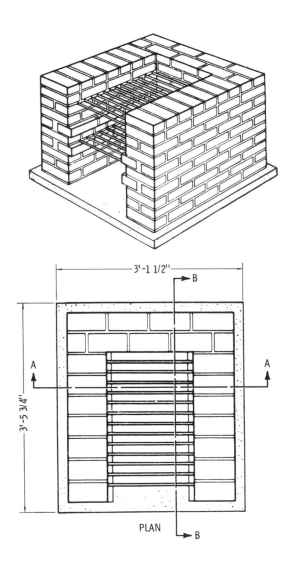

**Fig. 31. Complete dimensions for building a**

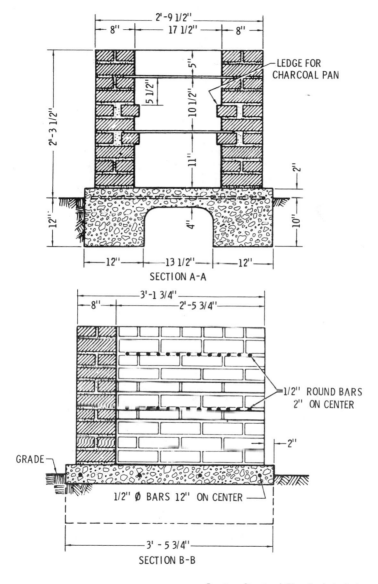

2'-9 1/2"
8" — 17 1/2" — 8"

5"

LEDGE FOR
CHARCOAL PAN

5 1/2"

10 1/2"

2'-3 1/2"

11"

2"

12"

4"

10"

12" — 13 1/2" — 12"

SECTION A-A

3'-1 3/4"
8" — 2'-5 3/4"

1/2" ROUND BARS
2" ON CENTER

2"

GRADE

1/2" Ø BARS 12" ON CENTER

3' - 5 3/4"

SECTION B-B

Courtesy Structural Clay Products Inst.

**barbecue pit of brick and a heavy concrete base.**

The concrete base is a 1:2:3½ mix. That is, the material proportions are 1 part portland cement, 2 part graded sand, and 3½ parts graded aggregate. The masonry mortar is a 1:0.25:3 mix, or 1 part portland cement, ¼ part hydrated lime, and 3 parts sand. Because of the total amount of materials needed, it will be more economical to purchase them in bulk.

Here is the total bill of materials for this particular barbecue grill:

| | |
|---|---|
| Portland cement | 3 sacks |
| Graded sand | 9 cu. ft. |
| Graded aggregate or gravel | 6 cu. ft. |
| Hydrated lime | 1 sack |
| Brick | 250 |
| 3-ft. lengths, ½" bars. | 4 |
| 2-ft. lengths, ½" bars. | 26 |

Two sacks of cement will be used for the concrete and one sack for the mortar. If the ground is firm enough, no forms will be needed for the concrete base below ground level. A form 4¾" × 37½" (inside dimensions) should be made for that part of the base above ground, to assure smooth sides.

Dig out a rectangular hole to the dimensions mentioned above, leaving a 13½" mound of dirt in the center. This mound saves on the amount of concrete needed. Mix the total amount of concrete in a power mixer adding water according to Tables given in the Volume on Concrete. About 17 gallons of water will be needed and this should be precisely measured. Pour the concrete into the hole up to the ground level. Lay the 3-ft. rods in place at 12" intervals. Pour the balance of the concrete up to the top of the forms in place. This should bring the base approximately 2" above ground level. Carefully smooth and trowel the surface for a flat even top. Allow 48 hours for thorough setting of the concrete before starting the brick work.

Carefully review the sketches of Fig. 31 and note that the fourth and sixth courses of brick have their inside tier slightly protruding inside the pit to support the lower row of rods and provide a ledge for the charcoal pan. Outside of this, the laying up of the brick is standard, using ½" mortar joints. The outside edges of the brick structure should fall just 2" inside the edges of the concrete base. To make sure of this it may be wise to dry-lay the first course of brick on all sides. Then pencil-mark the outer edges for a guide. Another way is to drive stakes into the ground and use string guides on all four sides.

Mix an amount of mortar that can be handled within a 2-hour work session. Lay a bed of mortar on the concrete base for the first course of brick, using the pencil marks or string guide to assure straight sides. Because of the short wall sizes, it may not be necessary to use the taut line method described in earlier chapters, but a straight board should be at hand to check the level of each course as it goes up.

Butter about five bricks at a time and put them in place tapping them into position. After the fourth course is laid, place the 2-ft. rods in place over the protruding ledge of brick and space them parallel 2" apart. Carefully place mortar around them to hold them in place as the brick courses continue on up. Do not overlook the protruding brick at the sixth course. Above the eighth course, place the second set of rods and mortar around them. Complete the brick work, with the top two sides a course of all headers.

Be sure to trowel off excess mortar within 15 minutes after laying, to prevent its setting up too hard to remove. Tool all joints firmly and clean off any feathers. To protect the base from the fallen mortar, place plastic sheets around the edges of the brick at the base line to catch the debris. Otherwise, scrape off fallen mortar within 25 minutes after it has fallen onto the concrete base.

## CHAPTER 14

# Plastering

The final surfaces of interior walls are usually made of plaster or plasterboard. Plaster walls generally have a hard smooth finish that is easily painted or papered. It is (to some extent) fire retarding and has some sound deadening qualities. The plaster is applied to a base which is attached to wood studding of residential structures, which is usually 2"×4" lumber, or to the metal studs of many industrial buildings, as shown in Fig. 1. It may also be cemented to brick or masonry walls.

Two methods are used to apply plaster to a wall. The older method is called "lath and plaster," in which plaster, in plastic form, is applied by hand to properly spaced horizontally mounted furring strips. When applied in a thick coat, the plaster is forced into the spaces between the furring strips which forms a bond. The horizontally mounted wood furring strips have been replaced, to a large extent, by metal screen lathing similar to that used for stucco.

The "lath and plaster" method requires a tremendous amount of hand labor and considerable time because of the three coats applied and the drying time between coats. Since World War II, this method has been almost entirely replaced by the plasterboard method, in which 4 ft. × 8 ft., 10 ft., or 12 ft. plasterboard sheets are nailed or screwed to the wall studs. Plasterboard has a number of advantages over the "lath and plaster" method. It eliminates the need to mix plaster on the job site which saves

considerably on the amount of labor involved. Moreover, plasterboard is available in a large number of designs to fit about any
special requirement of interior wall finishing. They are made in

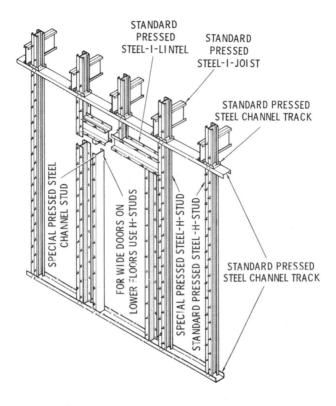

Fig. 1. Illustrating one type of metal wall and ceiling structure designed to hold
plaster board.

thicknesses from ¼″ to ¾″. There are many suppliers of plasterboard throughout the country and some make prefinished
plasterboard to simulate wood or textured cloth finishes.

Most of this chapter will be devoted to the installation of
plasterboard. The "lath and plaster" method will be described
only briefly.

## PLASTER CONTENT

Plaster is generally cement, pure white in color, and includes a number of minerals. Most contain the mineral gypsum which is hydrated calcium sulfate. Some plasters with a smoother surface for the finish coat contain lime, which is calcium carbonate. Fine sand is often used in plaster but not for the finish layer. Other minerals are included in smaller quantities, which alter the characteristics slightly, to meet certain requirements. For "lath and plaster" methods, plaster is supplied in bags as a chalk-like white powder. When mixed with water, it is plastic and workable. When the water evaporates, what remains is a rock-like hard plaster.

Plasterboards include a paper backing which helps to give the boards support for shipping and handling. This paper backing also gives a smooth finish for paint or wallpaper in drywall construction.

## LATH AND PLASTER

If you were to cut into the walls of older homes you would find wood furring strips supporting a thick coat of plaster. A cutaway view is shown in Fig. 2. The wood furring strips are 4 ft. long, to fit studs 16" on center, 1½" wide, and ¼" thick. They are installed with a ⅜" space between each lath.

Wood furring strips have been replaced by metal lathing, in the limited use today of the "lath and plaster" method. Metal lathing is die cut from flat stock sheets then pulled apart to form a pattern like that shown in Fig. 3. Expanded metal lathing has edges turned outward, which make excellent keys for holding the plaster.

Plaster is supplied in bags with the necessary ingredients already mixed. It requires only the addition of water which is added on the job. The amount of water required is marked on the bag. Plaster must be mixed in clean wooden boxes. Mix only as much as can be applied within an hour or hydration will begin to take place and the plaster will become too hard to handle with ease. Each time a new batch is to be mixed, the box must

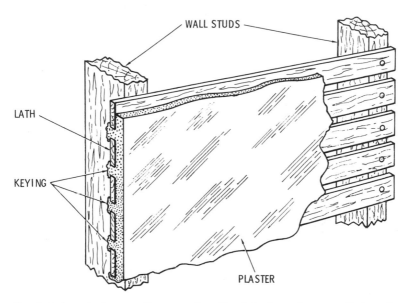

WALL STUDS

LATH

KEYING

PLASTER

Fig. 2. Lath and plaster wall construction. Wood furring strips are nailed to the wall studs and plaster is applied in several coats.

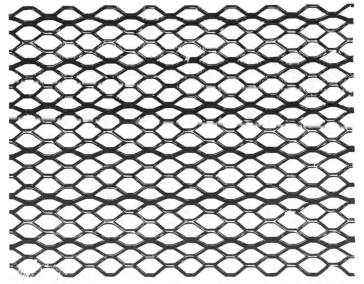

Fig. 3. Expanded metal screening like this is applied to the wall instead of wood furring strips.

277

first be thoroughly washed out. Leave the box clean at the end of the day ready for use the next day.

Plaster is carried to the work on a hand held, square wooden platen, and applied to the lathing with a rectangular-trowel. It must be firmly imbedded into the lathing so there is a firm keying into and around the edges of the lath strips.

Plasters are usually applied in three coats which are termed in order of application as follows:

1. Scratch coat.
2. Second or brown coat.
3. Finish or set coat.

*Scratch Coat*—This coat should be made approximately ⅜″ thick measured from the face of the backing and carried to the full length of the wall or the natural breaking points such as doors or windows. Before the scratch coat begins to harden, however, it should be cross-scratched to provide a mechanical key for the second or brown coat.

*Brown Coat*—The brown coat should be approximately the same thickness as that of the scratch coat. Before applying the brown coat, dampen the surface of the scratch coat evenly by means of a fog spray to obtain uniform suction. This coat may be applied in two thin coats, one immediately following the other. Such a method may prove helpful in applying sufficient pressure to ensure a proper bond with the base coat.

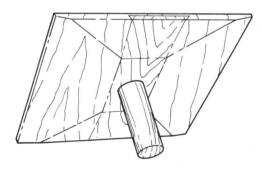

Fig. 4. A wood hawk used to carry the plaster material to the wall or ceiling.

Bring the brown coat to a true even surface then roughen with a wood float or cross-scratch it lightly to provide a bond for the finish coat. Damp-cure the brown coat for at least two days then allow it to dry.

*Finish Coat*—The brown coat (as mentioned above) should be dampened for at least two days before application of the finish coat. Begin moistening as soon as the brown coat has hardened sufficiently, applying the water in a fine fog spray. Avoid soaking

Fig. 5. How plaster is applied to the wall showing the use of the hawk and the trowel.

279

the wall but give it as much water as will readily be absorbed.

## APPLYING THE PLASTER

The assortment of tools used by the plasterer are very similar to those employed by the bricklayer. Essential plastering tools are as follows:

*Hawk*—This tool is usually made of hard pine or cedar and is usually about 13″ or 14″ square (Fig. 4). It is held in the left hand, as shown in Fig. 5, forming a small "hand table" which holds a supply of plaster. The plasterer conveys this plaster from the hawk to the work where he spreads it over the surface to be plastered as shown in the illustration.

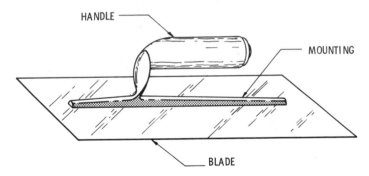

Fig. 6. The trowel which is used to apply plaster is generally made of 24-gauge polished steel.

*Trowel*—As distinguished from the bricklayers' trowel, the plasterers' trowel is rectangular in shape, as shown in Fig. 6. The handle is attached to a mounting which stiffens the blade. The trowel is light, so that the tool is easily used. Trowels are classed as:

1. Browning.
2. Finishing.

The browning trowel is used for rough coating and has a heavier blade than that used on the finishing trowel, otherwise the construction of both are the same.

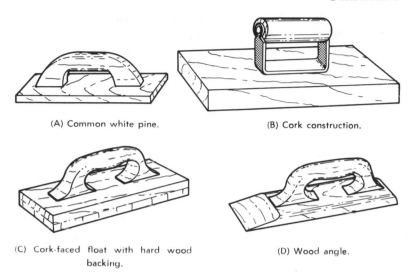

(A) Common white pine.

(B) Cork construction.

(C) Cork-faced float with hard wood backing.

(D) Wood angle.

Fig. 7. Several types of wooden floats.

*Float*—The common form of float consists of a piece of hard pine board 10″ or 12″ × ⅝″ to ⅞″ having a wooden handle, preferably of hard wood screwed to the back. Because of the great friction, the face of a float soon wears off and becomes thin; hence, there is usually an adjustable handle fastened with bolts which can be fixed to new face pieces as they are required. Floats are applied in smoothing and finishing with a rotary motion sometimes reversed as left to right and vice versa. Various types of floats are shown in Fig. 7.

*Darby*—This tool is simply a flat straight strip of wood (or

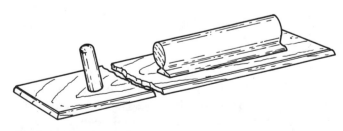

Fig. 8. An ordinary wooden darby used to level large areas of plaster.

281

metal) provided with handles to enable the workman to level up and straighten large surfaces as they are put on.

The tool is held by both hands and moved with a sliding up and down diagonal and horizontal motion to level off by rubbing and pressing any lumps or high spots which may be left after applying the mortar with the trowels. This work is very laborious, especially on ceilings or any job above the line of the shoulders. The tool is also essential in preserving an even thickness of each coat. Fig. 8 shows an ordinary wooden darby.

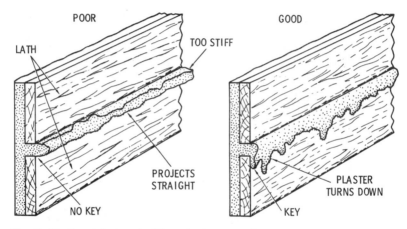

Fig. 9. Good and bad embedding of plaster on furring strips. The plaster must form a key behind the strips to hold well.

It is important that the first coat of plaster have the right consistency, to establish a firm key onto the lath. If the plaster is too thick it will stand out behind the lathing material but not grab securely. A thinner plaster tends to turn down behind the lathing material and form a key and lock into place. This is illustrated in Fig. 9 with wood lathing. The same reasoning applies to metal lathing, although keying to expanded metal lathing is more secure even with stiff plaster material.

Each coat must be thoroughly dry before applying the next coat. While the second coat is fogged with a spray of water before applying the finish coat, the second coat must be allowed to dry before fogging.

It is often desirable to obtain a hard glossy surface on the finish coat. This is done by brushing water on the surface, using a large painter's brush, then floating again with a hardwood float. If this is done a couple of times, the surface will take on a very hard finish.

While the description given above is brief for "lath and plaster," it can readily be seen how much labor is involved. This is why this kind of plastering has given way almost exclusively to the use of plasterboard.

## PLASTERBOARD

Plasterboard (sometimes referred to as drywall or wallboard) is available in solid sheets made of fireproof material. Standard width is usually 4 ft., with a few types in 2-ft. widths. Lengths are from 6 ft. to 16 ft. and are available with thicknesses from ¼" to ¾". Edges are tapered to permit smooth edge finishing, although some boards can be purchased with square edges.

The most common length is 8 ft. to permit wasteless mountings to the wall studs. This particular size will fit standard 8-ft. ceiling heights when vertically mounted. However, recommended mounting for easier handling is horizontal. Two lengths, one above the other, fit the 8-ft. ceiling heights, when mounted horizontally.

In addition to regular wallboard, many other types are available for special purposes. The descriptions which follow are based on those from the NATIONAL GYPSUM CO., who supplied considerable information and all of the illustrations which follow, for this chapter. Similar boards may be obtained from other manufacturers. Check your local supplier for his catalog on your needs.

Regular wallboard comes in thicknesses of ¼", ⅜", ½", and ⅝". The ¼" board is used in two or three layer wallboard construction and generally has square edges. The most commonly used thickness is ⅜" which can be obtained in lengths up to 16 ft. All have a smooth cream-colored paper covering that takes any kind of decoration.

Insulating (foil-backed) wallboards have aluminum foil which is laminated to the back surface. The aluminum foil creates a vapor barrier and provides reflected insulation value. It can be used in a single-layer construction or as a base layer in two-layer construction. Thicknesses are ⅜", ½", and ⅝", with lengths from 6 ft. to 14 ft. All three thicknesses are available with either square or tapered edges.

Wallboard with a specially formulated core, which provides increased fire-resistance ratings when used in recommended wall and ceiling systems, is made by many companies. NATIONAL GYPSUM CO. calls their product *Fire-Shield* which achieves a one-hour fire rating in single-layer construction over wood studs. It is manufactured in ½" and ⅝" thicknesses with lengths from 6 ft. to 14 ft., with tapered edges.

Some suppliers have a lower cost board called backer board. These are used for the base layer in two-layer construction. Thicknesses are ⅜", ½", and ⅝", with a width of 2 ft. as well as the usual 4 ft. Length is 8 ft. only. The edges are square but the 2-ft. wide, in ½", and ⅝" thickness can be purchased with tongue-and-groove edges.

Another type of backer board has a vinyl surface. It is used as a waterproof base for bath and shower areas. The size is 4 ft. × 11 ft. which is the right size for enclosing around a standard bathtub. It is available in ½" and ⅝" thicknesses with square edges.

A moisture-resistant board is specially processed for use as a ceramic tile base. Both core and facing paper are treated to resist moisture and high humidity. Edges are tapered and the regular tile adhesive seals the edges. The boards are 4 ft. wide with lengths of 8 ft. and 12 ft.

Finding increased use is vinyl-covered decorator plasterboard which eliminates the need for painting or wallpapering. The vinyl covering is available in a large number of colors and patterns to fit many decorator needs. Many colors in a fabric like finish plus a number of wood grain appearances can be obtained. Only mild soap and water are needed to keep the finish clean and bright. Usual installation is by means of an adhesive, which eliminates nails or screws except at the top and bottom where decorator nails are generally used. The square edges are butted together (Fig. 10). They are available in ½" and ⅜" thicknesses, 4 ft. wide, and 8 ft., 9 ft., and 10 ft. long.

Courtesy National Gypsum Co.

Fig. 10. Modern home interior design is using more and more of the vinyl-finish plasterboard.

A similar vinyl covered plasterboard, called monolithic, has an extra width of vinyl along the edges. The boards are installed with adhesive or nails. The edges are brought over the fasteners and pasted down then cut flush at the edges. This method hides the fasteners. Extruded aluminum bead and trim accessories, covered with matching vinyl, can be purchased to finish off inside, outside, and ceiling corners, for vinyl covered plasterboard.

## Plasterboard Ratings

The principal manufacturers of plasterboard maintain large laboratories for the testing of their products for both sound absorption ability and fire retardation. They are based on established national standards that have been industry accepted and all follow the same procedure. Tests for sound absorption result in figures of merit and those for fire retardation on the length

285

of time a wall will retard a fire. Both vary depending on the material of the wallboard, the layers and thickness, and the method of wall construction.

## Sound Absorption

Drywall construction systems are rated for Sound Transmission Class (STC) and floor to ceiling systems in Impact Noise Rating (INR). The ASTM E90-66T procedure for STC figures for walls is a measurement of sound transmission loss taken from 125 to 4000 hertz. It is measured at 16 third-octave frequencies with the STC curve plotted to reflect the overall performance at all frequencies tested. An older method based on ASTM E90-61T uses ½-octave measurements but the STC figure is nearly the same.

## Fire Retardation

ASTM Standard E119, Fire Tests of Building Construction and Materials, is the standard by which fire retardation is measured. Tests made by this standard are generally recognized by building code authorities and fire insurance rating bureaus. The degree to which systems prevent the spread of fire or damaging heat is indicated in intervals of time. If a construction assembly contains the fire and heat for two hours during the test, it is given a two hour fire resistance rating.

Table 1 gives the ratings of some of the wall assemblies as catalogued by NATIONAL GYPSUM CO. The capitalized wallboard names shown in the charts are brand names of the various board materials made by various companies. Note the importance of the wall construction, in addition to the plasterboard types, thicknesses, and layers used.

Plasterboard is easily cut to size. If whole width or lengths are to be cut from a board, score the paper side deeply, place the board over a straight edge or edge of a work table with the paper side up. Strike the overhanging piece and it will break off, something like you score and break glass. For odd shaped pieces, use a wood saw which goes through plasterboard with ease. Cutouts for electrical fixtures and switches are made by drilling a large hole and cutting out the piece with a key-hole saw.

286

# Table 1. Fire Retardation and Sound Transmission Rating
## PARTITIONS — WOOD FRAMING (load-bearing)

| | FIRE RATING | REF. | STC | REF. | DESCRIPTION |
|---|---|---|---|---|---|
| SINGLE LAYER | 45-min. | U.L. Design No. 1 — 45 m n. | 34 | NGC 2161 | ½" Fire-Shield Gypsum Wallboard, nailed both sides 2" x 4" studs, 16" o.c. |
| | 1-hour | U.L. Design No. 5 — 1 hr. | 35 | NBS 240 | 5/8" Fire-Shield Gypsum Wallboard or Fire-Shield M-R Board nailed both side 2" x 4" wood studs, 16" o.c. |
| | 1-hour | U.L. Design No. 25 — 1 hr. | 37 | NG 246 FT | 5/8" Fire-Shield Gypsum Wallboard nailed both sides. 2" x 4" wood studs, 24" o.c. |
| | 1-hour | F.M. Design WP.9C — 1 hr. | 37 | Based on NG 246-FT | 5/8" Fire-Shield Monolithic Durasan, vertically applied to 2" x 4" studs spaced 24" o.c. secured at joints with 6d nails spaced 7" o.c. and at intermediate studs with 3/8" x 3/8" bead of MC Adhesive. |
| SINGLE LAYER (resilient) | 1-hour | Based on O.S.U. T-3376 & U... Design No. 5 — 1 hr. | 45 | TL 63-13 Riverbank | 5/8" Fire-Shield Gypsum Wallboard, screw applied to Resilient Furring Channel, spaced 24" o.c. one side only, on 2" x 4" studs spaced 16" o.c. Other side 5/8" Fire-Shield Gypsum Wallboard nailed direct to studs. |
| | 1-hour | Based on O.S.U. T-3376 | 52 | NG 137-FT | 5/8" Fire-Shield Gypsum Wallboard, screw applied to Resilient Furring Channel, spaced 24" o.c. one side only, on 2" x 4" studs spaced 16" o.c. Other side 5/8" Fire-Shield Gypsum Wallboard screw attached at 16" spacing. 3" Fiberglas in stud cavity. |
| | 1-hour | O.S.U. T-3376 | 45 | NGC 2046 | 5/8" Fire-Shield Gypsum Wallboard, screw applied to resilient furring channels 24" o.c. nailed to both sides of 2" x 4" studs spaced 16" o.c. |

## Table 1 PARTITIONS — WOOD FRAMING (cont.)

| | FIRE RATING | REF. | STC | REF. | DESCRIPTION |
|---|---|---|---|---|---|
| **DOUBLE LAYER** | 1-hour | F.M. Design WP-147-1 hr. | 45 | NGC 2321 | ½" Fire-Shield Wallboard or Durasan laminated to ¼" gypsum wallboard nailed to both sides 2" x 4" studs spaced 16" o.c. |
| | 2-hour | Based on U.L. Design No. 4 — 2 hr. | 41 | NBS 241 | ⅝" Fire-Shield Gypsum Wallboard base layer nail applied to 2" x 4" wood stud spaced 16" o.c. Face layer ⅝" Fire-Shield Gypsum Wallboard laminated and nail applied. |
| **EXTERIOR WALLS** | 1-hour | F.M. Design WP-78 — 1 hr. U.L. Design | | | ⅝" Fire-Shield Gypsum Wallboard nailed horizontally to inside face of 2" x 4" wood studs 16" o.c. ½" gypsum sheathing nailed to outside face of studs. Siding ⅜" Woodrock. |
| | 2-hour | No. 23 — 2 hr. | | | Two layers ⅝" Fire-Shield Gypsum Wallboard nailed horiz. or vert. to inside face of 2" x 4" wood studs 16" o.c. ½" gypsum sheathing nailed to outside face of studs, brick veneer facing. |
| **DOUBLE LAYER with Deciban Sound Deadening Board** | Non-rated | | 46 | G & H No. 6 | ½" Deciban nail applied both sides 2" x 4" wood studs, 16" o.c. Face layer ½" Gypsum Wallboard laminated. |
| | Non-rated | | 50 | G & H No. 20 | ½" Deciban nail applied both sides 2" x 4" wood studs, 16" o.c. fire-topped Face layer. ⅝" Gypsum Wallboard laminated. |
| | 1-hour | U.L. Design No. 17 — 1 hr. | 53 | NG 213 FT | ½" Deciban nail applied both sides 2" x 3" wood studs, staggered 16" o.c. on 2" x 3" plates spaced 1" apart. Face layer ⅝" Fire-Shield Gypsum Wallboard nail applied. |
| | 1-hour | U.L. Design No. 26 — 1 hr. | 49 | NGC 1009 | ½" Deciban nail applied both sides 2" x 3" wood studs, staggered 24" o.c. on 2" x 3" plates spaced 1" apart. Face layer ½" Fire-Shield Gypsum Wallboard nail applied. |

## Table 1 PARTITIONS — STEEL FRAMING (cont.)

| | FIRE RATING | REF. | STC | REF. | DESCRIPTION |
|---|---|---|---|---|---|
| SINGLE LAYER 1⅝" STUDS | 1-hour | O.S.U. T-3296 | 39 | TL-64-244 | ⅝" Fire-Shield Gypsum Wallboard screw attached vertically to both sides 1⅝" screw studs, 24" o.c. |
| | 1-hour | Based on O.S.U. T-3296 | 42 | *Based on NGC 2184 | ⅝" Fire-Shield Gypsum Wallboard screw attached vertically to both sides 1⅝" screw studs, 24" o.c. with 1" Fiberglas in cavity. |
| SINGLE LAYER 2½" STUDS | 1-hour | Based on O.S.U. T-3296 | 41 | NG 149 FT | ⅝" Fire-Shield Gypsum Wallboard screw attached vertically to both sides 2½" screw studs, 24" o.c. |
| | 1-hour | Based on O.S.U. T-3296 | 46 | *Based on NGC 2182 | ⅝" Fire-Shield Gypsum Wallboard screw attached vertically to both sides 2½" screw studs, 24" o.c. with 3" Fiberglas in cavity. |
| | 1-hour | F.M. Design WP-51 | 45 | NGC 2179 | ½" Fire-Shield Gypsum Wallboard screw attached vertically to both sides 2½" screw studs 24" o.c., 2" mineral wool in stud cavity. |
| SINGLE LAYER 3⅝" STUDS | 1-hour | F.M. Design WP-45 | 41 | Based on TL-61-215 | ⅝" Fire-Shield Gypsum Wallboard screw attached horizontally to both sides 3⅝" screw studs 24" o.c. Wallboard joints staggered. |
| | 1-hour | Based on O.S.U. T-1770 | 46 | TL-66-143 | ⅝" Fire-Shield Gypsum Wallboard screw attached vertically to both sides 3⅝" screw studs, 24" o.c. with 3" Fiberglas in cavity. |
| | 45-min. | Based on F.M. Design WP-51 | 45 | NGC 2146 | ½" Fire-Shield Gypsum Wallboard screw attached vertically to both sides 3⅝" screw studs 24" o.c., 2" Fiberglas in cavity. |
| | 1-hour | Based on F.M. Design WP-51 | 45 | NGC 2149 | ½" Fire-Shield Gypsum Wallboard screw attached vertically to both sides 3⅝" screw studs 24" o.c., 2" mineral wool in stud cavity. |
| | 1-hour | O.S.U. T-1770 | 41 | TL-61-215 | ⅝" Fire-Shield Gypsum Wallboard screw attached vertically to both sides 3⅝" screw studs, 24" o.c. |

## PARTITIONS — STEEL FRAMING (continued)

| | | FIRE RATING | REF. | STC | REF. | DESCRIPTION |
|---|---|---|---|---|---|---|
| UNBALANCED | 2½" STUDS | 1-hour | F.M. Design WP-66 | 44 | Based on NGC 2248 | ½" Fire-Shield (Monolithic Durasan) vertically applied to 2½" screw stud. Double layer one side single layer on the other. Base layer screw attached, face layer and single layer screwed at edges, adhesively attached along center. |
| | | 1-hour | Based on F.M. Design WP-66 | 43 | NGC 2248 | ½" Fire-Shield Gypsum Wallboard screw attached vertically to both sides 2½" screw studs spaced 24" o.c. second layer screw attached vertically to one side only. |
| | | 1-hour | Based on F.M. Design WP-66 | 50 | NGC 2253 | ½" Fire-Shield Gypsum Wallboard screw attached vertically to both sides 2½" screw studs spaced 24" o.c. second layer screw attached vertically to one side only and 3" Fiberglas in cavity. |
| | | 1½-hour | Based on O.S.U. T-3240 | 44 | *Based on NGC 2248 | ⅝" Fire-Shield Gypsum Wallboard screw attached vertically to both sides 2½" screw studs spaced 24" o.c. second layer screw attached vertically to one side only. |
| | | 1½-hour | Based on O.S.U. T-3240 | 50 | *Based on NGC 2253 | ⅝" Fire-Shield Gypsum Wallboard screw attached vertically to both sides 2½" screw studs spaced 24" o.c. second layer screw attached vertically to one side only and 3" Fiberglas in cavity. |
| | 3⅝" STUDS | 1-hour | Based on F.M. Design WP-66 | 44 | NGC 2323 | ½" Fire-Shield Gypsum Wallboard screw attached vertically to both sides 3⅝" screw studs spaced 24" o.c. second layer screw attached vertically to one side only. |
| | | 1-hour | Based on F.M. Design WP-66 | 51 | *Based on NGC 2253 | ½" Fire-Shield Gypsum Wallboard screw attached vertically to both sides 3⅝" screw studs spaced 24" o.c. second layer screw attached vertically to one side only and 3" Fiberglas in cavity. |
| | | 1½-hour | O.S.U. T-3240 | 47 | TL-64-245 | ⅝" Fire-Shield Gypsum Wallboard screw attached vertically to both sides, 3⅝" screw studs 24" o.c. Second layer laminated vertically and screwed to one side only. |

## Table 1 PARTITIONS — STEEL FRAMING (cont.)

| | FIRE RATING | REF. | STC | REF. | DESCRIPTION |
|---|---|---|---|---|---|
| UNBALANCED 3⅝" STUDS | 1½-hour | Based on O.S.U. T-3240 | 53 | NG 243 FT | ⅝" Fire-Shield Gypsum Wallboard screw attached vertically to both sides, 3⅝" screw studs 24" o.c. Second layer laminated vertically and screwed to one side only and 2" Fiberglas or min. wool in cavity. |
| DOUBLE LAYER 2½" STUDS | 1-hour | F.M. Design WP-156 | 45 | NGC 2328 | ½" Fire-Shield Wallboard or Durasan laminated to ¼" wallboard screw attached both sides 2½" screw studs spaced 24" o.c. |
| | 1-hour | Based on F.M. Design WP-152 | 53 | NGC 2318 | ½" Fire-Shield Wallboard or Durasan laminated to ¼" wallboard screw attached both sides 2½" screw studs spaced 24" o.c. with 2" Fiberglas in cavity. |
| | 2-hour | O.S.U. T-3370 | 46 | NGC 2250 | Two layers ½" Fire-Shield Gypsum Wallboard screw attached vertically both sides 2½" screw studs spaced 24" o.c. vertical joints staggered. |
| | 2-hour | F.M. Design WP-47 | 46 | NGC 2250 | First layer ½" Fire-Shield Gypsum Wallboard screw attached vertically both sides 2½" screw studs spaced 24" o.c. Second layer screw attached horizontally both sides. |
| | 2-hour | Based on O.S.U. T-3370 | 53 | NGC 2252 | Two layers ½" Fire-Shield Gypsum Wallboard screw attached vertically both sides 2½" screw studs spaced 24" o.c. vertical joints staggered and 3" Fiberglas in cavity. |
| | 2-hour | Based on F.M. Design WP-47 O.S.U. T-1771 | 54 | *Based on NGC 2252 | First layer ⅝" Fire-Shield Gypsum Wallboard screw attached vertically both sides 2½" screw studs spaced 24" o.c. Second layer screw attached horizontally both sides and 3" Fiberglas in cavity. |

## Table 1 PARTITIONS — STEEL FRAMING (cont.)

| | FIRE RATING | REF. | STC | REF. | DESCRIPTION |
|---|---|---|---|---|---|
| DOUBLE LAYER 3⅝" STUDS | 2-hour | Based on O.S.U. T-3370 | 48 | NGC 2282 | Two layers ½" Fire-Shield Gypsum Wallboard screw attached vertically both sides 3⅝" screw studs spaced 24" o.c. vertical joints staggered. |
| | 2-hour | Based on O.S.U. T-3370 | 53 | NGC 2288 | Two layers ½" Fire-Shield Gypsum Wallboard screw attached vertically both sides 3⅝" screw studs spaced 24" o.c. vertical joints staggered and 3" Fiberglas in cavity. |
| | 2-hour | O.S.U. T-1771 | 49 | *Based on NGC 2282 | First layer ⅝" Fire-Shield Gypsum Wallboard screw attached vertically both sides 3⅝" screw studs spaced 24" o.c. Second layer laminated vertically both sides. |
| | 2-hour | Based on F.M. Design WP-47 | 55 | Based on NG 220 FT | First layer ⅝" Fire-Shield Gypsum Wallboard screw attached vertically both sides 3⅝" screw studs spaced 24" o.c. Second layer screw attached horizontally both sides and 3" Fiberglas in cavity. |

Courtesy National Gypsum Co.

*Sound test conducted using ½" F. S. Wallboard

## Table 2. Optimum Spacing of Spring Clips for Ceiling

### 25 GAUGE STUDS — MAXIMUM HEIGHTS

| Stud Spacing | 1⅝" Stud | | 2½" Stud | | 3¼" Stud | | 3⅝" Stud | | 4" Stud | |
|---|---|---|---|---|---|---|---|---|---|---|
| | ½" GWB | ⅝" GWB | ½" GWB | ⅝" GWB | ½" GWB | ⅝" GWB | ½" GWB | ⅝" GWB | ½" GWB | ⅝" GWB |
| 12" o.c. | 12'-0" | 12'-4" | 16'-2" | 16'-6" | 19'-6" | 19'-10" | 21'-0" | 21'-4" | 22'-0" | 22'-4" |
| 16" o.c. | 11'-0" | 11'-7" | 14'-8" | 15'-5" | 17'-10" | 18'-4" | 19'-5" | 19'-11" | 20'-8" | 20'-10" |
| 24" o.c. | 10'-0" | 10'-10" | 13'-5" | 14'-3" | 15'-10" | 16'-7" | 17'-3" | 18'-2" | 18'-5" | 19'-2" |

### 20 GAUGE STUDS — MAXIMUM HEIGHTS

| Stud Spacing | 2½" Stud | | 3¼" Stud | | 3⅝" Stud | | 4" Stud | |
|---|---|---|---|---|---|---|---|---|
| | ½" WB | ⅝" WB | ½" WB | ⅝" WB | ½" WB | ⅝" WB | ½" WB | ⅝" WB |
| 12" o.c. | 18'-9" | 19'-0" | 22'-8" | 22'-11" | 24'-8" | 24'-10" | 26'-7" | 26'-10" |
| 16" o.c. | 17'-9" | 18'-0" | 21'-7" | 21'-9" | 23'-5" | 23'-7" | 25'-3" | 25'-6" |
| 24" o.c. | 15'-9" | 16'-0" | 18'-11" | 19'-2" | 20'-5" | 20'-8" | 22'-0" | 22'-3" |

Courtesy National Gypsum Co.

## CONSTRUCTION WITH PLASTERBOARD

Several alternate methods of plasterboard construction may be used, depending on the application and desires of the customer, or yourself if you are the homeowner. Most residential homes use 2" × 4" wall studs and single-layer plasterboard walls are easily installed. Custom built homes, commercial buildings, and party walls between apartments should use double-layer plasterboard construction. It provides better sound insulation and fire retardation. For the greatest protection against fire hazards, steel frame partitions, plus plasterboard, provide an all noncombustible system of wall construction. All wood or the all steel construction apply to both walls and ceilings.

Plasterboard may also be applied directly to either insulated or uninsulated masonry walls. Plasterboard may be fastened in place by any of several methods such as, nails, screws, or adhesives. In addition, there are special resilient furrings and spring clips, both providing added sound deadening.

## Single Layer on Wood Studs

The simplest method of plasterboard construction is a single layer of plasterboard nailed directly to the wood studs and ceiling joists (Fig. 11). For single-layer construction, ⅜″, ½″, or ⅝″ plasterboard is recommended.

The ceiling boards should be installed first then the wall boards. Install plasterboard perpendicular to the studs for minimum joint treatment and greater strength. This applies to the ceiling as well. Either nails, screws, or adhesive may be used to fasten the plasterboard. Blue wallboard nails have annular rings for better grip than standard nails and the screws have *Phillips* heads for easy installation with a power driver. In single-nail installations, as shown in the illustration of Fig. 11, the nails should be spaced

Courtesy National Gypsum Co.

Fig. 11. The most common interior finishing today uses plasterboard, known as drywall construction.

not to exceed 7″ on the ceilings and 8″ on the walls. An alternate method, one which reduces nail popping, is the double-nail method. Install the boards in the single-nail method first, but, with nails 12″ apart. Then, drive a second set of nails about 1½″ to 2″ from the first (Fig. 12), from the center out, but not at

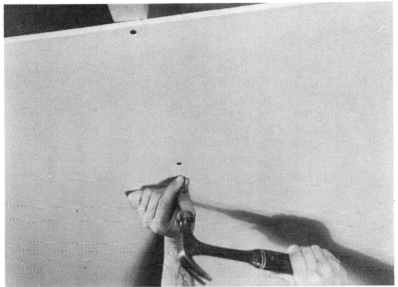

Fig. 12. In the double-nail method of fastening wallboard, the first set of nails are put in place and a second set of nails are driven in place about 1½″ to 2″ from the first.

the perimeter. The first series of nails are then struck again to assure the board being drawn up tight.

Use 4d cooler type nails for ⅜″ regular foil backed or backer board if used, 5d for ½″ board, and 6d for ⅝″ board.

Screws are the preferred method of fastening plasterboard, since they push the board up tight against the studding and will not loosen. Where studs and joists are 16″ on center, the screws can be 12″ apart on ceilings and 16″ apart on walls. If the studs are 24″ on center, the screws should be not over 12″ apart on the walls. The illustration in Fig. 13 shows a power screwdriver

295

in use. Strike the heads of all nails, and screws, to just below the surface of the board. The dimples will be filled in when joints and corners are finished.

A number of adhesives are available for installing plasterboard. Some are quick-drying, others are slower. Adhesives can be purchased in cartridge or bulk form, as shown in Fig. 14. The adhesive is applied in a serpentine bead, as shown in Fig. 15, to the facing edges of the studs and joists. Place the wallboard in position and nail it temporarily in place. Use double-headed nails or nails through a piece of scrap plasterboard. When the adhesive has dried, the nails can be removed and the holes filled when sealing the joints.

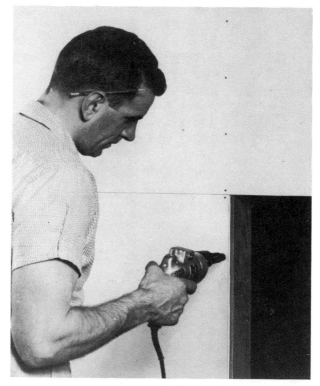

Courtesy National Gypsum Co.

Fig. 13. Wallboard fastened to studs with a power screwdriver.

Courtesy National Gypsum Co.

**Fig. 14. Adhesives are available either in bulk or in cartridge form.**

Plasterboards arc butted together but not forced into a tight fit. The treatment of joints and corners is covered later. The adhesive method is ideal for prefinished wallboard, although special nails with colored heads can be purchased for the decorator boards. Do not apply more adhesive than can permit installation within 30 minutes.

## Two Layer Construction

As mentioned, two layers of plasterboard improves sound deadening and fire retardation. The first layer of drywall or plasterboard is applied as described before. Plasterboard may be less expensive used as a backing type board. Foil backed or special sound reducing board may also be used. Nails need only be struck and screws driven with their heads just flush with the surface of

Fig. 15. Using a cartridge to apply a bead of adhesive to the wall studs.

the board. The joints will not be given special treatment since they will be covered by the second layer.

The second layer is cemented to the base layer. The facing layer is placed over the base layer and temporarily nailed at the top and bottom. Temporary nailing can be done with either double-headed nails or blocks of scrap wood or plasterboard under the heads. The face layer is left in place until the adhesive is dry.

To make sure of good adhesion, lay bracing boards diagonally from the center of the facing layer to the floor. Prebowing of the boards is another method. Lay the plasterboards finish face down across a 2″ × 4″ for a day or two. Let the ends hang free.

Joints of boards on each layer should not coincide but should be separated by about 10″. One of the best ways of doing this is to install the base layer horizontally and the finish layer vertically.

When using adhesive, a uniform temperature must be maintained. If construction is in the winter, the rooms should be heated to somewhere between 55°F and 70°F, and kept well ventilated.

Double-layer construction, with adhesive, is the method used with decorator type vinyl finished panelling except that special matching nails are used at the base and ceiling lines and left permanently in place.

Fig. 16 shows the basic double-layer construction, with details for handling corners, and an alternate method of wall construction for improved sound deadening.

## Other Methods of Installation

Sound transmission through a wall can be further reduced if the vibrations of the plasterboard can be isolated from the studs or joists. Two methods are available to accomplish this. One uses metal furring strips whose edges are formed in such a way as to give them flexibility. The other is by means of metal push-on clips with bowed edges also for flexibility, used on ceilings only.

Fig. 17 shows the appearance and method of installing resilient furring channels. They are 12 ft. long strips of galvanized steel and include predrilled holes spaced every inch. This permits nailing to studs 16" or 24" on center. *Phillips* head self-tapping screws are power driven through the plasterboard and into the surface of the furring strips.

As shown in Fig. 17, strips of 3" × ½" plasterboard are fastened to the sole and plate at top and bottom to give the plasterboard a solid base. For best sound isolation, the point of intersection between the wall and floor should be caulked prior to application of the baseboard.

On ceiling joists, use two screws at each joist point to fasten the furring strips. Do not overlap ends of furring strips, leave about a ⅜" space between ends. Use only ½" or ⅝" wallboard with this system.

Suspending plasterboard ceilings from spring clips is a method of isolating the vibrations from the ceiling joists and floor above. Details are shown in Fig. 18.

The push-on clips are placed on 1" × 2" nominal size wood-furring strips. The clips are then nailed to the sides of the ceiling

299

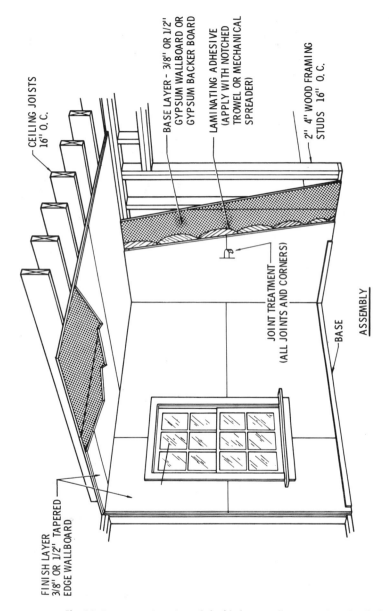

CEILING JOISTS 16" O. C.

BASE LAYER – 3/8" OR 1/2" GYPSUM WALLBOARD OR GYPSUM BACKER BOARD

LAMINATING ADHESIVE (APPLY WITH NOTCHED TROWEL OR MECHANICAL SPREADER)

2" 4" WOOD FRAMING STUDS 16" O. C.

JOINT TREATMENT (ALL JOINTS AND CORNERS)

BASE

ASSEMBLY

FINISH LAYER 3/8" OR 1/2" TAPERED EDGE WALLBOARD

Fig. 16. A cross-section view of double-layer wall construction, details for

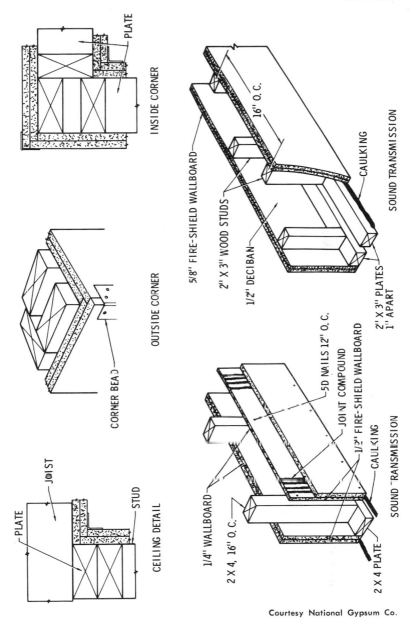

INSIDE CORNER

PLATE

5/8" FIRE-SHIELD WALLBOARD

16" O. C.

2" X 3" WOOD STUDS

1/2" DECIBAN

CAULKING

SOUND TRANSMISSION

2" X 3" PLATES 1" APART

OUTSIDE CORNER

CORNER BEAD

CEILING DETAIL

JOIST

PLATE

STUD

5D NAILS 12" O. C.

JOINT COMPOUND

1/2" FIRE-SHIELD WALLBOARD

CAULKING

1/4" WALLBOARD

2 X 4, 16" O. C.

2 X 4 PLATE

SOUND TRANSMISSION

Courtesy National Gypsum Co.

handling corners, and special wall construction for sound deadening.

301

joists with short annular ringed or cooler type nails. With furring strips installed, they will be against the nailing edge of the joists.

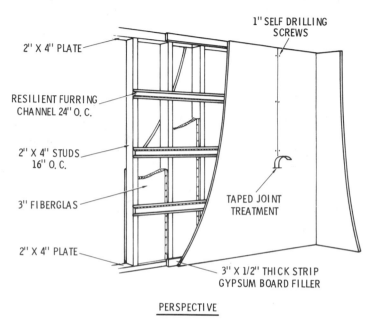

2" X 4" PLATE

RESILIENT FURRING CHANNEL 24" O. C.

2" X 4" STUDS 16" O. C.

3" FIBERGLAS

2" X 4" PLATE

1" SELF DRILLING SCREWS

TAPED JOINT TREATMENT

3" X 1/2" THICK STRIP GYPSUM BOARD FILLER

PERSPECTIVE

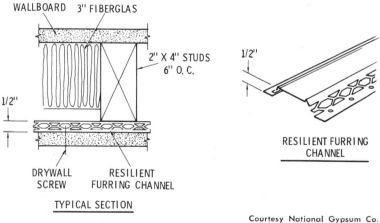

WALLBOARD    3" FIBERGLAS

2" X 4" STUDS 6" O. C.

1/2"

1/2"

DRYWALL SCREW

RESILIENT FURRING CHANNEL

TYPICAL SECTION

RESILIENT FURRING CHANNEL

Courtesy National Gypsum Co.

Fig. 17. Resilient furring strips, with expanded edges, may be installed to isolate the plasterboard from the stud.

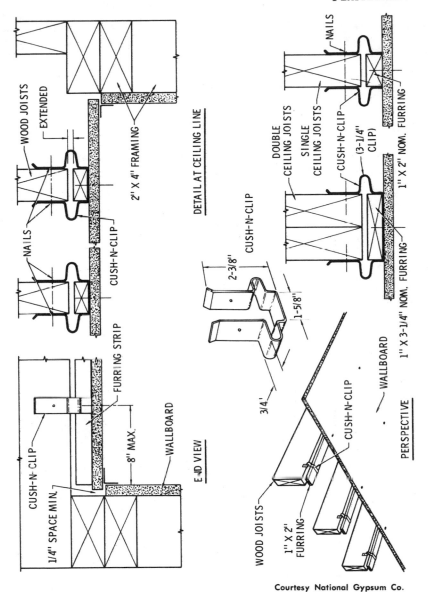

WOOD JOISTS

EXTENDED

2" X 4" FRAMING

NAILS

CUSH-N-CLIP

FURRING STRIP

CUSH-N-CLIP

1/4" SPACE MIN.

8" MAX.

WALLBOARD

END VIEW

DETAIL AT CEILING LINE

NAILS

DOUBLE CEILING JOISTS

SINGLE CEILING JOISTS

CUSH-N-CLIP

(3-1/4" CLIP)

1" X 2" NOM. FURRING

1" X 3-1/4" NOM. FURRING

CUSH-N-CLIP

2-3/8"

1-5/8"

3/4"

WALLBOARD

PERSPECTIVE

WOOD JOISTS

1" X 2" FURRING

CUSH-N-CLIP

Courtesy National Gypsum Co.

Fig. 18. Details for installing spring clips to ceiling joist. Clips suspend plasterboard from joist to provide isolation from noise vibrations.

This provides a solid foundation for nailing the plasterboard to the clips. The weight of the plasterboard after installation will stretch the clips to a spring position.

The wood furring strips must be of high quality material so they will not buckle, twist, or warp. Nails for attaching the wallboard should be short enough so they will not go through the furring strips and into the joist edges. The wallboard must be held firmly against the strips while it is being nailed. Expansion joints must be provided every 60 ft. or for every 2400 sq. ft. of surface.

It is essential that the right number of clips be used on a ceiling, depending on the thickness of the wallboard and whether single or double layered. The spring or efficiency of the clips is affected by the weight. Table 2 shows clip spacing for various ceiling thicknesses and layers.

## Tile Underlayment

At least two types of plasterboard are available as backing material for use in tiled areas where moisture protection is important, such as tub enclosures, shower stalls, powder rooms, kitchen-sink splash boards, and locker rooms. One is a vinyl-covered plasterboard and the other is a specially designed board material to prevent moisture penetration.

The vinyl-covered board is 4 ft. x 11 ft. the right length for a tub enclosure. By scoring it and snapping it to length, the vinyl covering can be a continuous covering all around the tub and no corner sealing is required. This is shown in one of the sketches in Fig. 19. This board has square edges and is nailed or screwed to the studs without the need to countersink the nails or screws. The waterproof tile adhesive is applied and the tile is installed over the board. This board is intended for full tile treatment and is not to extend beyond the edges of the tile.

Unlike vinyl-surfaced board, the moisture resistant board may be extended beyond the area of the tile. The part extending beyond the tile may be painted with latex, oil-based paint, or papered. It has tapered edges and is installed and treated in the same manner as regular plasterboard. Corners are made waterproof by the tile adhesive. The sketches in Fig. 19 show details for the installation of either board.

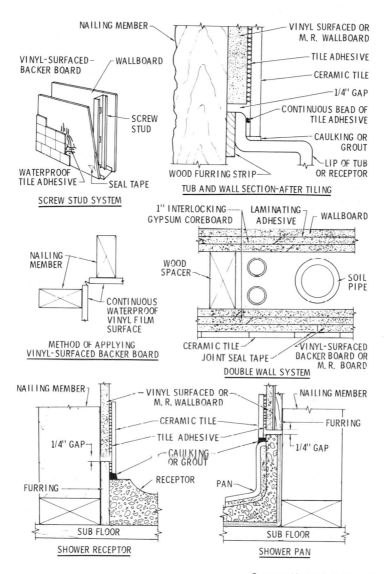

Courtesy National Gypsum Co.

**Fig. 19. Details for installing vinyl-locked and moisture-resistant wallboard for bath and shower use.**

305

## Plasterboard over Masonry

Plasterboard may be applied to inside masonry walls in any one of several methods: directly over the masonry using adhesive cement; over wood or metal furring strips fastened to the masonry; to urethane or polystyrene insulated walls by furring strips over the insulation; or by lamination directly to the insulation.

Regular or prefinished plasterboard may be laminated to unpainted masonry walls such as concrete or block interior partitions and to the interior of exterior walls above or below grade. While nearly all of the adhesive available may be used either above or below grade, the regular joint compounds are recommended for use only above grade. Exterior masonry must be waterproofed below grade and made impervious to water above grade.

The masonry must be clean and free of dust, dirt, grease, oil, loose particles, or water soluble particles. It must be plumb, straight, and in one plane. Fig. 20 shows the method of applying the adhesive to masonry walls. Boards may be installed either horizontally or vertically. Ceiling wallboard should normally be applied last to allow nailing temporary bracing to the wood joists. The wallboard should be installed with a clearance of ⅛" or more from the floor, to prevent wicking. If there are expansion joints in the masonry, cut the wallboard to include expansion joints to match that of the masonry.

The sketches of Fig. 21 show the installation of wallboard to masonry with furring strips. Furring strips may be wood or U-shaped metal as used for foam insulation. The furring strips are fastened to the masonry with concrete nails. They may be mounted vertically or horizontally but there must be one horizontal strip along the base line. The long dimension of the wallboards are to be perpendicular to the furring strips. Furring strips are fastened 24" on center. The wallboard is attached to the furring strips in the usual way. Use self-drilling screws on the metal furring strips and nails or screws on the wood strips.

Insulation may be applied between the plasterboard and the masonry, using urethane foam sheets or extruded polystyrene. Plasterboard is then secured to the wall either with the use of

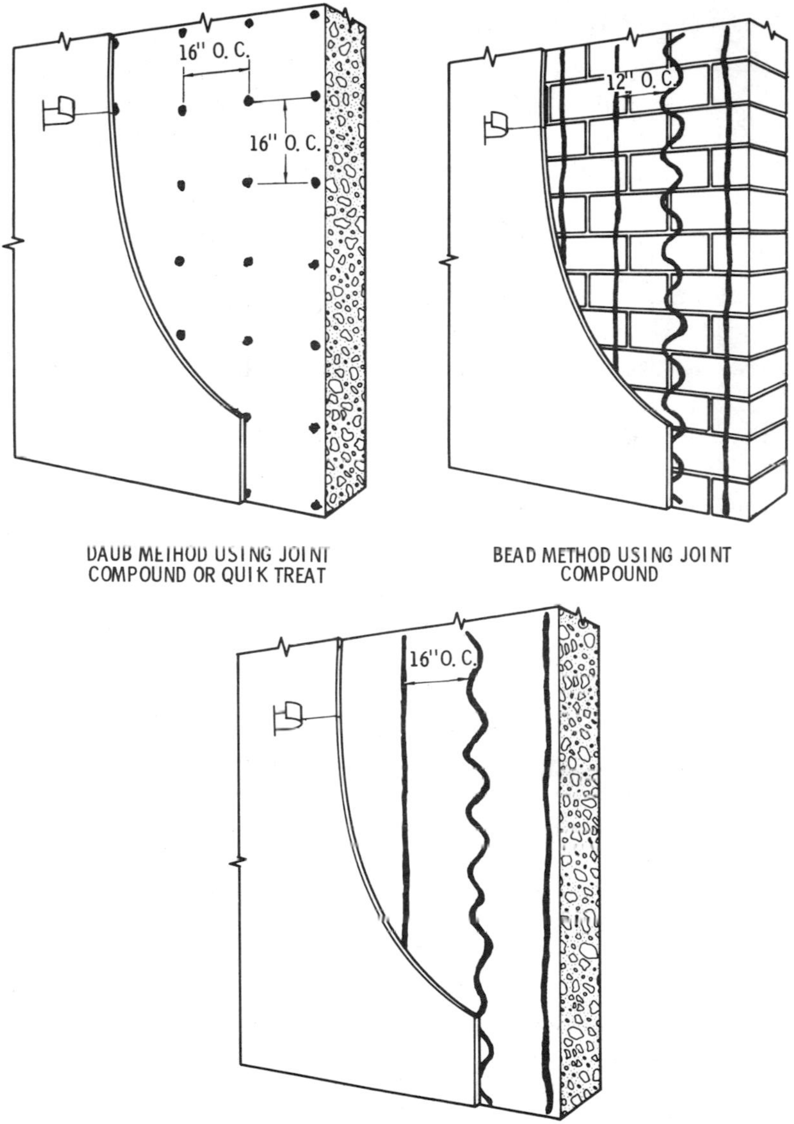

DAUB METHOD USING JOINT
COMPOUND OR QUIK TREAT

16" O. C.

16" O. C.

BEAD METHOD USING JOINT
COMPOUND

12" O. C.

16" O. C.

BEAD METHOD USING MC ADHESIVE
OR BLACK ADHESIVE

Courtesy National Gypsum Co.

Fig. 20. Method of applying adhesive directly to masonry walls.

307

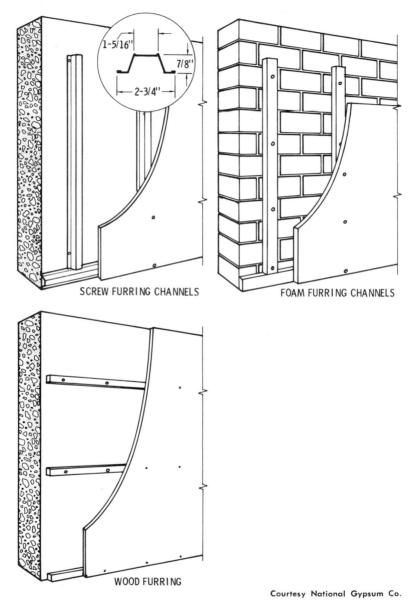

1-5/16"

7/8"

2-3/4"

SCREW FURRING CHANNELS

FOAM FURRING CHANNELS

WOOD FURRING

Courtesy National Gypsum Co.

Fig. 21. Illustrating three types of furring strips that are used between masonry walls and plasterboard.

furring strips over the insulation or by laminating directly to the insulation.

Special U-shaped metal furring strips are installed over the insulation. This is shown in Fig. 22. The insulation pads may

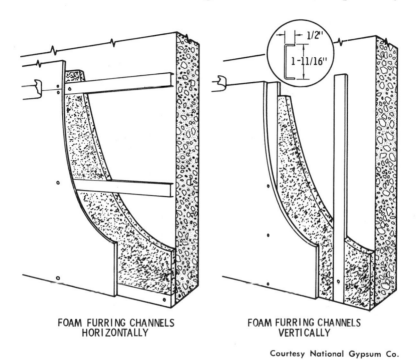

FOAM FURRING CHANNELS
HORIZONTALLY

FOAM FURRING CHANNELS
VERTICALLY

Courtesy National Gypsum Co.

Fig. 22. U-shaped furring channels installed horizontally or vertically over foam insulating material

be held against the wall while the strips are installed or they can be held in place with dabs of plasterboard adhesive. Use a fast drying adhesive. If some time is to elapse before the furring strips and plasterboard are to be applied, dot the insulation with adhesive every 24″ in both directions on the back of the insulation pads.

The metal furring strips are fastened in place with concrete nails. Place them a maximum of 24″ apart, starting about 1″ to 1½″ from the ends. The strips may be mounted vertically or horizontally, as shown in Fig. 22. Fasten the wallboard to the

Courtesy National Gypsum Co.

**Fig. 23. Special self-drilling screws are power-driven through the plasterboard and into the metal furring strip.**

furring strips with a power driver (Fig. 23), using self-drilling screws. Screws must not be any longer than the thickness of the wallboard plus the ½ " furring strip. Space screws 24" on center for ½ " and ⅝" board, 16" on center for ⅜" board.

Plasterboard may be laminated directly to the foam insulation. The sketches in Fig. 24 show how this is done for both horizontal and vertical mounted boards. Install wood furring strips onto the masonry wall, for the perimeter of the wallboard. The strips should be 2" wide and 1/32" thicker than the foam insulation. Include furring where the boards join, as shown in the left hand sketch of Fig. 24.

Apply a ⅜" diameter bead over the back of the foam insulation and in a continous strip around the perimeter. Put the bead dots about 16" apart. Apply the foam panels with a sliding motion and hand press the entire panel to ensure full contact with the wall surface. For some adhesives, it is necessary to pull the panel off of the wall to allow flash-off of the solvent. Then reposition the panel. Read the instructions with the adhesive purchased.

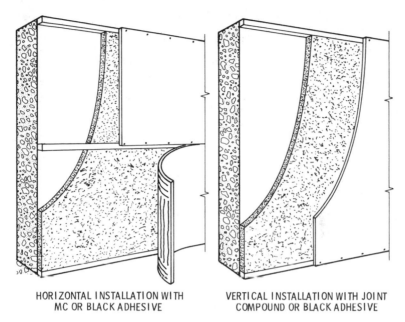

HORIZONTAL INSTALLATION WITH
MC OR BLACK ADHESIVE

VERTICAL INSTALLATION WITH JOINT
COMPOUND OR BLACK ADHESIVE

Courtesy National Gypsum Co.

Fig. 24. Plasterboard may be installed against the foam insulation with adhesive.

## Table 3. Maximum Spacing of Joist or Supporting Channel

### For ½" and ⅝" Single Layer Wallboard

| FURRING MEMBER | FURRING MEMBER SPACING | | |
|---|---|---|---|
| | 24" o.c. | 16" o.c. | 12" o.c. |
| Resilient Furring Channel | 2' 0" | 2' 0" | 2' 0" |
| Furring Channel | 4' 0" | 4' 6" | 5' 0" |
| 1⅝" Screw Studs* | 5' 0" | 5' 6" | 6' 0" |
| 2½" Screw Studs | 6' 0" | 6' 6" | 7' 0" |
| 3⅝" Screw Studs | 8' 0" | 8' 6" | 9' 0" |
| 4" Screw Studs | 8' 6" | 9' | 9' 6" |

*Position 1⅝" studs with legs against framing. Other width studs
as illustrated opposite.

Courtesy National Gypsum Co.

## Table 4. Door and Frame Selector (Type of Door Frame)

| Door Weight | Gauge Jamb Studs | Bracing Over Header | Knock Down Alum. | Knock Down Steel | Fixed Steel | Requires Mechanical Closure | *Height Stud Size 1⅝" | 2½" | 3⅝" | 4" |
|---|---|---|---|---|---|---|---|---|---|---|
| Up To 50 lbs. | 25 | | x | | | | NA** | 10' | 14' | 15' |
| | 25 | | | x | | | NA | 10' | 14' | 15' |
| | 25 | | | | x | | NA | 10' | 14' | 15' |
| | 25 | x | x | | | | 10' | 12' | 16' | 17' |
| | 25 | x | | x | | | 10' | 12' | 16' | 17' |
| | 25 | x | | | x | | 10' | 12' | 16' | 17' |
| | 20 | x | x | | | | — | 16' | 21' | 22' |
| | 20 | x | | x | | | — | 16' | 21' | 22' |
| | 20 | x | | | x | | — | 16' | 21' | 22' |
| 50 lbs. To 80 lbs. | 25 | x | | | x | x | 12' | 10' | 14' | 15' |
| | 25 | x | | | x | | | 10' | 14' | 15' |
| | 25 | x | | x | | | | 10' | 14' | 15' |
| | 25 | x | x | | | x | 10' | 12' | 14' | 15' |
| | 20 | | x | | | x | | 10' | 14' | 15' |
| | 20 | | | x | | | | 10' | 14' | 15' |
| | 20 | | | | x | | | 10' | 14' | 15' |
| | 20 | x | | x | | | | 12' | 16' | 17' |
| | 20 | x | | | x | | | 12' | 16' | 17' |
| | 20 dbl. | x | | x | | | | 16' | 21' | 22' |
| | 20 dbl. | | | | x | | | 16' | 21' | 22' |
| 80 lbs. To 120 lbs. | 25 | x | | | x | | | 12' | 16' | 17' |
| | 20 | x | x | | | x | | 12' | 16' | 17' |
| | 20 | | | x | | x | | 12' | 16' | 17' |
| | 20 dbl. | x | | | x | | | 16' | 21' | 22' |

*See partition height table for stud spacing.
**NA—Not allowed.

Courtesy National Gypsum Co.

Coat the back of the wallboards and press it against the foam insulation. Nail or screw the boards to the furring strips. The nails or screws must not be too long or they will penetrate the furring strips and press against the masonry wall. The panels must clear the floor by ⅛". About any type of adhesive may be used with urethane foam but some adhesives cannot be used with polystyrene.

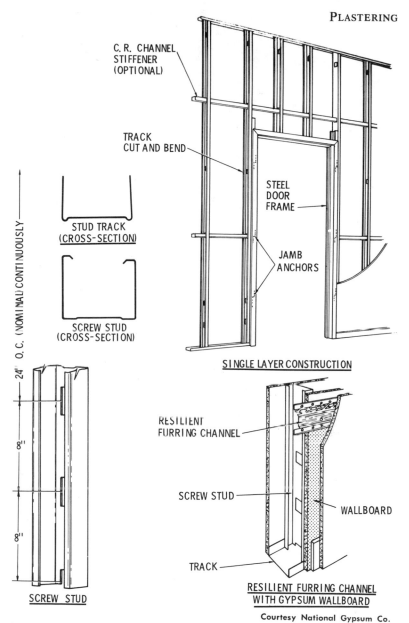

C. R. CHANNEL
STIFFENER
(OPTIONAL)

STUD TRACK
(CROSS-SECTION)

SCREW STUD
(CROSS-SECTION)

TRACK
CUT AND BEND

STEEL
DOOR
FRAME

JAMB
ANCHORS

SINGLE LAYER CONSTRUCTION

24" O. C. (NOMINAL) CONTINUOUSLY

8"

8"

SCREW STUD

RESILIENT
FURRING CHANNEL

SCREW STUD

WALLBOARD

TRACK

RESILIENT FURRING CHANNEL
WITH GYPSUM WALLBOARD

Courtesy National Gypsum Co.

Fig. 25. Details of metal wall construction using metal studs and tracks. This type
of wall construction becomes an all noncombustible interior wall.

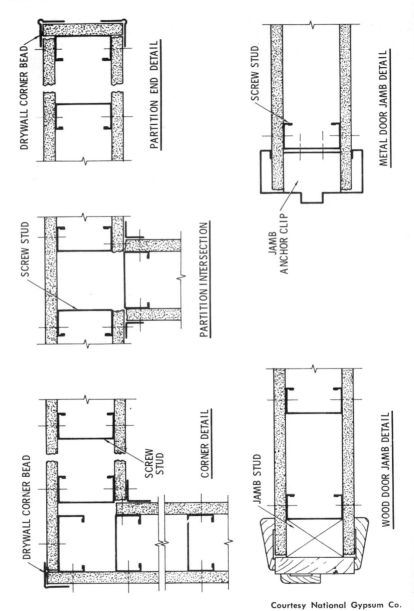

DRYWALL CORNER BEAD

PARTITION END DETAIL

SCREW STUD

PARTITION INTERSECTION

DRYWALL CORNER BEAD

SCREW STUD

CORNER DETAIL

SCREW STUD

METAL DOOR JAMB DETAIL

JAMB ANCHOR CLIP

JAMB STUD

WOOD DOOR JAMB DETAIL

Courtesy National Gypsum Co.

Fig. 26. Details for intersections and jambs using metal wall construction.

## Table 5. Allowable Carrying Loads for Anchor Bolts

| TYPE FASTENER | SIZE | ALLOWABLE LOAD ½" WALLBOARD | 5/8" WALLBOARD |
|---|---|---|---|
| HOLLOW WALL SCREW ANCHORS | ⅛" dia. SHORT | 50 LBS. | —— |
| | 3/16" dia. SHORT | 65 LBS. | —— |
| | ¼", 5/16", 3/8" dia. SHORT | 65 LBS. | —— |
| | 3/16" dia. LONG | —— | 90 LBS. |
| | ¼", 5/16", 3/8" dia. LONG | —— | 95 LBS. |
| COMMON TOGGLE BOLTS | ⅛" dia. | 30 LBS. | 90 LBS. |
| | 3/16" dia. | 60 LBS. | 120 LBS. |
| | ¼", 5/16", 3/8" dia. | 80 LBS. | 120 LBS. |

Courtesy National Gypsum Co.

Also, in applying prefinished panels, be careful on the choice of adhesive. Some of the quick-drying types are harmful to the finish. Read the instructions on the adhesive before you buy.

### FIREPROOF WALLS AND CEILINGS

For industrial applications, walls and ceilings may be made entirely of noncombustible materials, using galvanized steel wall and ceiling construction and faced with plasterboard. Assembly is by self-drilling screws, driven by a power screwdriver with a *Phillips* bit.

### WALL PARTITIONS

Construction consists of U-shaped track which may be fastened to existing ceilings, or the steel member ceilings, and to the floors.

315

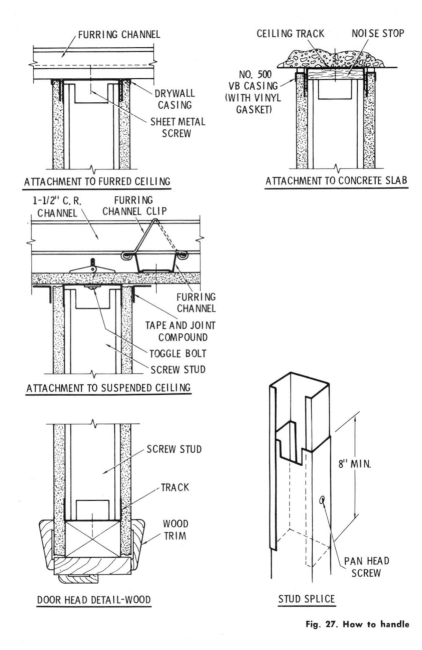

FURRING CHANNEL

DRYWALL CASING

SHEET METAL SCREW

ATTACHMENT TO FURRED CEILING

CEILING TRACK    NOISE STOP

NO. 500 VB CASING (WITH VINYL GASKET)

ATTACHMENT TO CONCRETE SLAB

1-1/2" C.R. CHANNEL    FURRING CHANNEL CLIP

FURRING CHANNEL

TAPE AND JOINT COMPOUND

TOGGLE BOLT

SCREW STUD

ATTACHMENT TO SUSPENDED CEILING

SCREW STUD

TRACK

WOOD TRIM

DOOR HEAD DETAIL-WOOD

8" MIN.

PAN HEAD SCREW

STUD SPLICE

Fig. 27. How to handle

316

U-shaped steel studs are screwed to the tracks. Also available are one-piece or three-piece metal door frames. The three-piece frames are usually preferred by contractors since they permit finishing the entire wall before the door frames are installed.

The sketches in Fig. 25 show details of wall construction as well as the cross section of the track and stud channels. For greater sound deadening, double-layer board construction with resilient

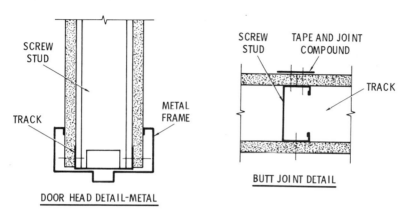

DOOR HEAD DETAIL-METAL

BUTT JOINT DETAIL

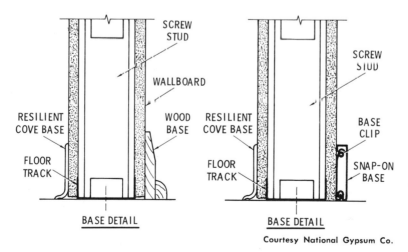

BASE DETAIL

BASE DETAIL

Courtesy National Gypsum Co.

ceiling and base finishing.

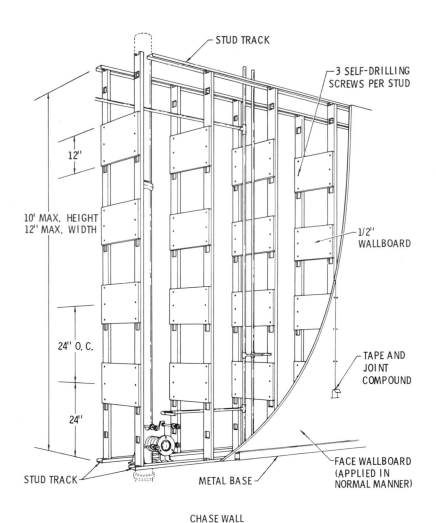

STUD TRACK

3 SELF-DRILLING
SCREWS PER STUD

12"

10' MAX. HEIGHT
12" MAX. WIDTH

1/2"
WALLBOARD

24" O. C.

TAPE AND
JOINT
COMPOUND

24"

STUD TRACK

METAL BASE

FACE WALLBOARD
(APPLIED IN
NORMAL MANNER)

CHASE WALL

Fig. 28. Deep-wall construction where space is needed for

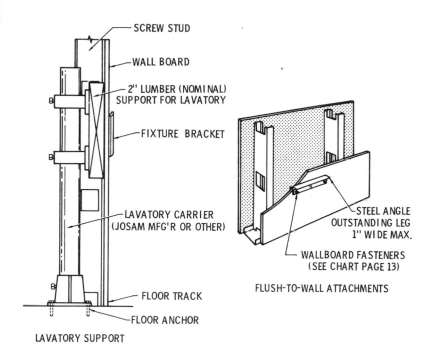

SCREW STUD

WALL BOARD

2" LUMBER (NOMINAL)
SUPPORT FOR LAVATORY

FIXTURE BRACKET

LAVATORY CARRIER
(JOSAM MFG'R OR OTHER)

FLOOR TRACK

FLOOR ANCHOR

LAVATORY SUPPORT

STEEL ANGLE
OUTSTANDING LEG
1" WIDE MAX.

WALLBOARD FASTENERS
(SEE CHART PAGE 13)

FLUSH-TO-WALL ATTACHMENTS

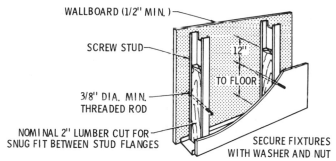

WALLBOARD (1/2" MIN.)

SCREW STUD

12"

TO FLOOR

3/8" DIA. MIN.
THREADED ROD

NOMINAL 2" LUMBER CUT FOR
SNUG FIT BETWEEN STUD FLANGES

SECURE FIXTURES
WITH WASHER AND NUT

FOR WALL HUNG FURNITURE
(BOTH SIDES OF PARTITION)
ALLOWABLE 60 FT. LBS. PER FASTENER- (2'-0" O.C. STUD SPACING)

Courtesy National Gypsum Co.

various reasons such as plumbing and heating pipes.

furring strips between the two layers is recommended. This is shown in a cutaway view in the lower right hand corner of Fig. 25. Heavier material and wider studs are required for high wall construction. Table 3 lists the recommended gauge of steel and stud widths for walls of various heights.

Figs. 26 and 27 show details for intersecting walls, jambs, and other finishing needs. Table 4 lists door frame specifications. Chase walls are used (Fig. 28), where greater interior wall space is needed (between the walls) for equipment.

Fig. 29 shows how brackets are attached for heavy loads. Table 5 lists the allowable load for bolts installed directly to the plaster board.

## STEEL FRAME CEILINGS

Three types of furring members are available for attaching plasterboard to ceilings. They are screw-furring channels, resilient screw-furring channels, and screw studs. Self-drilling screws attach the wallboard to the channels. These are illustrated in Fig. 30. Any of the three may be attached to the lower chord of steel joists or carrying channels in suspended ceiling construction. Either special clips or wire ties are used to fasten the channels. Fig. 31 shows the details in a complete ceiling assembly.

## SEMISOLID PARTITIONS

Complete partition walls may be made of all plasterboard, at a considerable savings in material and time over the regular wood and plasterboard types. These walls are thinner than the usual 2" × 4" stud wall, but they are not load-bearing walls.

Fig. 32 shows cross-section views of the all plasterboard walls, with details for connecting them to the ceiling and floor. Also shown is a door frame and a section of the wall using the baseboard. Partitions may be 2¼", 2⅝", or 2⅞" thick, depending on the thickness of the wallboard used and the number of layers. The center piece is not solid, but a piece of 1" or 1⅝" plasterboard about 6" wide acting as a stud element.

Fig. 33 shows how the wall is constructed. The boards are vertically mounted, so their length must be the same distance as from the floor to the ceiling, but not exceeding 10 ft. The layers are prelaminated on the job, then raised into position.

Place two pieces of wallboard on a flat surface with face surfaces facing each other. These must be the correct length for the height

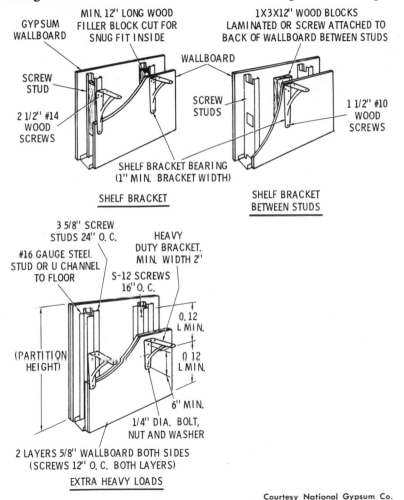

GYPSUM WALLBOARD

MIN. 12" LONG WOOD FILLER BLOCK CUT FOR SNUG FIT INSIDE

1X3X12" WOOD BLOCKS LAMINATED OR SCREW ATTACHED TO BACK OF WALLBOARD BETWEEN STUDS

WALLBOARD

SCREW STUD

SCREW STUDS

2 1/2" #14 WOOD SCREWS

1 1/2" #10 WOOD SCREWS

SHELF BRACKET BEARING (1" MIN. BRACKET WIDTH)

SHELF BRACKET

SHELF BRACKET BETWEEN STUDS

3 5/8" SCREW STUDS 24" O. C.

HEAVY DUTY BRACKET. MIN. WIDTH 2"

#16 GAUGE STEEL STUD OR U CHANNEL TO FLOOR

S-12 SCREWS 16" O. C.

0. 12 L MIN.

(PARTITION HEIGHT)

0 12 L MIN.

6" MIN.

1/4" DIA. BOLT, NUT AND WASHER

2 LAYERS 5/8" WALLBOARD BOTH SIDES (SCREWS 12" O. C. BOTH LAYERS)

EXTRA HEAVY LOADS

Courtesy National Gypsum Co.

**Fig. 29. Recommended method for fastening shelf brackets to plasterboard.**

of the wall. Cut two studs 6" wide and a little shorter than the length of the large wallboards. Spread adhesive along the entire length of the two plasterboard studs and put one of them, adhesive face down, in the middle of the top large board. It should be 21" from the edges and equidistant from the ends. Set the other stud, adhesive face up flush along one edge of the large plasterboard.

Place two more large boards on top of the studs, with edge of the bundle in line with the outer edge of the uncoated stud. Temporarily place a piece of plasterboard under the opposite edge for support. In this system each pair of boards will not be directly over each other, but alternate bundles will protrude. Continue the procedure until the required number of assemblies are obtained. Let dry, with temporary support under the overhanging edges. Fig. 33 shows the lamination process.

To raise the wall, first install a 24" wide starter section of wallboard with one edge plumbed against the intersecting wall. Spread adhesive along the full length of the plasterboard stud of

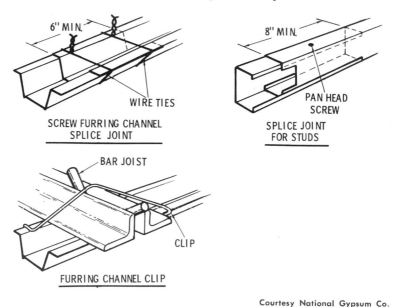

Courtesy National Gypsum Co.

Fig. 30. Metal ceiling channels may be fastened to metal joists by wire ties or special clips.

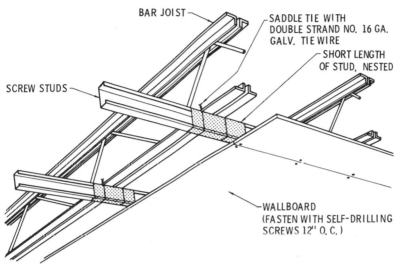

BAR JOIST

SADDLE TIE WITH
DOUBLE STRAND NO. 16 GA.
GALV. TIE WIRE

SHORT LENGTH
OF STUD, NESTED

SCREW STUDS

WALLBOARD
(FASTEN WITH SELF-DRILLING
SCREWS 12" O.C.)

SCREW STUDS IN CEILING SYSTEMS

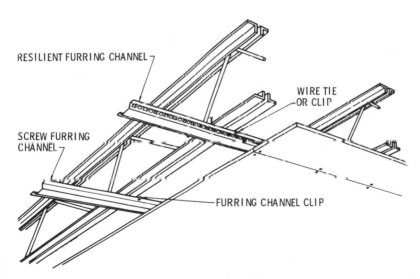

RESILIENT FURRING CHANNEL

WIRE TIE
OR CLIP

SCREW FURRING
CHANNEL

FURRING CHANNEL CLIP

FURRING CHANNELS

Courtesy National Gypsum Co.

Fig. 31. Complete details showing two methods of mounting wallboard to
suspended ceiling structures.

323

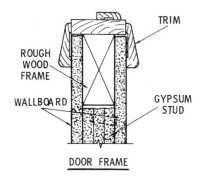

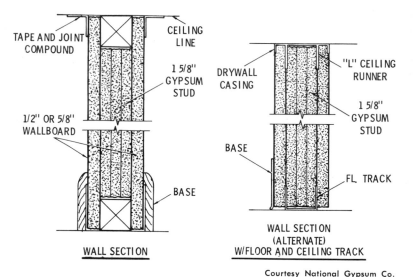

Courtesy National Gypsum Co.

**Fig. 32. Cross section view of a semisolid all plasterboard wall.**

one wall section and erect it opposite to the 24″ starter section. The free edge of the starter section should center on the stud piece. Apply adhesive to the plasterboard stud of another section and erect it adjacent to the starter panel. Continue to alternate sides as you put each section in place.

Some plasterboard manufacturers make thick solid plasterboards for solid partition walls. Usually they will laminate two pieces of 1″ thick plasterboard to make a 2″ thick board. Chase walls, eleva-

LAMINATING PANEL ASSEMBLIES

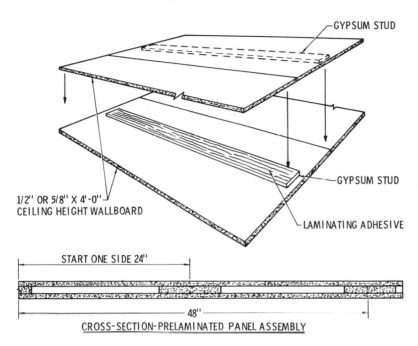

GYPSUM STUD

GYPSUM STUD

1/2" OR 5/8" X 4'-0"
CEILING HEIGHT WALLBOARD

LAMINATING ADHESIVE

START ONE SIDE 24"

48"

CROSS-SECTION-PRELAMINATED PANEL ASSEMBLY

Courtesy National Gypsum Co.

**Fig. 33. Plasterboards are laminated together with wide pieces of plasterboard acting as wall studs.**

tor shafts, and stair wells usually require solid and thick walls which can be of all plasterboard at reduced cost of construction. There is no limit to the thickness that can be obtained, depending on the need.

## JOINT FINISHING

Flat and inside corner joints are sealed with perforated tape embedded in joint compound and with finishing coats of the same compound. Outside corners are protected with a metal bead, nailed into place and finished with jointing compound, or a special metal-backed tape, which is also used on inside corners.

Fig. 34. The first step in finishing joints between plasterboard.

Fig. 35. Place perforated tape over the joint and embed it into the jointing
compound.

Two types of jointing compound are generally available—regular, which takes about 24 hours to dry, and quick-setting, which takes about 2½ hours to dry. The plastering mason must make the decision on which type to use, depending on the amount of jointing work he has to do and when he can get around to subsequent coats.

Begin by spotting nail heads with jointing compound. Use the broad knife to smooth out the compound. Apply compound over the joint (Fig. 34). Follow this immediately by embedding the perforated tape over the joint (Fig. 35). Fig. 36 is a closeup view showing the compound squeezed through the perforation of the tape for good keying. Before the compound dries, run the broad knife over the tape to smooth down the compound and to level the surface (Fig. 37).

After the first coat has dried, apply a second coat (Fig. 38) thinly and feather it out 3" to 4" on each side of the joint. Also apply a second coat to the nail spots. When the second coat has dried, apply a third coat also thinly. Feather it out to about 6" or

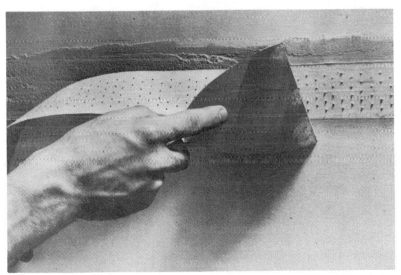

Courtesy National Gypsum Co.

Fig. 36. Closeup view showing how a properly embedded tape will show beads of the compound through the perforations.

7" from the joint (Fig. 39). Final nail spotting is also done at this time.

## INSIDE CORNERS

Inside corners are treated in the same way as flat joints, with one exception. The tape must be cut to the proper size and creased down the middle. Apply it to the coated joint (Fig. 40) and follow with the treatment mentioned above, but to one side at a time. Let the joint dry before applying the second coat of compound and the same for the third coat.

Courtesy National Gypsum Co.

**Fig. 37. Using a broad knife to smooth out the compound and to feather edges.**

## OUTSIDE CORNERS

Outside corners need extra reinforcement because of the harder knocks they may take by the family. Metal corner beads (Fig. 41) are used. Nail through the bead into the plasterboard and framing. Apply joint compound over the beading, using a broad knife, as shown in Fig. 42. The final treatment is the same as for other

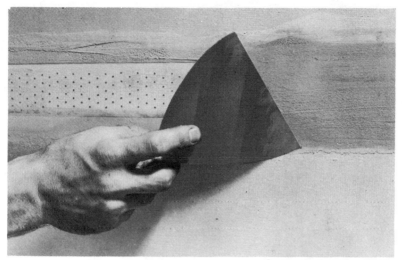

Fig. 38. Applying second coat of compound over perforated tape after first coat has dried. This coat must be applied smooth with a good feathered edge.

Fig. 39. The final coat is applied with a wide knife carefully feathering the edges. A wet sponge will eliminate any need for further smoothing when dry.

329

joints. The first coat should be about 6" wide and the second coat about 9". Feather out the edges and work the surface smooth with the broad knife and a wet sponge.

## PREFINISHED WALLBOARD

Prefinished wallboard is surfaced with a decorative vinyl material. Since it is not painted or papered after installation, in order to maintain a smooth and unmarred finish, its treatment is slightly different than that of standard wallboard. In most installations, nails and screws are avoided (except at top and bottom) and no tape and joint compound are used at the joints.

Courtesy National Gypsum Co.

Fig. 40. Inside corners are handled in the same manner as the flat joints.

Three basic methods are used to install prefinished wallboard.

1. Nailing to 16″ on center studs or to furring strips but using colored and matching nails available for the purpose.
2. Cementing to the studs or furring strips with adhesive, nailing only at the top and bottom. These nails may be matching colored nails or plain nails, which are covered with matching cove molding and base trim.

Courtesy National Gypsum Co.

Fig. 41. Outside corners are generally reinforced with a metal head. It is nailed in place going through the plasterboard into the stud.

3. Laminating to a base layer on regular wallboard or to old wallboard in the case of existing wall installations.

Before installing prefinished wallboard, a careful study of the wall arrangement should be made. Joints should be centered on architectural features such as fireplaces, windows, etc. End panels

Fig. 42. Applying compound over the corner head.

should be of equal width. Avoid narrow strips as much as possible.

Decorator wallboard is available in lengths to match most wall heights without further cutting. It should be installed vertically, and should be about ⅛" shorter than the actual height, so it will not be necessary to force it into place. Prefinished wallboards have square edges and are butted together at the joints, with or without the vinyl surface lapped over the edges.

As with standard wallboard, prefinished wallboard is easily cut into a narrow piece by scoring and snapping. Place the board on a flat surface with the vinyl side up. Score the vinyl side with a dimension about 1" wider than the width of the panel (Fig. 43). Turn vinyl surface face down and score the back edge to the actual dimension desired. In both cases use a good straight board as a

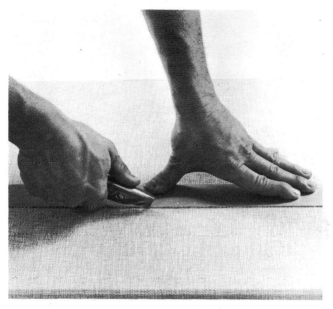

Fig. 43. When cutting vinyl-finished wallboard the cut should be about 1 inch wider than the desired width. This is to allow an inch of extra vinyl for edge treatment.

straightedge. Place the board over the edge of a long table and snap the piece off (Fig. 44). This will leave a piece of vinyl material hanging along the edge. Fold the material back and tack it into place onto the back of the wallboard (Fig. 45).

Cutouts are easily made on wallboard with a fine-toothed saw. Where a piece is to be cut out, as for a window, saw along the narrower cuts, then score the longer dimension and snap off the piece (Fig. 46). Circles are cut out by first drilling a hole large enough to insert the end of the keyhole saw (Fig. 47). Square cutouts for electrical outlet boxes need not be sawed but can be punched out. Score through the vinyl surface, as shown in Fig. 48. Give the area a sharp blow and it will break through.

## INSTALLING PREFINISHED WALLBOARD

Prefinished wallboard may be nailed to studs or furring strips

Fig. 44. Score the back of the wallboard to- the actual width desired leaving a 1-inch width of vinyl.

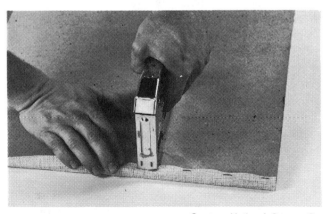

Fig. 45. Fold the 1-inch vinyl material over the edge of the wallboard and tack in place. This will provide a finished edge without further joint treatment.

334

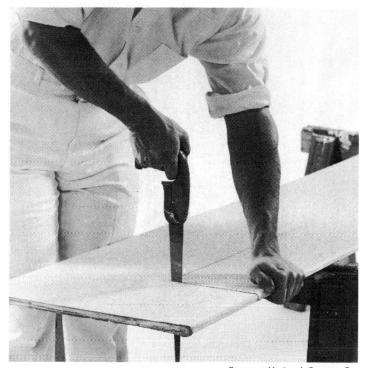

Courtesy National Gypsum Co.

**Fig. 46. Cutting vinyl-covered wallboard for various openings.**

with decorator type or colored nails. In doing so, however, the job must be done carefully so the nails make a decorative pattern. Space them every 12″ and not less than ⅜″ from the panel edges (Fig. 49). When nailing directly to the studs, be sure the studs are straight and flush. If warped, they may require shaving down at high spots or shimming up at low spots. To avoid extra work, carpenters should be instructed, on new construction, to select the best 2″ × 4″ lumber and do a careful job of placing it. Where studs are already in place, it may be easier to install furring strips horizontally and shim them during installation (Fig. 50). Use 1″ × 3″ wood and space them 16″ apart. Over an existing broken plaster wall, or solid masonry, install furring strips as shown in Fig. 51. Use concrete nails to fasten the furring strips on solid masonry.

335

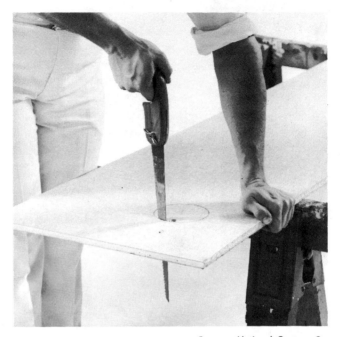

Fig. 47. Circle cutouts are made by first drilling a hole large enough to insert a key hole saw.

The most acceptable method of installing prefinished wallboard is with adhesive, either to vertical studs or horizontal furring strips, or to existing plasterboard or solid walls. In order to get effective pressure over the entire area of the boards for good adhesion, the panels must be slightly bowed. This is done in the manner shown in Fig. 52. A stock of wallboards is placed either face down over a center support, or face up across two end supports. The supports can be a 2″ × 4″ lumber, but if they are in contact with the vinyl finish, they must be padded to prevent marring. It may take one day or several days to get a moderate bow, depending on the weather and humidity.

The adhesive may be applied directly to the studs (Fig. 53) or to furring strips (Fig. 54). Where panel edges join, run two adhesive lines on the stud, one for each edge of a panel. These lines should be as close to the edge of the 2″ × 4″ stud as possible to prevent the adhesive from oozing out between the panel joints. For

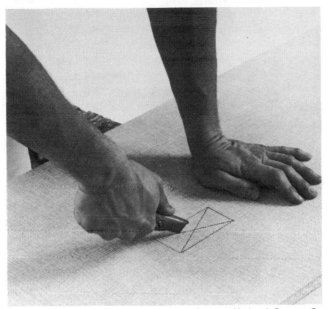

Fig. 48. For rectangular cutouts, score deeply on the vinyl side for the outline of the cutout. Tap the section to be removed.

the same reason, leave a space of 1″ with no adhesive along the furring strips, where panel edges join.

Place the panels in position with a slight sliding motion and nail the top and bottom edges. Be sure long edges of each panel are butted together evenly. Nail to sill and plate at top and bottom only. The bowed panels will apply the right pressure for the rest of the surface.

The top and bottom nails may be matching colored nails or finished with a cove and wall trim. Special push-on trims are available which match the prefinished wall. Inside corners may be left with panels butted but one panel must overlap the other. Outside corners must include solid protection. For both inside corners, if desired, and for outside corners, snap-on trim and bead

337

matching the panels can be obtained (Fig. 55). They are applied by installing retainer strips first (vinyl for inside corners and steel for outside corners), which holds the finished trim material in place.

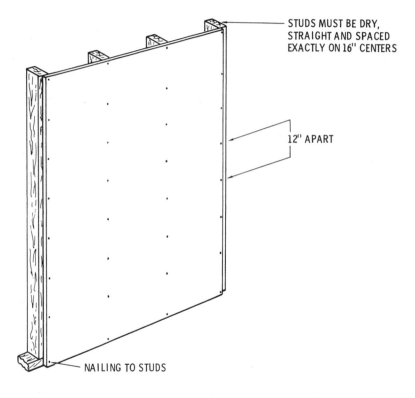

STUDS MUST BE DRY, STRAIGHT AND SPACED EXACTLY ON 16" CENTERS

12" APART

NAILING TO STUDS

Courtesy National Gypsum Co.

**Fig. 49. Prefinished walls may be nailed directly to studs as shown.**

Prefinished panels may be placed over old plaster walls or solid walls by using adhesive. If on old plaster, the surface must be clean and free of dust or loose paint. If wallpapered, the paper must be removed and walls completely washed. The new panels are bowed, as described before, then lines of adhesive are run down the length of the panels about 16″ apart (Fig. 56). Keep edge lines ¾″ to 1″ from the edges. Apply the boards to the old surface with a slight

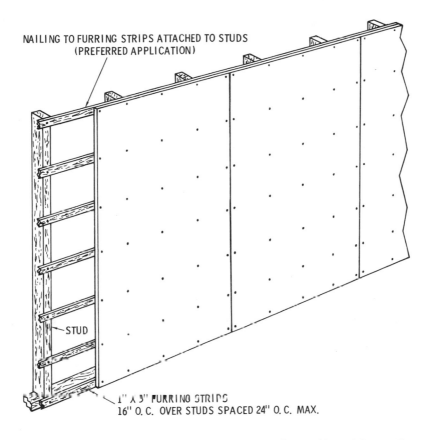

NAILING TO FURRING STRIPS ATTACHED TO STUDS (PREFERRED APPLICATION)

STUD

1″ X 3″ FURRING STRIPS 16″ O. C. OVER STUDS SPACED 24″ O. C. MAX.

Courtesy National Gypsum Co.

Fig. 50. Wood furring strips may be installed over wall studs that are not straight.

sliding motion and fasten at top and bottom with 6d nails, or matching colored nails. If boards will not stay in proper alignment, add more bracing against the surface and leave for 24 hours. The top and bottom may be finished with matching trim, as explained before.

## FAST INDUSTRIAL WALL CONSTRUCTION

Plasterboard materials are available that generally give a pro-
duction-line speed to the installation of drywalls. They are based

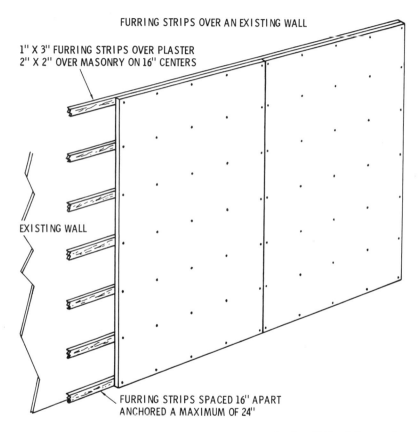

FURRING STRIPS OVER AN EXISTING WALL

1" X 3" FURRING STRIPS OVER PLASTER
2" X 2" OVER MASONRY ON 16" CENTERS

EXISTING WALL

FURRING STRIPS SPACED 16" APART
ANCHORED A MAXIMUM OF 24"

Courtesy National Gypsum Co.

**Fig. 51. Wood furring strips installed over solid masonry or old existing walls.**

on the use of thermosetting materials that are welded rather than
cemented at the joints. One manufacturer calls it their *Thermoweld*
system. With this system, a wall may be joint sealed and the finish
applied, all in less than an hour. The special panel boards are
available in ⅜" and ½" thick with lengths up to 16 ft.

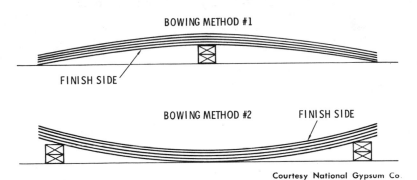

BOWING METHOD #1

FINISH SIDE

BOWING METHOD #2    FINISH SIDE

Courtesy National Gypsum Co.

**Fig. 52. Bowing wallboard for the adhesive method of installation.**

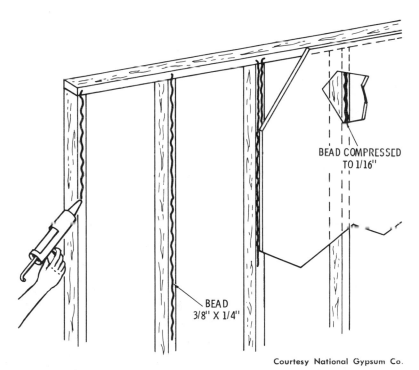

BEAD COMPRESSED
TO 1/16"

BEAD
3/8" X 1/4"

Courtesy National Gypsum Co.

**Fig. 53. Adhesive applied directly to the wall studs. The adhesive is applied in a wavy line the full length of the stud.**

341

LEAVE 1" SPACE AT
JOINT OF PANELS

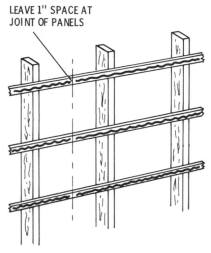

Fig. 54. Adhesive applied directly to
the wood furring strips.

Courtesy National Gypsum Co.

Courtesy National Gypsum Co.

Fig. 55. Snap-on matching trim is available for prefinished wallboard.

The walls are installed in the usual way, with adhesive as the preferred method. Within 24 hours, the wall is dry and set and finishing can be done quickly. If preferred, walls may be nailed or screwed (Fig. 57) to the studs and it is easier to do if applied before the walls go up.

A special thermosetting tape is applied to the joints with a hot

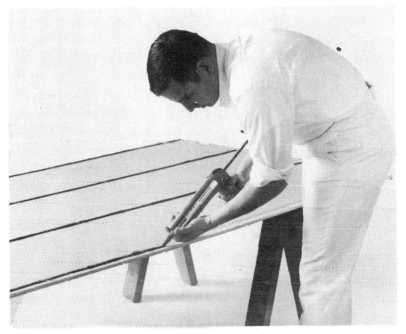

Courtesy National Gypsum Co.

Fig. 56. Applying adhesive to prefinished wallboard to be installed over old plaster walls.

tool like the one shown in Fig. 58. Cut the tape to the proper length and tack the end of the tape to the starting position with the iron. In a matter of 10 seconds the weld has set hard enough to run the balance of the tape over the joint with the iron. Immediately after, the tape can be bedded with a special fast-drying joint compound made specifically for this system. Use a 6″ drywall

343

Fig. 57. Illustrating how special wallboard for thermosetting joint treatment is first secured to the wall studs before the wall is raised into place.

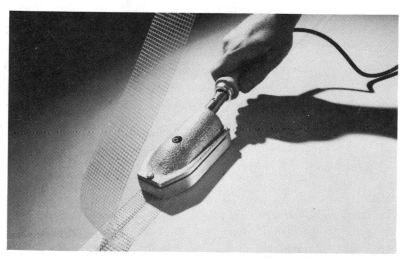

Fig. 58. Applying a special thermosetting tape to joints with a hot iron.

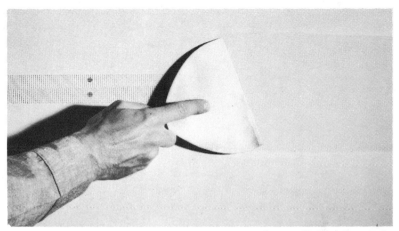

Fig. 59. Applying special joint compound over thermosetting tape.

Fig. 60. For inside corners a metal-backed tape is folded and applied over a base of thermosetting joint compound.

345

Courtesy National Gypsum Co.

Fig. 61. Bedding in the tape with a 4-inch broad knife.

finishing trowel (Fig. 59). Keep the joint as narrow as possible covering the tape and feathering the edges.

For inside corners, brush a thinner consistency of the same adhesive over the intersection of the walls, at least 2″ on each side. Cut a length of tape and fold it carefully down the middle and place it in contact with the wall surfaces (Fig. 60). Use a 4″ knife to set the tape (Fig. 61). Allow approximately 30 minutes for the adhesive to harden, if time permits. Apply another coat with the 4″ knife, as described for flat joints. Feather out the edges carefully.

Outside corners are handled in the same way, except a thicker consistency of adhesive is used. The tape has a metal backing which provides the protection needed. Butter the corner with the adhesive before applying the tape (Fig. 62), then apply the tape by hand with metal side against the board. Apply the second coat, feathered out at the edges.

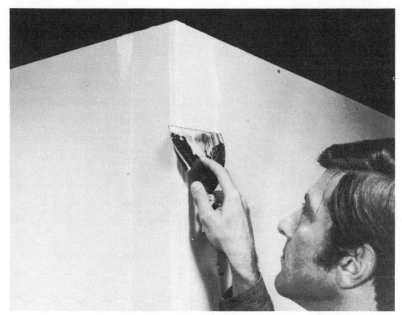

Courtesy National Gypsum Co.

**Fig. 62. Outside corners are finished in the same manner as inside corners.**

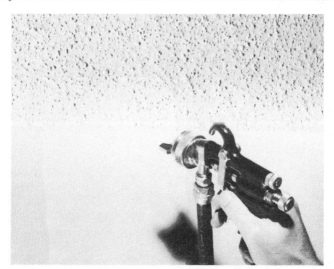

Courtesy National Gypsum Co.

**Fig. 63. Spraying a finish can be done immediately after finishing the joints.**

347

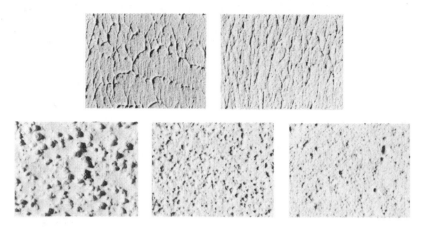

Courtesy National Gypsum Co.

**Fig. 64. Some examples of spray coatings that can be applied to ceilings and to walls.**

Final finishing is by spraying the walls and ceilings (Fig. 63), with a textured coating. A number of textures are available, some of which are shown in Fig. 64.

## CHAPTER 15

# Stone And Rock Masonry

With most of the crust of the earth composed of stone or rock (or rock-like materials), it is no wonder there is a large amount of this material used in masonry construction. It is probably one of the oldest construction materials known to man. The earliest solid dwellings known to man were natural caves. The cliff dwellings of the Southwest Indians date back thousands of years. Their homes were hand-hewn out of soft rock material on the sides of cliffs. The abundance of rock made a natural choice for early man to pick up loose pieces and pile them rock-upon-rock to build a wall against enemy invasion or to keep out wild animals. Such use led to cutting rock into more usable shapes which then could be stacked more precisely and more substantially into buildings, tombs, pyramids, etc.

The current use of stones and rocks for construction is usually based on:

1. The abundance of the material in the area.
2. The desire to attain a rustic appearance.

More commonly found abroad, than in this country, are fences of rock around a ranch or farm made from the rocks cleared from the land. They are simply piled on the ground without mortar. Because of the tremendous amount of hand labor involved, modern farms and ranches in this country find it more economical to construct post and wire fences. Rock and stone are carefully chosen, cut and polished to a luster, and used for home and building front facings.

**Table 1. Approximate Weight and Strength of Stone**

| Kind of Stone | Weight lbs. per cu. ft. | Crushing strength lbs. per sq. in. | Shearing strength lbs. per sq. in. |
|---|---|---|---|
| Sandstone ................................. | 150 | 8000 | 1500 |
| Granite .................................... | 170 | 15,000 | 2000 |
| Limestone ................................ | 170 | 6000 | 1000 |
| Marble .................................... | 170 | 10,000 | 1400 |
| Slate ...................................... | 175 | 15,000 | |
| Trap Rock ................................ | 185 | 20,000 | |

## TYPES OF STONE

There are roughly two types of stone. One type is granite and basalts which is called siliceous. They are hard, usually round in shape, and found in great abundance on the earth surface. They are usually cut or split to usable shapes by machine, but many are found with flat surfaces on one or two sides and, by careful selection, may be used as is for wall construction. The term used when building with this type of stone is called "rubble construction" (Fig. 1). Limestone, shale, and sandstone, are the other type and are stratified in their natural form, and are, therefore, easy to split into flat pieces. They are considered calcareous argillacious (claylike) materials. While this type of stone is easier to work with, it does have one drawback. Because of its stratified makeup, it is subject to earlier deterioration in climates of extreme cold and wetness. Moisture can get into the crevices and, on freezing, break away edge pieces a little at a time. Building with this type of stone is called "ashlar construction."

## KINDS OF STONE

Table 1 lists the weight and strengths of various types of stone.

A Random bond

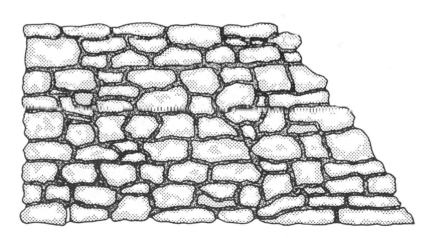

(B) Course bond.

Fig. 1. The appearance of rubble construction.

351

It must be borne in mind that the figures for strength are only approximate. Stones of the same kind from different parts of the country can vary considerably in strength. For those interested in a more detailed description of the makeup of various stone types, the following will be found interesting:

*Limestone*—Limestones consist chiefly of calcium carbonate with small proportions of other substances. They are often classified under four heads: Compact limestones consist of carbonate of lime, either pure or in combination with clay and sand. Granular or oolitic limestones consist of grains of carbonate clay. The grains are egg shaped (hence the name "oolite") and vary in size from tiny particles to grains as large as peas. Shelly limestones consist almost entirely of small shells, cemented together by carbonate of lime. Magnesian limestones are composed of carbonates of lime and magnesia in varying proportions and usually also contain small quantities of silica, iron, and alumina. The hardest and closest grained of these are capable of taking a fine polish. Limestones should be used with care since they are uncertain in their behavior and usually more difficult to work than sandstones. As a general rule they do not stand the action of fire well.

*Sandstone*—Sandstones are composed of grains of sand held together by a cementing substance to form a compact rock. The cementing medium may be silica, alumina, carbonate of lime, or an oxide of iron. Those stones that have a siliceous cement are the most durable. Sandstones vary more in color than limestones, the color being largely due to the presence of iron. Cream, brown, gray, pink, red, light and dark blue, and drab are common colors. The texture of sandstones varies from a fine, almost microscopic, grain to one composed of large particles of sand. It will generally be found that the heaviest, densest, least porous, and most lasting stones are those with a fine grain.

*Granite*—Granites are igneous rocks formed by volcanic action and are of all geological ages. Granite is composed of quartz, felspar, and mica intimately compacted in varying proportions to form a hard granular stone. Quartz is the principal constituent and imparts to the rock the qualities of durability and strength. Stones containing a large proportion of quartz are hard and difficult to work. Felspar of an earthly nature is opaque in appearance and is liable to decay; it should be clear and almost transparent. The characteristic color of the granite is generally due to this substance, but the stone is often affected by the nature of the mica it contains, whether it is light or dark in tint. Granite is the hardest, strongest, and most durable of building stones, and is difficult and costly to work. When polished, many varieties present a beautiful and lasting surface. By reason of its strength and toughness this stone is often used for foundations, bases, columns, curbs and paving, and in all positions where great strength is required.

*Slate*—Slate used for roofing and other purposes in building is a fine-grained and compact rock composed of sandy clay which has been more or less metamorphosed by the action of heat and tremendous pressure. Such rocks were originally deposited in the form of sediment by the sea or river, afterward becoming compacted by the continual heaping up of superincumbent material.

Fig. 2. The stone facing of this wall has the appearance of solid rock construction, but the facing stones are shallow and used for its rustic western look.

Fig. 3. An expertly built stone wall used for fencing between home lots. Note the random rubble type of construction capped with a layer of brick

Fig. 4. Because of the slope of the land on which this home is built, some form of retaining wall is needed to prevent soil erosion during rains. Natural stone carefully selected and cut forms a retaining wall which is both attractive and functional.

Owing no doubt to some sliding motion having at some time taken place, slatey rocks are capable of being split into thin sheets which are trimmed to the various marketable sizes. A good slate is hard, tough and nonabsorbent. It will give out a metallic ring if struck and when trimmed it will not splinter nor will the edges become ragged. Slates range in color from purple to gray and green.

Fig. 5. The entrance to a restaurant with walls veneered with flat cut and polished stone.

## ROCK AND STONE USES

Rocks and stones are used for construction or for facing to achieve a rustic appearance (Fig. 2). Construction is usually confined to boundary walls or fencing (Fig. 3); earth retaining walls (Fig. 4), dams, etc. Complete housing or building structures are seldom made of stone exclusively. Veneer stone is mortar-set against an existing building and adds no support to the structure (Fig. 5). Various color and texture combinations can be made by careful selection of polished stone (Fig. 6). Facing stone may be small round (Fig. 7) or flat pieces, usually highly polished. The small round stones are carefully selected for uniformity of size and shape. Flat rock is generally factory cut and polished. This

355

Fig. 6. By careful selection and polishing, the stones are made to vary in color and texture.

Fig. 7. An older building which has been remodeled by installing round stone veneer to the front.

type is flat with little depth and must be set in with great care as to pattern to retain a flat surface, and for cleanliness of the finished work.

356

Most solid structures are in the form of walls either self-supporting or for earth retaining. Either rubble or ashlar construction is
used, with ashlar predominating because of the ease with which
the rock is split. Rubble construction requires careful selection of
rocks with flat sides or purchasing the rock with factory cut sides.
Concrete block can also be purchased with one side treated to
look like natural rock. Such blocks are easier to lay up and require
much less mortar than natural stone.

Rocks may be laid up dry, or with mortar, with the latter preferred. While dry construction is somewhat obsolete, there is one
example of modern dam construction using no mortar. In Ciudad
de Juarez in Mexico, a water retaining dam was recently built with
stones so carefully cut and laid that no mortar was used, and there
is no leak in the dam. Mortar construction is generally the same
as for laying up brick or concrete blocks. The mortar ingredients
are about the same. A considerable amount of mortar is usually
required, because of the irregularity of the stone faces. The experienced mason or homeowner, if he builds his own, will fill voids

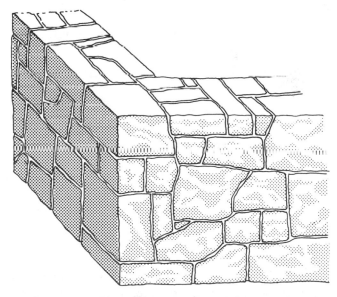

Fig. 8. Random course rubble wall construction. It takes carefully cut stones to
make mortar lines as fine as shown here.

between rocks with smaller stones as much as possible, to reduce the amount of mortar needed. Factually, the stones are stronger than the mortar.

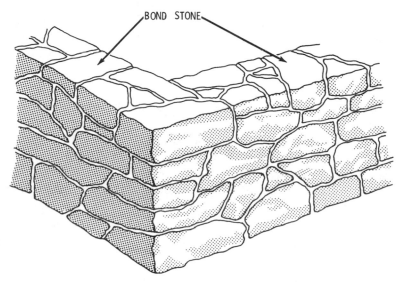

Fig. 9. Illustrating the use of long stones as headers to bond the wall transversely.

## CONSTRUCTION CONSIDERATIONS

With the exception of stones laid on the ground without mortar, stone walls or rough fencing require a firm foundation, preferably of concrete, as with brick or concrete wall construction. Without a solid foundation, heaving of the earth as a result of freezing and thawing will crack the wall and require frequent repairs. Refer back to Volume 1 of this library for detailed instructions on footing construction. In general, a trench should be dug below the frost line and have a width about twice that of the wall to be built. Pour concrete up to just below the level of the ground. Allow it to cure for 48 hours before beginning the stone wall construction.

Determine the pattern desired and the construction method to be used then order stones or rocks to fit. Random rubble masonry has the most rustic appearance but may require more care in setting up a desirable pattern. Ashlar construction begins to approach the system of brick laying in that there is some resemblance of course-upon-course construction. Half way between these two is the random coursed rubble construction probably the most popular pattern used. The stones generally have a somewhat flat face but the nearly straight mortar lines identifying the courses is altered (Fig. 8).

A proportion of the stones should be long enough to reach from the front of the wall to the back. These stones will act as

Fig. 10. Loose rock and a drain pipe were installed behind this stone retaining wall before the earth was filled in.

headers, as with brick, and are necessary for good wall strength (Fig. 9). Stones should be small enough for easy handling. Considering that a piece only 1 cu. ft. in size weighs over 150 lbs., hand laying makes size selection important. Where larger sizes are specified, contractors should place the stones with power equipment, equipped with rock handling tongs. For random masonry, include a quantity of small stones to be used to fill between large spaces and save on the cost of mortar.

In constructing an earth retaining wall, there must be a back fill of stone and a drain pipe properly placed (Fig. 10). It is important to provide water drainage, to avoid moisture from collecting behind the wall which could seep into the mortar. This could weaken the mortar and cause crumbling. All stones and rocks should be washed and allowed to drain dry before using. Any dust on the stones prevents proper cementing of the mortar to the stone. All necessary material should be on hand before starting to lay a stone wall—tools, stones of all sizes, and plenty of mortar ingredients. Remember, much more mortar will be used for stone walls than for brick or concrete-block masonry.

Fig. 11. Nearly all stones have a cleavage line. Stones are more easily broken, when necessary, by breaking with a chisel at the cleavage line.

## LAYING A STONE MASONRY WALL

The strongest mortar is regular sand and concrete—consisting of 1 part portland cement and 3 parts sand, plus water. However, this mortar does have some shrinkage and lacks the workability of mortar cement. For ease of laying, use a portland cement-lime-sand mix, the same as that used for laying bricks. Regular portland cement tends to stain stones and rocks, which effect can be lessened by the use of white portland cement in the mortar.

With the foundation installed and all materials and tools on hand, lay a bed of mortar over the foundation to take the first course of stones. The bed of mortar must be thick, to fill all crevices of the bottom stones. If necessary, include small stones. Each stone should be laid with its broadest face horizontal. Place the larger stones for the bottom courses, both for strength and better appearance. Porous stones should be dampened before placing, to prevent too much water absorption from the mortar. If necessary to reset a stone, lift it clear of its position and reset with new mortar. Remember the importance of good bonding.

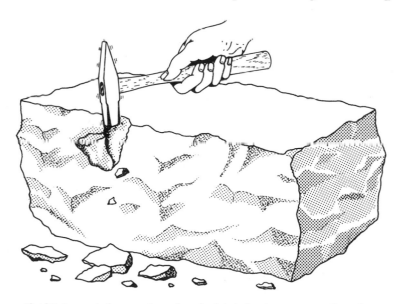

Fig. 12. A masons hammer is used on the job to break away protruding edges.

Place long stretcher stones about every 6 to 10 sq. ft. of wall. Offset adjacent header stones above and below it.

If alignment of the wall is not important, the courses of stone may be laid and aligned by sight. For precise alignment, drive a stake at each end of the wall and stretch a string across as a gauge for a straight line. Move the string up the stakes as the courses are laid. The top course of stones should present a flat appearance. This may require some readjustment of the course below to fit the top course. Save flat-faced stones for the top course.

It is frequently necessary to cut some stones on the job. Nearly all stones have cleavage lines. By placing a large chisel at the cleavage line, a few strokes of a small sledge should break the stone at or near this line as shown in Fig. 11. A mason's hammer may be used to chip away protruding pieces from stones (Fig. 12). Wear face goggles when doing this.

Finally, tool the mortar joints with a stick or jointing tool. Clean away excess mortar. Use a wet sponge to clean off the face of stones which have mortar spots. If mortar is left it will be difficult to remove when hard, and may stain the stone.

## CHAPTER 16

# How To Read Blue Prints

Whether the mason is his own contractor, working for a contractor, or is an apprentice, it is important that he know how to read and follow a blue print for the structure he is working on. In order to do his job properly it is not necessary for the mason to know how to draw a blue print, but only to read one. The mason must know what work he is to do on a structure, and where it is to be done.

Blue prints are made by the architect of the structure, or by members of his staff. In some cases the architect oversees the work itself, or it is turned over to a general contractor. In any case there is someone with whom the mason can communicate if there are any questions about details. Blue print details and symbols have been standardized and, once understood, there is usually no problem in proceeding with the work required.

## DEVELOPING THE BLUE PRINT

Start with a small block of wood, $1'' \times 2'' \times 4''$. Look at it, and compare it with the top illustration of Fig. 1. The illustration is called an orthographic view of the object. It differs from an actual view as parallel lines are drawn truly parallel, whereas when the object itself is viewed the parallel lines (AB, EF, DC, and HG) seem to taper to a vanishing point. This is the same effect as when the object is photographed. While an orthographic view is not as actually seen, it does permit the use of equal dimensions where such dimensions exist.

The lower part of Fig. 1 is a projection of the orthographic view, in which each plane of the object is shown as flat illustrations on a sheet of paper. The elevation view is the height and width of the object, and the end view is as named. The plan view is looking straight down on the object.

Fig. 2 is an equivalent drawing, but of a simple structure such as a barn. The plan view shown here is that of the roof of the struc-

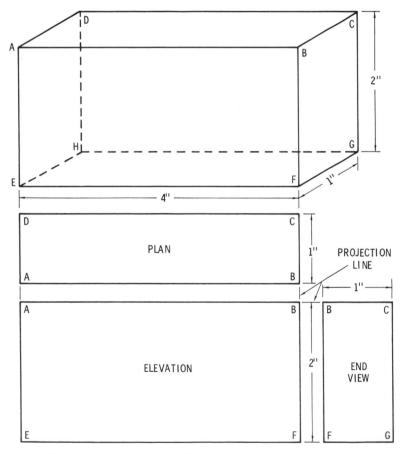

Fig. 1. Projecting an orthographic view of a wood block to flat planes.

ture. The plan view could also be the floor line of the structure by omitting the line AB. It is the "plan" view that is used most in architectural blue prints, and it is in this view that other details are included. In a multistory structure, there would be a plan view of each floor. The drawing would include details of equipment to be supplied by the contractor, or by the subcontractors, such as mason contractors, electrical contractors, plumbing contractors, etc.

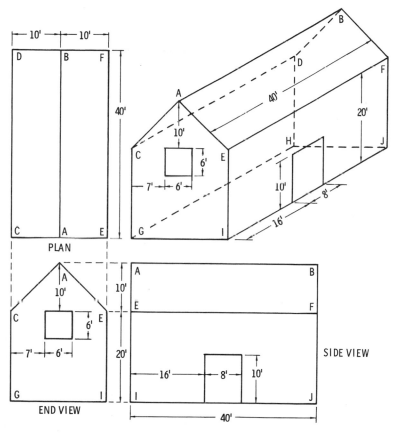

**Fig. 2. Steps in projecting an orthographic view of a barn to plane views. In construction blue prints, the plane view is the most important.**

The architect will discuss a structure with the customer, and will make some rough hand drawings during the discussion. Back at his office the hand sketches will be made to look a little more formal, but will not include dimensions, equipment, electrical and plumbing details. It will locate the rooms, doors, windows, stairs and other important features (Fig. 3).

Further discussions will finalize dimensions showing equipment and other considerations. The architect will then return to the drawing board to make the final blue prints. Fig. 4 shows a print with

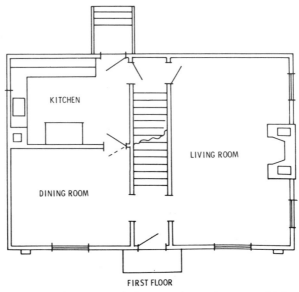

FIRST FLOOR

Fig. 3. The first ruled drawings made by an architect show essential features, but leaving out many details until they are finalized with the customer.

everything in except dimensions, which are promptly added. It is from a print like this, with dimensions, that contractors do their work. Fig. 5 shows a floor plan of a basement of a home, with all dimensions shown.

A set of blue prints for a home or building consists of many drawings. There will be elevations views, end views, and plan views for each floor as well as the roof. In addition, special structural details will be shown separately, but keyed to the main plan view. Fig. 6

shows the details of a basement wall, footing and floor. This print would be used by the excavator and concrete mason. Fig. 7 shows details of the wall construction. It is used by the brick mason, the plasterer, and the carpenter.

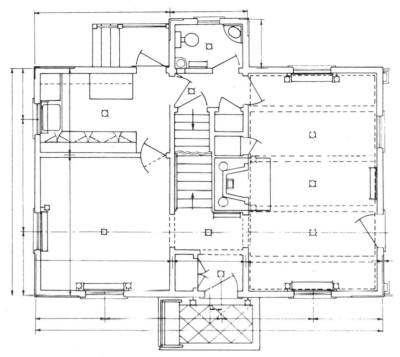

Fig. 4. Plan view of the first floor of a residence. All details are now shown, except dimensions.

## SCALED DIMENSIONS

All blue prints are drawn to scale. That is, ½ " of print is equal to 1 ft. of actual construction, or some other ratio. The scale ratio is given on the print. Should a dimension be questioned it is easy to check with an architect's scale ruler. The one shown in Fig. 8 has three edges, and has 11 proportionate scales from 3" to 1 ft., down to 3/32" to 1 ft., in addition to a standard 12" rule. Many scales are obtained by reading from both ends of the ruler. The beginning end of each scale includes scaled inches.

## STANDARD SYMBOLS

The symbols used by architects to represent details in a blue print have become standardized, and masons must be acquainted with them. The use of symbols prevents the cluttering of prints with small details that may not show clearly.

Fig. 9 shows the standard symbols pertaining to walls and openings, of importance to masons. The distance between parallel lines

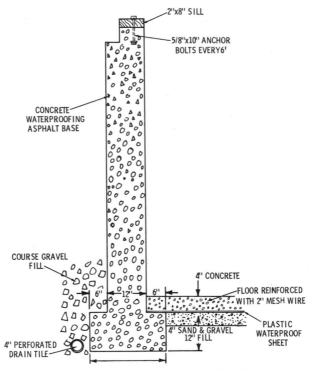

Fig. 5. Plan view of a basement, now including dimensions.

is the scaled thickness of the walls. The actual construction details would be shown in separate drawings, as mentioned above, except where such construction is assumed standard in the industry and dictated by building codes, either national or local.

Fig. 10 shows the standard symbols dictating the material to be used in construction. These have been agreed upon by the A.S.A.

368

and A.S.M.E. societies, which do testing and have set standards for the building trades.

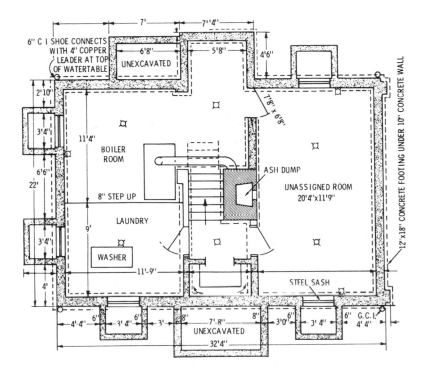

**Fig. 6. Details of a basement wall, floor, and footing.**

## SPECIFICATIONS

By definition, a specification is a definite, particularized, and complete statement setting forth the nature and construction of the object to which it relates; as applied to the building trades, specifications describe briefly, yet exactly, each item in a list of the materials required to complete a contract for building the entire project.

Great care should be used when writing specifications to avoid misunderstandings and disputes. Each item entering into the con-

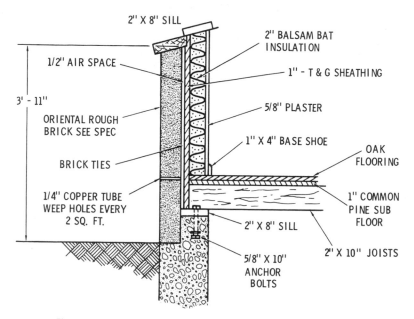

Fig. 7. Details of floor, and inside and outside of wall construction.

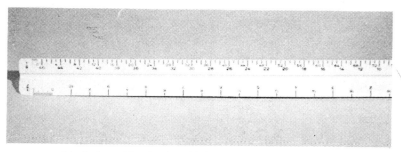

Fig. 8. An architect's rule, with fractions of an inch to a foot.

struction should be defined and described with such precision that there can be no chance of misunderstanding or double interpretation. The language should be simple and brief. For the guidance of architects in writing specifications, the American Institute of Architects has prepared a number of *Standard Documents,* and these should be carefully studied and consulted by the architect

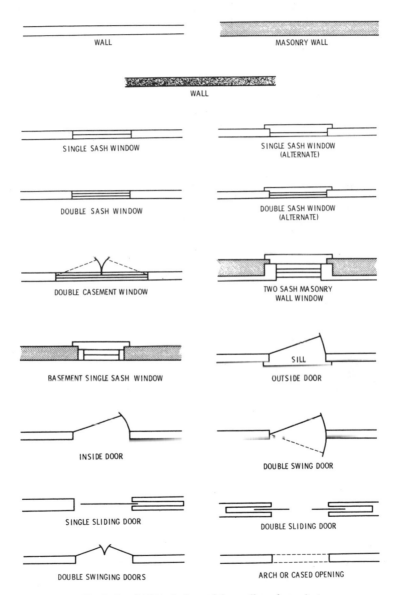

**Fig. 9. Standard symbols used for walls and openings.**

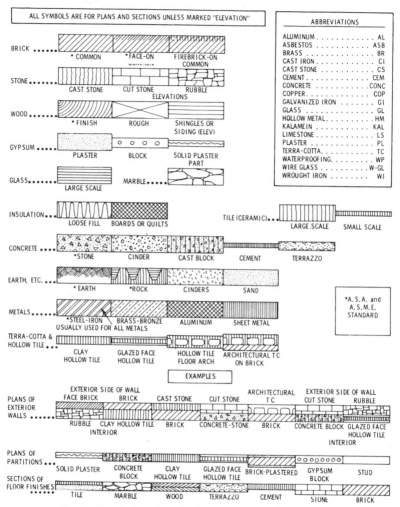

**Fig. 10. Standard symbols for the material in walls and floors.**

when writing specifications for building and construction of any size project.

Specifications should refer to the contract form of which they are to become a part. This saves repetition of statements with regard to liability of contractor, owner, etc. The following is an example of specifications as ordinarily prepared by an architect.

# Index

373

# INDEX

# The Audel® Mail Order Bookstore

Here's an opportunity to order the valuable books you may have missed before and to build your own personal, comprehensive library of Audel books. You can choose from an extensive selection of technical guides and reference books. They will provide access to the same sources the experts use, put all the answers at your fingertips, and give you the know-how to complete even the most complicated building or repairing job, in the same professional way.

## Each volume:

- **Fully illustrated**

- **Packed with up-to-date facts and figures**

- **Completely indexed for easy reference**

## APPLIANCES

### AIR CONDITIONING
Domestic, commercial, and automobile air conditioning fully explained in easily understood language. Troubleshooting charts aid in diagnosing and repairing system troubles. **Cat. No. 23159   Price: $6.95**

### HOME APPLIANCE SERVICING, 3rd Edition
A practical book for electric & gas servicemen, mechanics & dealers. Covers the principles, servicing, and repairing of home appliances. **Cat. No. 23214   Price: $8.50**

### HOME REFRIGERATION AND AIR CONDITIONING, 2nd Edition
Covers basic principles, servicing, operation, and repair of modern household refrigerators and air conditioners. Automotive air conditioners are also included. **Cat. No. 23133   Price: $8.95**

### OIL BURNERS, 3rd Edition
Provides complete information on all types of oil burners and associated equipment. Discusses burners—blowers—ignition transformers—electrodes—nozzles—fuel pumps—filters—controls. Installation and maintenance are stressed. **Cat. No. 23277   Price: $6.95**

*Use the order coupon on the back page of this book.*

# AUTOMOTIVE

## AUTO BODY REPAIR FOR THE DO-IT-YOURSELFER

Shows how to use touch-up paint; repair chips, scratches, and dents; remove and prevent rust; care for glass, doors, locks, lids, and vinyl tops; and clean and repair upholstery. Softcover. **Cat. No. 23238  Price: $5.95**

## AUTOMOTIVE LIBRARY—2 Vols.
**Cat. No. 23198  Price: $15.95**

### AUTOMOBILE GUIDE, 3rd Edition

A practical reference for auto mechanics, servicemen, trainees, and owners Explains theory, construction, and servicing of modern domestic motorcars. **Cat. No. 23192  Price: $10.25**

### AUTO ENGINE TUNE-UP, 2nd Edition

This popular guide shows you exactly how to tune your car engine for extra power, gas economy and fewer costly repairs. **Cat. No. 23181  Price: $6.75**

---

### CAN-DO TUNE-UP™ SERIES

Each book in this series comes with an audio tape cassette. Together they provide an organized set of instructions that will show you and talk you through the maintenance and tune-up procedures designed for your particular car. All books are softcover.

---

## AMERICAN MOTORS CORPORATION CARS

(The 1964 thru 1974 cars covered include: Matador, Rambler, Gremlin, and AMC Jeep (Willys).) **Cat. No. 23843  Price: $7.95**
**Cat. No. 23851** Without Cassette  **Price: $4.95**

## CHRYSLER CORPORATION CARS

(The 1964 thru 1974 cars covered include: Chrysler, Dodge, and Plymouth) **Cat. No. 23825  Price: $7.95**
**Cat. No. 23846** Without Cassette  **Price: $4.95**

## FORD MOTOR COMPANY CARS

(The 1964 thru 1974 cars covered include: Ford, Lincoln, and Mercury.) **Cat. No. 23827  Price: $7.95**
**Cat. No. 23848** Without Cassette  **Price: $4.95**

## GENERAL MOTORS CORPORATION CARS

(The 1964 thru 1974 cars covered include: Buick, Cadillac, Chevrolet, Oldsmobile, and Pontiac.) **Cat. No. 23824  Price: $7.95**
**Cat. No. 23845** Without Cassette  **Price: $4.95**

## PINTO AND VEGA CARS,

1971 thru 1974. **Cat. No. 23831  Price: $7.95**
**Cat. No. 23849** Without Cassette  **Price: $4.95**

## TOYOTA AND DATSUN CARS,

1964 thru 1974. **Cat. No. 23835  Price: $7.95**
**Cat. No. 23850** Without Cassette  **Price: $4.95**

## VOLKSWAGEN CARS

(The 1964 thru 1974 cars covered include: Beetle, Super Beetle, and Karmann Ghia.) **Cat. No. 23826  Price: $7.95**
**Cat. No. 23847** Without Cassette  **Price: $4.95**

---

*Use the order coupon on the back page of this book.*

### DIESEL ENGINE MANUAL, 3rd Edition

A practical guide covering the theory, operation, and maintenance of modern diesel engines. Explains diesel principles—valves—timing—fuel pumps—pistons and rings—cylinders—lubrication—cooling system—fuel oil and more. **Cat. No. 23199** **Price: $8.50**

### GAS ENGINE MANUAL, 2nd Edition

A completely practical book covering the construction, operation, and repair of all types of modern gas engines. **Cat. No. 23245** **Price: $7.95**

### OUTBOARD MOTORS & BOATING, 3rd Edition

Provides the information you need to maintain, troubleshoot, repair, and adjust all types of outboard motors. Explains the basic principles of outboard motors and the functions of the various engine parts. Softcover. **Cat. No. 23279** **Price: $6.95**

# BUILDING AND MAINTENANCE

### ANSWERS ON BLUEPRINT READING, 2nd Edition

Covers all types of blueprint reading for mechanics and builders. This book reveals the secret language of blueprints, step by step in easy stages. **Cat. No. 23041** **Price: $6.50**

### BUILDING A VACATION HOME

From selecting a building site to driving in the last nail, this book explains the entire process, with fully illustrated step-by-step details. Includes a complete set of drawings for a two-story vacation and/or retirement home. Softcover. **Cat. No. 23222** **Price: $7.95**

### BUILDING MAINTENANCE, 2nd Edition

Covers all the practical aspects of building maintenance. Painting and decorating; plumbing and pipe fitting; carpentry; heating maintenance; custodial practices and more. (A book for building owners, managers, and maintenance personnel.) **Cat. No. 23278** **Price: $7.50**

### GARDENING & LANDSCAPING

A comprehensive guide for homeowners and for industrial, municipal, and estate groundskeepers. Gives information on proper care of annual and perennial flowers; various house plants; greenhouse design and construction; insect and rodent controls; and more. **Cat. No. 23229** **Price: $7.95**

### CARPENTERS & BUILDERS LIBRARY, 4th Edition (4 Vols.)

A practical, illustrated trade assistant on modern construction for carpenters, builders, and all woodworkers. Explains in practical, concise language and illustrations all the principles, advances, and shortcuts based on modern practice. How to calculate various jobs. **Cat. No. 23244** **Price: $24.50**

    Vol. 1—Tools, steel square, saw filing, joinery cabinets. **Cat. No. 23240** **Price: $6.50**

    Vol. 2—Mathematics, plans, specifications, estimates. **Cat. No. 23241** **Price: $6.50**

    Vol. 3—House and roof framing, laying out, foundations. **Cat. No. 23242** **Price: $6.50**

    Vol. 4—Doors, windows. stairs, millwork, painting. **Cat. No. 23243** **Price: $6.50**

---

*Use the order coupon on the back page of this book.*

## CARPENTRY AND BUILDING

Answers to the problems encountered in today's building trades. The actual questions asked of an architect by carpenters and builders are answered in this book. **Cat. No. 23142   Price: $7.50**

## DO-IT-YOURSELF ENCYCLOPEDIA

An all-in-one home repair and project guide for all do-it-yourselfers. Packed with step-by-step plans, thousands of photos, helpful charts. **Cat. No. 23207   Price: $13.50**

## HEATING, VENTILATING, AND AIR CONDITIONING LIBRARY (3 Vols.)

This three-volume set covers all types of furnaces, ductwork, air conditioners, heat pumps, radiant heaters, and water heaters, including swimming-pool heating systems. **Cat. No. 23227   Price: $22.50**

### Volume 1

Partial Contents: Heating Fundamentals . . . Insulation Principles . . . Heating Fuels . . . Electric Heating System . . . Furnace Fundamentals . . . Gas-Fired Furnaces . . . Oil-Fired Furnaces . . . Coal-Fired Furnaces . . . Electric Furnaces. **Cat. No. 23248   Price: $7.95**

### Volume 2

Partial Contents: Oil Burners . . . Gas Burners . . . Thermostats and Humidistats . . . Gas and Oil Controls . . . Pipes, Pipe Fitting, and Piping Details . . . Valves and Valve Installations. **Cat. No. 23249   Price: $7.95**

### Volume 3

Partial Contents: Radiant Heating . . . Radiators, Convectors, and Unit Heaters . . . Stoves, Fireplaces, and Chimneys . . . Water Heaters and Other Appliances . . . Central Air Conditioning Systems . . . Humidifiers and Dehumidifiers. **Cat. No. 23250   Price: $7.95**

## HOME MAINTENANCE AND REPAIR: Walls, Ceilings, and Floors

Easy-to-follow instructions for sprucing up and repairing the walls, ceiling, and floors of your home. Covers nail pops, plaster repair, painting, paneling, ceiling and bathroom tile, and sound control. Softcover. **Cat. No. 23281   Price: $5.95**

## HOME PLUMBING HANDBOOK

A complete guide to home plumbing repair and installation. Softcover. **Cat. No. 23239   Price: $8.95**

## HOME WORKSHOP & TOOL HANDY BOOK

Tells how to set up your own home workshop (basement, garage, or spare room) and explains the various hand and power tools (when, where, and how to use them). **Cat. No. 23208   Price: $6.50**

## MASONS AND BUILDERS LIBRARY—2 Vols.

A practical, illustrated trade assistant on modern construction for bricklayers, stonemasons, cement workers, plasterers, and tile setters. Explains all the principles, advances, and shortcuts based on modern practice—including how to figure and calculate various jobs. **Cat. No. 23185   Price: $13.95**

Vol. 1—Concrete, Block, Tile, Terrazzo. **Cat. No. 23182   Price: $7.50**

Vol. 2—Bricklaying, Plastering, Rock Masonry, Clay Tile. **Cat. No. 23183   Price: $7.50**

---

*Use the order coupon on the back page of this book.*

## PLUMBERS AND PIPE FITTERS LIBRARY—3 Vols.

A practical, illustrated trade assistant and reference for master plumbers, journeymen and apprentice pipe fitters, gas fitters and helpers, builders, contractors, and engineers. Explains in simple language, illustrations, diagrams, charts, graphs, and pictures, the principles of modern plumbing and pipe-fitting practices. **Cat. No. 23255  Price $19.95**

Vol. 1—Materials, tools, roughing-in. **Cat. No. 23256  Price: $6.95**

Vol. 2—Welding, heating, air-conditioning. **Cat. No. 23257  Price: $6.95**

Vol. 3—Water supply, drainage, calculations. **Cat. No. 23258  Price: $6.95**

## PLUMBERS HANDBOOK

A pocket manual providing reference material for plumbers and/or pipe fitters. General information sections contain data on cast-iron fittings, copper drainage fittings, plastic pipe, and repair of fixtures. Softcover. **Cat. No. 23246  Price $5.50**

## QUESTIONS AND ANSWERS FOR PLUMBERS EXAMINATIONS,

### 2nd Edition

Answers plumbers' questions about types of fixtures to use, size of pipe to install, design of systems, size and location of septic tank systems, and procedures used in installing material. Softcover. **Cat. No. 23285  Price: $5.50**

## TREE CARE MANUAL

The conscientious gardener's guide to healthy, beautiful trees. Covers planting, grafting, fertilizing, pruning, and spraying. Tells how to cope with insects, plant diseases, and environmental damage. Softcover. **Cat. No. 23280  Price: $8.95**

## UPHOLSTERING

Upholstering is explained for the average householder and apprentice upholsterer. From repairing and regluing of the bare frame, to the final sewing or tacking, for antiques and most modern pieces, this book covers it all. **Cat. No. 23189  Price: $6.95**

## WOOD FURNITURE: Finishing, Refinishing, Repairing

Presents the fundamentals of furniture repair for both veneer and solid wood. Gives complete instructions on refinishing procedures, which includes stripping the old finish, sanding, selecting the finish, and using wood fillers. **Cat. No. 23216  Price: $7.50**

# ELECTRICITY/ELECTRONICS

## ELECTRICAL LIBRARY

If you are a student of electricity or a practicing electrician, here is a very important and helpful library you should consider owning. You can learn the basics of electricity, study electric motors and wiring diagrams, learn how to interpret the NEC, and prepare for the electrician's examination by using these books. **Cat. No. 23293  Price: $40.00**

Electric Motors, 3rd Edition. **Cat. No. 23264  Price: $7.95**

Guide to the 1975 National Electrical Code. **Cat. No. 23223  Price: $8.95**

House Wiring, 3rd Edition. **Cat. No. 23224  Price: $6.50**

Practical Electricity, 3rd Edition. **Cat. No. 23218  Price: $7.50**

Questions and Answers for Electricians Examinations, 5th Edition. **Cat. No. 23225  Price: $6.50**

Wiring Diagrams for Light and Power, 3rd Edition. **Cat. No. 23232  Price: $6.95**

## ELECTRICAL COURSE FOR APPRENTICES AND JOURNEYMEN

A study course for apprentice or journeymen electricians. Covers electrical theory and its applications. **Cat. No. 23209  Price: $7.50**

---

*Use the order coupon on the back page of this book.*

## ELECTRONIC SECURITY SYSTEMS

Protect your home and business. Such objects as sensors and encoders, indicators and alarms, electrical control and alarm circuits, security communications and security system installations are covered. **Cat. No. 23205  Price: $6.95**

## RADIOMANS GUIDE, 4th Edition

Contains the latest information on radio and electronics from the basics through transistors. **Cat. No. 23259  Price: $7.50**

## TELEVISION SERVICE MANUAL, 4th Edition

Provides the practical information necessary for accurate diagnosis and repair of both black-and-white and color television receivers. **Cat. No. 23247  Price: $7.95**

# ENGINEERS/MECHANICS/ MACHINISTS

### MACHINISTS LIBRARY, 2nd Edition

Covers modern machine-shop practice. Tells how to set up and operate lathes, screw and milling machines, shapers, drill presses, and all other machine tools. A complete reference library. **Cat. No. 23174  Price: $19.50**

**Vol. 1**—Basic Machine Shop. **Cat. No. 23175  Price: $6.75**

**Vol. 2**—Machine Shop. **Cat. No. 23176  Price: $6.75**

**Vol. 3**—Toolmakers Handy Book. **Cat. No. 23177  Price: $6.75**

## MECHANICAL TRADES POCKET MANUAL

Provides practical reference material for mechanical tradesmen. This handbook covers methods, tools, equipment, procedures, and much more. Softcover. **Cat. No. 23215  Price: $4.50**

## MILLWRIGHTS AND MECHANICS GUIDE, 2nd Edition

Practical information on plant installation, operation, and maintenance for millwrights, mechanics, maintenance men, erectors, riggers, foremen, inspectors, and superintendents. **Cat. No. 23201  Price: $11.95**

## POWER PLANT ENGINEERS GUIDE, 2nd Edition

The complete steam or diesel power-plant engineers' library. **Cat. No. 23220  Price: $10.50**

## QUESTIONS & ANSWERS FOR ENGINEERS AND FIREMANS EXAMINATIONS, 2nd Edition

An aid for stationary, marine, diesel & hoisting engineer's examinations for all grades of licenses. A new concise review explaining in detail the principles, facts, and figures of practical engineering. **Cat. No. 23217  Price: $7.95**

## WELDERS GUIDE, 2nd Edition

This new edition is a practical and concise manual on the theory, practical operation, and maintenance of all welding machines. Fully covers both electric and oxy-gas welding. **Cat. No. 23202  Price: $11.95**

## SHEET METAL WORKERS HANDY BOOK, 2nd Edition

Presents the fundamentals of sheet metal work layout in clear and simple language. **Cat. No. 23235  Price: $6.95**

*Use the order coupon on the back page of this book.*

# FLUID POWER

### PNEUMATICS AND HYDRAULICS, 3rd Edition

Fully discusses installation, operation, and maintenance of both HYDRAULIC AND PNEUMATIC (air) devices. **Cat. No. 23237   Price: $7.95**

### PUMPS, 2nd Edition

A detailed book on all types of pumps from the old-fashioned kitchen variety to the most modern types. Covers construction, application, installation, and troubleshooting. **Cat. No. 23167   Price: $8.95**

# HOBBY

### COMPLETE COURSE IN STAINED GLASS

Written by an outstanding artist in the field of stained glass, this book is dedicated to all who love the beauty of the art. Ten complete lessons describe the required materials, how to obtain them, and explicit directions for making several stained glass projects. 80 pages; 8½ x 11; softbound. **Cat. No. 23287   Price: $4.95**

### THE COMPLETE HOME CARPENTER

A colorfully illustrated guide that will inspire you to create practical and professional-looking furniture for your home. Contains forty-six chapters of explicit instructions and helpful "dos and don'ts." 222 pages; hardbound. **Cat. No. 52066   Price: $14.95**

## BUILD YOUR OWN AUDEL DO-IT-YOURSELF LIBRARY AT HOME!

Use the handy order coupon today to gain the valuable information you need in all the areas that once required a repairman. Save money and have fun while you learn to service your own air conditioner, automobile, and plumbing. Do your own professional carpentry, masonry, and wood furniture refinishing and repair. Build your own security systems. Find out how to repair your TV or Hi-Fi. Learn landscaping, upholstery, electronics and much, much more.

# HERE'S HOW TO ORDER

1. Enter the correct catalog number(s) of the book(s) you want in the space(s) provided.

2. Print your name, address, city, state and zip code, clearly.

3. Detach the order coupon below and mail today to:

## Theodore Audel & Company
4300 West 62nd Street
Indianapolis, Indiana 46206
**ATTENTION: ORDER DEPT.**

All prices are subject to change without notice.

----------------------------------------------------------------

# ORDER COUPON

Please rush the following book(s).

Write book catalog numbers at left.
(Numbers are listed with titles.)

NAME _____

ADDRESS _____

CITY _____ STATE _____ ZIP _____

☐ Payment Enclosed _____
   (No Shipping and          Total
   Handling Charge)

☐ Bill Me (Shipping and Handling Charge will be added)

Add local sales tax where applicable.

237

Litho in U.S.A.